28°

Cambridge Human Geography

PROPERTY COMPANIES AND THE CONSTRUCTION INDUSTRY IN BRITAIN

Cambridge Human Geography

PROPERTY COMPANIES AND THE CONSTRUCTION INDUSTRY IN BRITAIN

HEDLEY SMYTH

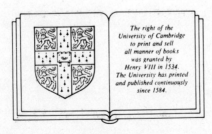

CAMBRIDGE UNIVERSITY PRESS

Cambridge

London   New York   New Rochelle
Melbourne   Sydney

Published by the Press Syndicate of the University of Cambridge
The Pitt Building, Trumpington Street, Cambridge CB2 1RP
32 East 57th Street, New York, NY 10022, USA
10 Stamford Road, Oakleigh, Melbourne 3166, Australia

First published 1985

Printed in Great Britain at The Bath Press, Avon

Library of Congress catalogue card number: 84–21408

British Library cataloguing in publication data
Smyth, Hedley
Property companies and the construction industry
in Britain. – (Cambridge human geography)
1. Construction industry – Great Britain
1. Title
338.4'7624'0941   HD9715.G72
ISBN 0 521 26512 6

Contents

Figures and tables

Figures

Tables

Preface

The aim of this book is to contribute to the formulation of an analysis of the built environment. My interest in the sphere arises from working in development and construction and from my first degree in geography at Sussex University. The material is both theoretical and empirical, and the work endeavours to engage the two in the historical chapters. The research was carried out at the School for Advanced Urban Studies, University of Bristol, between 1979 and 1982 for my doctorate, and was funded by the Social Science Research Council. This book is essentially an edited version of that thesis.

I wish to thank these institutions for their support and the friends and colleagues I have worked with over the years, all of whom have influenced me. The company directors and stockbrokers I interviewed as part of the research contributed more than can be adequately indicated by academic references. On the academic side, I wish especially to thank Sue Barrett for all her help and confidence in my work, Tom Davies and Robin Means for many stimulating discussions and the other postgraduate students who helped alleviate the isolation of research work. Sue and Tom along with Martin Boddy and Alan Murie provided valuable comments on drafts. I used their help and advice together with the views and information from other sources, drawing them all together in the way which most adequately makes sense of the phenomena I researched. The work is therefore my own and I am responsible for any errors of fact or misinterpretation of people's views. I would like to thank Brian Robson and Murray Stewart for encouraging me to write the book from the thesis.

I dedicate the book to the reader.

HEDLEY SMYTH
Bristol, 1984

Introduction

Planners, geographers, urban economists and others concerned with 'urban questions' have produced a considerable and valuable body of literature over the last decades. They have, however, ignored or neglected the agents who produce and control the built environment. This is a serious shortcoming and therefore the object of this study is to address this issue by focusing on property developers and construction contractors.

There will be differences between the approaches adopted in this work and other approaches. Some differences arise from different theoretical conceptions while others arise from different starting points in addressing 'urban questions'. However, the aim is to produce a study which will complement the existing literature as well as provide a challenge to broaden thinking.

A considerable amount of work has emanated from the sociological tradition in recent academic history. This study is not a sociological one, but the disaffection with the Chicago School of sociology[1] led some authors to be concerned with the redistribution of resources in a physical environment,[2] a concern which is relevant to this study. Other authors[3] went a step further to consider the redefinition of social relations as a necessity to achieve redistribution, the struggle over collective redistribution being one motor for changing social relations.[4] These academic traditions have recently become more fragmented,[5] one important component being concerned with the production of the built environment.[6] This work emanates from that academic development plus a personal career interest on the part of the author in construction and development. C. Wright Mills[7] predicted that academic work would become more fragmented and diffuse. This work tries to link back to a broad range of traditions, although the main thrust is economic rather than sociological. It is hoped that by linking traditions there will be useful material both implicitly and explicitly for social scientists.

Content and outline

The first main question addressed by the book concerns how the production and control of the built environment relate to the performance of the economy as a whole. In order to relate the built environment to the economy, an understanding of the operation of the economy is essential. A theoretical view of the economy is outlined in the first chapter. A materialist starting point is provided with theories of crisis considered as the pivot around which the production and control of the built environment relate. Four theories of crisis are considered. They are *profit squeeze, underconsumption*, the *tendency for the rate of profit to fall* and *over-production*. The chapter ends with a *synthesis* of the tendency for the rate of profit to fall and overproduction in this century.

The second main question addressed by the book concerns the characteristics and operation of the property and construction sectors. They both pose theoretical challenges because their appearance is distinctive. The few accounts of the construction industry have emphasised the description of the different characteristics without providing an explanation of them. In the case of the property sector there have been attempts to try to relate the activities to spheres or fractions of the economy despite the differences. Using crisis theory chapters 2 and 3 relate the characteristics of these two sectors to the economy, so providing a theoretical basis to explain how and when these sectors grow or decline and why these sectors exhibit different characteristics.

Chapter 2 concerns the property sector. In relating the sector to the economy a number of theoretical points are developed. It is argued that there is no urban rent theory, but that rentals for property have to be considered in three components, the ground rent for the land, the value of the building and the building rent. The introduction of building rent uses the differential and absolute categories applied to ground rent, but in the context of the built environment differential building rent II takes on an additional significance. The three components are then related to each other.

Chapter 3 takes the general theory, applying it to the construction sector. It is argued that the sector is not backward, as is usually thought, but is different because of its relationship to the market and its experience of crises of accumulation. This completes the theoretical arguments, which are used in subsequent chapters to describe and explain the activities of the property and construction sectors between 1939 and 1979 in Britain.

Most accounts of recent decades, particularly planning and welfare orientated works, acknowledge the importance of the second world war but the main thrust of these accounts frequently starts around 1945. This work considers the second world war to be a crucial period related closely to the theory of crisis, and therefore commences at the beginning of the war. The analysis in chapter 4 shows the concentration and diversifica- CHAP ④ tion of construction capital during the war and the relationship between these processes and the state.

Chapter 5 considers the reconstruction period, showing how the re- CHAP. ⑤ structuring of the construction sector during the war was a necessity for the physical and hence economic reconstruction of the nation state after the war. It also demonstrates that the destruction during the war was an essential feature for post-war property development and the emergence of a new property sector.

Chapter 6 encompasses the period of prosperity in the late 1950s and CHAP ⑥ during most of the 1960s. It shows that the renewal of capital accumulation created the demand for office and retail development not only due to the expansion of these sectors but also because the existing stock was outmoded. The construction sector experienced high workloads, particularly from public sector contracts, and the division of these markets between contractors is analysed.

By 1968 rates of profit in industry were showing signs of falling and there was an increase in labour unrest. The considerable state expenditure, a large portion of which was on construction work, had led to a considerable increase in fixed capital nationally, which through tax and inflation had a detrimental effect on industrial profit rates. Chapter 7 CHAP ⑦ deals with this first phase of economic crisis, but demonstrates that the experiences of both the property and construction sector were more favourable than many other sectors, not because they defy the general processes but because of their relation to the economy in the first phase of economic crisis.

The property sector received a stimulus from the need to speed up capital circulation, which had a spin off for construction too. The dependence of the world economy on oil led to the Middle Eastern states becoming wealthier following the 'oil crisis', which in turn stimulated a growing overseas construction market. This was very important for contractors at the time.

The conclusion analyses recent trends and provides some pointers for the future of the property and construction sectors.

I

Theories of crisis

The aim of this chapter is to outline an analysis of the whole economy, in particular an explanation for crises of capital accumulation. Materialist analysis offers some of the most sophisticated accounts of crises, but these too display weaknesses. Using a synthesis of accounts a position is produced which overcomes the weaknesses as applied to contemporary society.

First of all a brief summary of material analysis is provided. This is to remind or introduce readers to the basic propositions. It is not an explanation or justification of these tenets.

Materialism

The law of value

People naturally have the ability to work, to transform raw material into items which are more useful than in their raw state.[1] Production, therefore, is the creation of use values. The potential development of the brain has permitted people to conceive of items prior to their production and assemble the materials necessary to produce that conceived use value. This distinguishes people from other animals whereby a goal is set subordinating the means to the achievement of that end, and in so doing overturning the cause and effect relationship.[2]

This ability to produce use values allows the material basis of society to be increased, an ability which is enhanced by the social character of people.[3] The means can be further subordinated to the end if items are made to help in the production of other use values. Production can, therefore, be broken down into two departments, one which produces the means of production, the second which produces the means of consumption. This use of tools and machines to make other items further increases the ability to increase the material living standards of society. As production has become more sophisticated the importance of social relations between people increasingly established the way in which production has

4

been carried out. In all production there is an underlying concept of the amount of labour required to make each item. The labour expended by labourers is embodied into the final use values. It is the amount of labour time which is needed in the production of each item that gives the item its value. If people cooperate in production, more can be produced with less effort. A greater number of use values are produced, but the labour time, and hence the value, is reduced. The use of other tools and machinery enhances the process of producing more use values with a reduction in the required labour time.

Capitalism is characterised by a set of social relations which define it as a distinctive mode of production. The key social relations are between capital and labour. Capital is represented by individual capitalists and their management, by a company or corporation or by the state and its management. They comprise the capitalist class, who have gained control over the means of production, which is legally enshrined in the ownership of property. But the possession of the means to produce items is not sufficient to undertake production. The capitalists are dependent on others who have the ability and are willing to undertake the work. Those who work are dependent on earning a living to feed, clothe, house and support themselves and their dependants, and they therefore sell their ability to work, their labour power, to the capitalists in exchange for wages. To the capitalists the ability to work is simply another factor of production, a use value like a raw material or a piece of plant, and it becomes their responsibility to combine these factors in work and manage the work process. The workforce imparts its labour power and thus increases the material basis of society by producing items which have more value embodied in them than in their raw state. The capitalists pay for all items according to their cost of production. The workforce is not produced, but its ability to work has to be renewed each day, week and month, so it is paid the cost of reproduction of its labour power. This is the wage, but it does not correspond to the total value of its work. The additional value, or at least a substantial portion of it, is not paid to the workforce but is locked up in the final items produced. This portion of value, which contributes towards increasing the material basis of society, is the surplus value, and is owned by the capitalists because they have the right of ownership of all the items produced in their factories. The workforce, therefore, receives the value of its labour power which is socially established for its reproduction, while the capitalists receive the surplus value as a gift from the workforce by virtue of the capitalist ownership of the means and results of production. This is the nature of exploitation and is a social relation which is simultaneously antagonistic and one of mutual dependence, which gives capitalism its distinctive

and contradictory character, the needs of the dominant class being satisfied at the expense of the subordinate class.

Productive capital is aided by other capitalist agencies which perform
facilitative functions. Those that loan money capital help capitalists to
maximise their expansion of production with an amount of initial capital
in return for a share in the final profits in the form of an interest repayment. Landowners and building owners, as will be seen in chapter 3,
demand shares in the form of rent for the use of their land and buildings.
The rent is paid prior to the production, a point of confusion because it
appears the rent is paid for the land rather than for its use. There are
merchants, who perform the sales functions for the productive capitalist.
They too take a share of the surplus value. The state taxes surplus in order
to provide things that are not sufficiently profitable for private capital but
are essential to production and hence for the reproduction of capital as a
whole. The state also indirectly and sometimes directly controls capital.
The surplus value is shared between a number of individuals, agencies and
nations, and the capitalists undertaking production are prepared to concede these divisions of function because they neither have the capital nor
the expertise to carry out all these functions. There is a degree of cooperation, therefore, between all these capitalist agencies.

The appropriation of surplus value by the productive capitalist is not
sufficient to maintain production. The surplus value has to be realised
into the money form. The money pays for the wages, the renewing of raw
materials and plant, pays the interest and rent, leaving sufficient for the
capitalists to live and sufficient to accumulate for future expansion. In
order to realise surplus value into money the produced items are placed on
the market as commodities for sale. Purchasers will buy the commodities
for their usefulness in production or consumption. The ability to buy
these commodities is limited by their ability to pay. The price at which
commodities are sold is the exchange value, and the exchange completes
the circulation of capital through the realisation of surplus value. The
original capital advanced can be replaced and a portion is accumulated as
profit. The capitalist starts with money capital, itself a commodity produced for its use as a means of exchange, and ends the turnover with
money capital. From the viewpoint of the capitalist the usefulness of the
commodities produced is irrelevant providing they can be sold, the sole
objective being capital accumulation. Capitalists must operate within
this *law of value*, and accumulation is not therefore a direct function of
the amount of surplus value they each appropriate. The deviation of
prices from value affects the transformation of surplus value to profits.

Rates of profit have a tendency to average out between the producers in
one sphere or sector of production. Different capitalists carry out their

production at different levels of sophistication. Those with more plant and machinery and less labour will have a lower rate of profit compared to capitalists with a larger proportion of labour, which alone is productive of surplus value. Those with an average composition will yield an average rate of profit, the tendency being that others will sell their commodities in competition and thus yield an average rate of profit. Capitalists with high rates of profit will tend to transfer, through competition, some of their profits to those with lower profit rates so that an average rate is earned by all the capitalists in the end. Total profits still equal total value and an average rate of profit is formed within one sector.

This process also occurs between sectors and nations,[4] which operates to form a general rate of profit. The general rate of profit will not only reflect the level of sophistication of production but is also weighted according to the distribution of capital invested in each sector and nation. Should a general rate of profit be achieved, then capitalists will sell their commodities at their cost price plus an average rate of profit which is called the price of production.

The deviation of prices of production from value only helps to obscure the social relations based on the law of value. The deviations between price and value occur between individual capitalists, sectors and nations, the total value equalling the total prices of production for capital as a whole according to the theory, although these arguments are the subject of controversy.

Prices of production will tend to equal their respective values, thus producing an equalisation of the general rate of profit. This is induced through competition. Capitalists are not only competing to realise their surplus value, a process which forms the average and general rate of profit, but capital is also competing for investment outlets. Where above average rates of profit are being achieved capital will flow in at the expense of spheres where below average rates of profit are being achieved. This produces a tendency towards bringing all capitals into line in terms of their sophistication, in other words their ratio of plant to labour power, and so an average composition of capital and average profits will result. The formation of average profits equalises the general rate of profit to bring prices of production equal to their values in each sphere.

Where average profits are being earned, the market value of commodities will equal the value. Should demand increase, however, the price of the commodity demanded will rise above the market value. Under conditions of stability, this must mean the demand for another commodity goes down and the market price will fall below the value. The explanation for this lies not in the equation of supply and demand, but in the conception of value and total prices equalling total values. Supply and demand can only operate according to the total value produced and in circulation at one time and according to the total ability to pay, whether from wages or from realised value in the hands of capitalists, for commodities which are historically circulating.[5] An increase in the demand for a commodity will allow the producer to increase the rate of profit, in other words to receive a surplus profit over and above the average profit. This process will of course enter into the formation and equalisation of the general rate of profit (unless interrupted by the formation of absolute rent, which is discussed in chapter 2) through competition with regard to investment and with regard to sales.

The formation and equalisation of the general rate of profit are, however, constantly subject to change as new technologies, new machinery, new ways of working and new wage levels are introduced in the sphere of production, while interest rates and the absolute and relative demand for commodities change in the sphere of circulation. These dynamics of capital ensure that tendencies remain merely tendencies, rather than infinite laws.

Expanding capital accumulation

There are a number of ways in which production, and hence reproduction, can be expanded. The first way is through the use of labour. Capitalists can lengthen the work day or working week. This increases the overall value produced and thus increases the overall surplus value the capitalists appropriate. This assumes that wages are paid for the extra effort in the same ratio of value to surplus value or that the ratio is increased in the capitalists' favour. The way this operates can be disguised by reaching agreement on basic rates of pay versus overtime payments, and is further complicated when apparent rises in pay become reductions when related to the rate of inflation. A similar effect is achieved if the working day or week remains the same but more is produced in the same time. This intensification of labour can be obscured when basic wage rates are kept down but superficially excellent bonus schemes or piecework operate as the norm. There are, however, limits to these options because the lengthening of the working day or the intensification of labour comes up against physical and mental fatigue and resistance in the workforce. If these methods are pushed too hard then the reproduction of the workforce can be threatened, particularly when there is a shortage in the supply of labour, a situation which is most likely to arise if demand is high and expansion is in full flow.

An alternative is to employ more people in order to increase output. This again reaches limits according to the availability of labour and skills in the market place. A high demand for labour can push up wages and hence increase the value of labour power, placing it on a higher level of reproduction. This may be justified from the point of view of capital because the rate of capital accumulation can still be increased. Another limit may be reached by the restricted capacity to take on more labour, plant and machinery without constructing or renting another factory. The expansion must be a sustained one to justify this move for the capitalist. The operation of plant and machinery in existing premises limits the possibility of intensifying the use of labour because sophisticated machinery often dictates the method, speed and place of work. Even though machinery can limit the intensification of labour under existing conditions, it can provide for the expansion of production on a very large scale with new investment.

The use of machinery can involve expansion by using the same methods or can reconstitute the labour process by using different methods.[6] This expansion through investment in machinery has been referred to as increasing the sophistication of production, but this needs clarification because of its crucial importance to one crisis theory in particular and its bearing on the remainder.

All investments made by capitalists appear as different forms of capital from their point of view because all appear to contribute equally to the eventual realisation of profit and hence continued capital accumulation. This appearance gives capitalists the impression that it is the act of investment, and putting the investment to work, which produces the profit and therefore is the result of their own efforts. Investments in buildings, raw materials, machinery and wages are all capital expenditure. Labour power is exchanged for wages, but to capitalists labour power is a capital, variable capital, because its size and contribution can be changed according to the prevailing conditions. The variation will depend on demand in the market for commodities and on conditions for the commodity, labour power. Capitalists will be able to respond to these variations according to whether the workforce is employed casually, on a subcontract or contract basis.

Constant capital is the converse of variable capital comprising the means of production. Once investments have been made in buildings, raw materials and machinery capitalists are committed to using them unless they are to be written off or sold off. The degree of flexibility to manipulate these overheads becomes increasingly restricted the higher the level of investment in constant capital.

Constant capital is bought by capitalists for its use value in their production; however, each cycle of production does not use up all the constant capital. The raw materials are consumed in production. Electricity and other utilities are consumed while the buildings and machinery suffer wear and tear, thus yielding some of their use value, and therefore value, into the production process. The consumption of the means of production does not yield any additional surplus value to these capitalists, the surplus value already being realised by the producer of the means of production through sale to other capitalist users.[7] The constant capital which is not yielded up in one turnover of capital is fixed capital, although the use value of fixed capital will be yielded up in subsequent turnovers unless left to deteriorate naturally. Buildings and civil engineering works are amongst the most durable items of fixed capital, in contrast to coal or electricity which is rapidly or instantly consumed. Depending on the durability of fixed capital, allowances have to be made for the replacement of the constant capital consumed. Buildings and machinery will not be replaced for some time, but their replacement costs will be high and so capitalists will calculate the rate of depreciation, set up a sinking fund to ensure the money capital is available or arrange facilities to borrow money to replace them.

Constant capital is labour power expended in other production processes sold to the user at their value. The variable capital is labour power being expended in one production process, while the constant capital is labour already embodied in commodities. This can be conceived as living and dead labour respectively, the balance between the two being described as the organic composition of capital. The higher the investment in constant capital or dead labour compared to variable capital or living labour, the higher the organic composition of capital. The significance of increasing the organic composition of capital is that the material basis of society can be increased beyond that which can be achieved by intensifying labour, lengthening the working day or employing more variable capital. The potential for increasing the mass of surplus value increases with a rise in the organic composition, and hand in hand with this the rate of exploitation or rate of surplus value increases also.[8] This, then, is the basis for expanding capitalist production.

The entire process of expansion can be enhanced by speeding up the circulation of capital once it leaves the factory gates. There is also a relationship between constant and variable capital in the sphere of circulation, whether this is commerce, banking or functions performed by the state. The organic composition in these spheres will relate either to the organic composition of their respective production processes or to the total national composition of capital where specific production processes cannot be linked, as in the case of many state operations. The mutual dependence of production and circulation is important not only in producing and realising surplus value, but also in the composition of capital.

The quicker capital circulates, the quicker capital can be reinvested to stimulate further production on a higher scale of expansion.

The point of departure for the circulation of capital is the two main departments, department I producing the means of production, department II producing the means of consumption. Under simple reproduction the following scheme can be drawn up:

Department I $200c + 50v + 50s = 300$
Department II $100c + 25v + 25s = 150$

$$450$$

where c = constant capital
v = variable capital
s = surplus value

In this scheme department I must produce sufficient to replace its own constant capital and constant capital for department II, therefore the product of I equals in value the sum of the constant capital in the two departments with the constant capital of department II equalling the sum of v and s in department I. This also means that the product of department II equals the sum of v and s in both departments. This demonstrates the circulation of capital between the departments. It also indicates, however, that all that is produced is consumed in order to maintain reproduction. The wages paid to the workforce in both departments are consumed in the form of the product of department II and similarly for the capitalists once their constant capital is replaced. This relationship between production and circulation is complicated but not superseded by the intervention of landed, mercantile or commercial and loan capital.

Enlarged reproduction takes place if department I invests more money capital, perhaps facilitated by a loan, to increase the scale of production, the effects working their way through the whole scheme to produce expansion throughout. The scheme was used to show that capitalism is a possibility and that an equilibrium can be achieved. It indicates that this is the exception rather than the rule, equilibrium merely reproducing capital and not satisfying the *raison d'être* of capital, that is, continual capital accumulation. The tendency is always towards disequilibria, equilibrium of necessity being short term. The paradox of expanded reproduction is that the process of enlarging the scale of operations induces the conditions for the interruption of capital accumulation. Expansion induces crisis. It is here that the disagreements start: what is the cause of crises?

There are a number of variants of crisis theory, but in my opinion there are four principal analyses. These are profits squeeze theory, the theory of the tendency for the rate of profit to fall, underconsumption and overproduction theories. They embrace a range of causes from the purely economic to combinations of economic and political causes, emanating from both capitalist and working classes. Capital endeavours to individualise all social relations between capital and labour as relations between the employer and employee, but crisis theories which embrace political content argue that the political shows the ability of each class to act in accord with its interests. The restoration of capital accumulation requires restructuring, the measures being defined by the cause, so a political content will be necessary to complement the economic measures in those theories embracing the political. The success of restructuring depends on the form and implementation of the measures, but it also depends on how deep the crises are seen to penetrate into the reproduction of capitalist social relations and accumulation. The significance of crises varies in different theories from being mild disturbances in accumulation posing no real threat to the existence of capital, at least in purely economic terms, to precipitating an economic and perhaps political breakdown of the system which can only be succeeded by another mode of production. The transformation between modes is defined by the course of economic and political action and the form of organisations used for change, sowing the seeds for a new set of social relations on which the new mode is established.

Because this work primarily concerns capital the focus will be on the economic, but references to the political will be used where this is necessary for the understanding of the theories of crisis, particularly where the assumption that wages are constant is dropped. It would be impossible to discuss all the intricacies and variants of the different theories, even purely in economic terms, and so a degree of choice has been exercised in bringing to the fore the arguments considered important. Any omissions must therefore be seen as a reflection of what I have evaluated as being central to the core theories and their arguments.

Of the theories considered, profit squeeze, the tendency for the rate of profit to fall, underconsumption and overproduction, the former two originate in the sphere of production and the latter two are sited in the sphere of circulation. The dependence of production on the circulation process has been stressed, so the theories of underconsumption and overproduction are not only related to value but operate under its law. They do not lead to the abandonment of the theory of value. One possible confusion arising in the discussion of these theories is that elements of one theory appear in another, but where this arises elements should be considered as effects rather than the primary cause, although it must be appreciated that effects can become causal in their own right in the appropriate circumstances. This causality is a knock-on, or secondary, effect for the purposes of this discussion.

The theories of crisis will first be considered from the viewpoint of early, mainly nineteenth century, writers, the final criterion being whether the theories are appropriate for the period between 1939 and 1979 which this work considers.

The theory of profits squeeze

The theory of profits squeeze is commonplace with currency from many theoretical standpoints. But at its simplest, the demand and achievement of wage rises squeeze profits, inducing the rate of profit to fall. Conventional analyses consider this outcome of wage bargaining illegitimate because the workforce is thought to be paid more than the value of its work, whereas the radical perspective sees this as quite legitimate, because the workforce is simply demanding to be paid for the full fruits of its labour. The labourforce is endeavouring to capture from capital the surplus value it produces, but in so doing this brings into question the economic viability of capitalist enterprises where wage increases have successfully captured part of the surplus value.

This analysis was not used by Marx as a cause of crisis, although it was used in conjunction with other trends during crisis.[9] This does not necessarily mean the theory is inappropriate, and certainly in recent years it has gained a lot of currency. Perhaps the most notable and influential proponents of this theory have been Glyn and Sutcliffe.[10] They argue that the squeeze is a twofold process where profits are placed between the faces of a vice. They consider the total national income, which comprises profits and wages, and show that from one side there is a tendency for wages to increase continually during expanded reproduction. This hastens a crisis which comes about from international competition pushing from the other side preventing prices being raised to compensate for the increases in wages. The end result is a crisis caused by a profits squeeze: 'we conclude that the basic reason for the decline in the profit share was the squeezing of profit margins between money wage increases on the one hand and progressively more severe international competition on the other'.[11]

There are a number of courses of action open to capital to restructure and restore profits. Inflation can nullify the effects of strong wage bargaining. This course of action may not be led by individual capitalists who are facing severe international competition, but the state can and has stimulated inflation with the intended or unintended effects of reducing the purchasing power of wages. This has particularly been the case in the seventies since Glyn and Sutcliffe proposed their arguments. A second way to counteract a profits squeeze is to stimulate investment in constant capital even if this does follow a lull in investment. The investment in constant capital will be at the expense of variable capital and, therefore, will considerably weaken the power of the labourforce in relation to capital. This will take a number of forms. First, increasing the organic composition of capital will shake out further labour, which will result in increasing unemployment. This growing pool of reserve labour weakens the bargaining power of the remaining workforce. Second, the rise in the organic composition of capital will tend to reduce or dichotomise the skill requirements of the labourforce and overall potentially lower the wages for unskilled work in the long term.[12] In these ways the vice is loosened from one side and the profits squeeze is eased.

To counteract international competition a series of protectionist measures are recommended for national capital, the focal point being import controls. This releases the pressure of competition and permits prices to rise to counteract the squeeze and so the vice is eased from the other side too.

There are a number of questions that need to be raised about the profits squeeze theory. The first question asks to what extent this theory of crisis is historically specific. During a period of prosperity when profit rates are high and are complemented by a high demand for products, labour will find itself in an increasingly strong bargaining position, especially if the supply of labour is restricted for certain skills or in total. The relative prosperity could lead to high wage demands being made and capitalists being willing to grant them on the basis of their prosperity. Simultaneously the profit rates could be falling due to other factors, which had not worked their way through the entire system and therefore have not yet appeared as falling profit rates. This is of course presupposing another cause of crisis; however, Glyn and Sutcliffe were writing during the early seventies when the first stages of the current crisis were increasingly becoming apparent and this period had been precluded by a series of high wage awards. Subsequently the crisis has deepened but wage demands have not kept pace with inflation and therefore it becomes increasingly difficult to believe that the wage demands of the late sixties and early seventies have directly or indirectly caused the recession. This must be an invitation to question this theory.

The profits squeeze theory sees inflation in terms of price rises to counteract the squeeze, yet the fact that inflation has exceeded wage rises should give rise to an expectation of restored rates of profit. Certainly this has not occurred, and it has been argued that inflation induces high wage claims more than the reverse.[13]

There is no clear evidence that wages do squeeze profits. An increase in wages may put a temporary squeeze on one capitalist producer or sector, but in turn it increases the purchasing power of the working class. This is likely to increase the consumption of commodities from department II. This can stimulate a greater investment in constant capital and so increase the demand for the means of production, giving a boost to department I. The result will be an increase in turnover and the maintenance of, or even higher, total profits although an initial squeeze would have been felt before the beneficial effects for capital had worked their way through the scheme of reproduction. This argument is very familiar to Keynesians and is also prevalent in materialist analyses, which claim that the profits squeeze theory is invalid and harks back to the thoughts of Say, who was heavily criticised by Marx. As Kalecki states: 'It follows that no absolute shift from profits to wages occurs and the argument based on Say's law would thus prove fallacious – at least with regard to the short period considered.'[14]

It is possible that the labourforce will save its additional wages or buy its own homes. This does not take the money out of the system or therefore reduce the ability to consume. The money paid for a new house, for example, would comprise the value of the house plus a rental which is passed into the hands of the builder and developer who can in turn invest or consume elsewhere.[15]

Considering wage demands from the political viewpoint, a further problem arises. Increased wage demands may be rejected by capitalist employers, but the willingness of the labourforce to pursue the demands to the point where a profits squeeze will exist to the extent that capital is overthrown depends entirely on working class consciousness. From this side of the vice the theory is political and raises questions as to the origin of consciousness and hence political motivation which would be difficult to reconcile with regularity of crises in previous centuries, and their form and duration in this century. Why consciousness is stronger in one period than another remains an open question for this theory.

Turning to the pressure exerted on profits from competition, the theory encounters a problem as to how the competition relates to the crisis, because it is viewed from the shores of one group of nations, Britain. International competition is therefore seen as an external factor. But capitalism is a world system, and thus the same laws would logically be operating in other national economies. Protectionist policies, and in particular import controls, certainly cannot be seen as a solution or part solution to profits squeeze if all countries are reacting in the same way. International trade, and hence production, would cease. While profits squeeze theorists may be tempted by this idea, it must be remembered that this is proposed as a countertendency to the squeeze for capital. Even if protectionist policies are taken on a selective basis by some nations the effect is merely to export the squeeze by further intensifying competition in remaining markets and to export unemployment caused by the crisis. This solution for capital is far from a solution but merely a displacement, and since capital has in the past successfully restructured itself from crises then the cause defining the restructuring is brought into question.

The foregoing analysis has demonstrated that the squeeze on profits from the wages side is largely a myth which can under certain circumstances lead to further expansion rather than crisis. On the side of international competition the theory fails to take account of the dynamics of capital in the world economy. Its recipes, therefore, fall short of expectations. Profits can be squeezed in the short term and this can be significant if other causes of crises are present, so it can only be concluded that profits squeeze may be an effect but not a cause of crises.

The theory of underconsumption

The cause for the underconsumption theory of crisis is located in the sphere of circulation. Although this is the location of the cause, its origin goes back to production being based on the appropriation of surplus value. The nub of the cause is that surplus value has to be realised in the profit form for capitalism to be reproduced. The expanded production of commodities is initiated from department 1 and a disproportion is set up between the level of overall production and the level of consumption during periods of expansion as capitalists invest rather than consume and total wages do not match or compensate for this. Thus all the surplus value appropriated is not realised. This underconsumption of value, and hence surplus value, leads to a crisis.

Prior to this century the problem was not seen as a very serious one, crises of underconsumption and the resulting fall in profit rates being relatively easily overcome in the long term although short term problems were thought to persist. One commentator, Tugan-Baranovski,[16] believed that underconsumption could always be overcome if investment was high and in proportion to consumption in a continual spiral of expansion. Another commentator, Hilferding,[17] saw the problem purely as one of anarchy in the market place. The merger of industrial and loan capital to form finance or monopoly capital would remove the anarchy and competitiveness of the market. This would also remove the possibility of underconsumption with production being geared towards need, rather than the production of surplus value, which would be planned by a working class state.

There is disagreement today concerning the extent to which industrial and loan capital have merged, particularly in the case of Britain, but there is general agreement that the degree of coordination between these two functions is considerably aided by states nationally and internationally. The high degree of coordination or merger has not achieved the outcome Hilferding imagined[18] and so the relevance of his analysis is certainly questionable.

Underconsumption theories have regained a greater importance in recent decades. This resurgence can be seen as a mirror of traditional trends in economic analysis, notably Keynesian economics. Indeed Kalecki was developing very similar analyses to Keynes at the same time albeit from a radical perspective.[19] It grew in popularity and a number of authors have developed analyses from this position,[20] but perhaps the most well known and consequently influential exposition of the under-consumption theory was written by Baran and Sweezy.[21]

Baran and Sweezy take the notion of disproportionality under competitive capitalism and apply it to a capitalism which they see as being controlled by a monopoly capital. The monopoly is a fusion of banking and corporate business operating on a multinational scale, the most important base of operation being the United States. Their argument is that monopoly capitalism brings about rapid technological change, with high investments in constant capital, thus lowering the value of the total output but raising the total surplus value because the reduction in value permits a greater level of consumption in the economy.

Hand in hand with this total rise in the surplus value, rates of profit increase as new technologies open up new consumer markets. For example the growth in car ownership means people can live further from work in suburban housing where the space and ability to consume more are increased. In relation to the built environment Harvey has taken up this notion.[22]

The additional surplus can either be consumed, usually on luxury commodities, it can be wasted or it can be reinvested. There is, however, a contradiction in this process. Increasingly higher levels of investment have to be achieved and this increases the output. Consequently the total demand, or effective demand in Keynesian terms, has to grow in proportion to this. On the one hand individual capitalists are trying to minimise their own wage bills to reduce costs. Department II producers hope that department I producers keep their wages low so they can afford their constant capital commodities and each department II producer hopes that all other producers keep wages high in order to keep the demand for their goods high. This cannot be realistic for capital as a whole, so on the other hand capitalists are reliant on increasing investment to ever higher levels in order to realise and reabsorb the surplus value. Baran and Sweezy explain the contradiction like this:

if total income grows at an accelerating rate, then a larger and larger share is devoted to investment, total income must grow at an accelerating rate. What this implies, however, is nonsensical from an economic standpoint. It means that a larger and larger volume of producer goods would have to be turned out for the sole purpose of producing a still larger and larger volume of producer goods in the future. Consumption would be a diminishing proportion of output, and growth of capital stock would have no relation to the actual or potential expansions of consumption.[23]

The problem here is realising the value and surplus value. The workforce is unable to consume the entire product due to the disproportion between investment and consumption under expanded reproduction, so capital must consume its own surplus. If capital does this, however, it is no longer satisfactory for its own needs of accumulation. Once this situation is perceived it is argued that further investment will be discouraged and the rate of profit will fall. Surplus value will remain unrealised and as this changing situation takes hold income and employment will decline, hence reducing the demand further.

The reversal from expansion to contraction is witnessed by the production of too much surplus value and the underconsumption of the value. Underconsumption first appears as overaccumulation of money capital as previously realised surplus value is not reinvested in the expansion of production, but is hoarded or invested unproductively in investment goods or speculative ventures.

The means to forestall or overcome the problems of underconsumption is to promote consumption through consumer credit or through state induced demand led management. State promoted consumption can take a welfare form, a capital expenditure form or a luxury expenditure form on armaments. The former two may stimulate further consumption and investment, while the latter is a luxury as it absorbs surplus, and although it may have similar effects to other state promotions in economic terms, the use values produced are seen as external to the pure economics of capital. This does not mean that the use values produced are external politically, indeed the reverse.

State intervention in the form described shares much in common with Keynesian economics although this underconsumption thesis sees the restructuring merely as a device to take capital on to a higher level of operation, thus alleviating the problems rather than solving them, underconsumption being a crisis which cannot be avoided in the long term.

Criticisms have been made of this thesis of underconsumption. One of the most important is that the theory reverses the relationship between investment and employment, in other words the relationship between production and consumption. Baran and Sweezy argue that it is the shortfall in investment that causes the crisis in relation to demand in the economy. This view implies that increased investment will again lead to increased employment and hence consumption. It has been argued that the reverse is the case. The conditions for renewed investment are not the need to increase employment further but the need to increase unemployment further. It is through these measures that wages can be pushed below the value of labour power.[24] This may reduce the immediate market, but the resulting lower values of commodities and the re-establishment of the total appropriation and realisation of surplus value potentially can lead to a rise in the rate of profit again.

Associated with increased state expenditure has been an increase in the rate of inflation. This has been considered a necessary evil by Keynesians in the past but legitimate in employment terms. Underconsumptionists have appreciated the structural effects of inflation, that is, the crisis is not solved but only postponed; however, in the last decade the link between inflation and high employment has been severed with high unemployment going hand in hand with high inflation. This cannot be explained away as the result of the adoption of deflationary or monetarist type policies because unemployment has been increasingly rising since the late sixties. Quite the reverse; deflationary policies have been adopted as a result of the failure of inflationary ones, although their lack of success has also become increasingly obvious. This criticism of Keynesian economics is also a criticism of underconsumption crisis theory. High investment does not lead to the realisation of surplus value and to the revitalisation of expanded reproduction.

A final criticism, which strikes at the core of the underconsumption theory, is that its cause is cited as being the production of too much surplus value. This has never been, at least to my knowledge, a complaint expressed, however obliquely, by capitalists. The problem has been to maintain the rate of profit, meaning the ability to maintain productivity and appropriate surplus value within the factory and then to try to realise it. This notion that capital is too successful for its own good must be considered inappropriate, even if in the late sixties and early seventies the economy was still living off the fruits of the passing boom while the recession was becoming increasingly apparent, thus giving the underconsumption theory the appearance of some credibility. Events must be considered to have overtaken the underconsumption theory of crisis.

The theory of the tendency for the rate of profit to fall

All crisis theories tend to produce a fall in profit rates, but this theory was the one extensively developed by Marx[25] and has been given pride of place as the orthodox Marxist analysis. As a result most commentators refer back to the nineteenth century analysis of this tendency. Its possible relevance as a theory is dependent on its internal consistency, but its relevance also depends on whether the explanation is appropriate in the twentieth century. Certainly capitalism has not been superseded, but its very dynamics, of which crises have been a very important component, have brought about changes in the form and operations of capital even if the fundamental social relations remain the same. It is in this context that the theory will be considered.

The cause of the theory is sited in the sphere of production emanating from the organic composition of capital. It has been stated that the organic composition of capital will increase over time with constant capital replacing variable capital in order to increase productivity. This process is generated and spurred on by competition in the market place because an increase of constant capital at the expense of variable capital reduces the value of the commodities produced and therefore potentially increases the turnover of sales and the mass of profits. This occurs for capital as a whole despite the formation towards a general rate of profit and, indeed, it is the capitals with a high organic composition that benefit from the flow of surplus value between capitals.

The organic composition will tend to rise despite this competition because exploitation, measured as the rate of surplus value,[26] will increase. Seen from the capitalist point of view a more efficient use is being made of the labour power employed, thereby considerably improving productivity.

The increase in the organic composition, whether spurred on by competition or not, will lift capital on to an expanded scale of reproduction, but this very process sows the seeds of its own crisis. The rate surplus value is increased and the mass of profits is increased by virtue of the higher sales turnover made possible by the cheapening of the cost of living. The cost of the reproduction of labour power is reduced because the values of the commodities have been reduced, in other words a rise in the organic composition of capital initially allows more use values to be produced at less value. But the increase in the organic composition of capital has a detrimental effect on the rate of profit. A higher investment in constant capital increases the proportion of dead labour to living labour, living labour or variable capital being the capital component productive of surplus value for the capitalists.[27] At first this is not significant. The reduction in the cost of living permits the output from the greater productivity to be sold. Wages can be lowered without reducing the standard of living of the workforce. This not only increases the rate of surplus value but decreases the cost price in relation to the profit, and thus rates of profit are maintained in the short term. Capitalist production changes towards producing surplus value relatively rather than absolutely.

The point will be reached when the increase in the organic composition of capital is unable to achieve successive reductions in the cost of reproducing labour power and can no longer, therefore, reduce the cost price. Although the rate of surplus value is maintained in its increased form, profit rates will now begin to fall. Hence, the increase in the organic composition of capital produces the tendency for the rate of profit to fall. This is the contradictory nature of capitalism. Expansion produces crisis, too much capital is invested in relation to the rate of exploitation *vis-à-vis* the rate of profit.

The analysis is often said to stop at this point, and indeed as far as the cause is concerned this is correct, but in my opinion it is quite clear that the analysis goes on to explain that the cause of the tendency for the rate of profit to fall creates conditions of overproduction, whereby too much is produced in relation to the market. The significance of this is that it deepens the crisis and leads to a further decline in the rate of profit because of a reduction in the realisation of surplus value.

The reduction in labour power requirements, due to constant capital investment reducing the necessary labour time, means that fewer people are required and so demand is reduced in the consumption goods market. More importantly, though, is the competition between capitals as the rate of profit falls. They will endeavour to raise the mass of profits accumulated even at lower profit rates, and this involves price cutting. Some capitalists will achieve their aims and from their viewpoint these aims are appropriate but the long term total mass of profits is reduced for capital as a whole, a condition exacerbated by the devaluing of capital which will be discussed below in relation to restructuring. So, on the one hand there is an overproduction of commodities due to the rise in the organic composition and on the other an overpopulation in terms of the labour market and therefore of the ability of people to consume what is produced due to both the cause and effect of the crisis.

A disproportionality has come into existence between the manufacturing of the means of production and the ability to consume from the producers of the means of consumption. The process is summarised in the following way:

Since the aim of capital is not to administer to certain wants, but to produce profit, and since it accomplishes this purpose by methods which adapt the mass of production to the scale of production, not vice versa, a rift must continually ensue between the limited dimensions of consumption under capitalism and a production which forever tends to exceed this immanent barrier. Furthermore, capital consists of commodities, and therefore over-production of capital implies

over-production of commodities . . . It amounts therefore to demanding that countries in which capitalist production is not developed, should consume and produce
at a rate which suits the countries with capitalist production. If it is said that overproduction is only relative, this is quite correct; but the entire capitalist mode of
production is only a relative one, whose barriers are not absolute. They are absolute
only for this mode, i.e. on its own basis.[28]

The above passage contains within it some of the elements of restructuring
necessary to restore the rate of profit and hence capital accumulation.
These now need to be made explicit.

   The crisis throws labour out of work, adding to those already displaced
by the investments in constant capital. This increase in labour supply
potentially permits wages to be pushed below the value of labour power,
hence asking labour to reproduce itself at a lower cost. Coupled with this
can be the aim to increase the intensity of labour. These measures will
restore the rate of profit in part but are not sufficient because they could lead
to more overproduction on their own. The value of capital has to be
reduced in total, although some capitals will suffer from the devaluation
while other capitals remain relatively untouched. Competition to realise
surplus value induced by the tendency for the rate of profit to fall will create
the conditions for the least competitive capitals to be shaken out. Those
who do have the best credit facilities, the higher organic composition of
capital to benefit from the formation towards a general rate of profit, those
with diverse products and markets or unique specialisms, and those having
the ability to withstand severe price cutting, thus using their mass of profits
as a cushion and sacrificing short term profits, will survive. The remaining
companies may be shaken out. The surviving companies tend to be the large
capitalists, and therefore capital concentration is one result of this crisis
theory, which involves the devaluation of the capitals going out of
business.

   Large capitalist concerns may also have to devalue their fixed capital by
closing excess capacity, selling off assets cheaply or being forced to depreci-
ate plant in the prevailing conditions, all leading to a further devaluation of
capital. It can also be devalued simply by investing even more in constant
capital, hence lifting the crisis to another level.[29] The devaluation of fixed
capital by any of these means will help to reduce the price of commodities as
it passes as constant capital into commodities.

   Constant capital is, therefore, devalued, and although the concentration
of capital lifts the development of capital on to a higher level, the devaluation appears to restore the process down to a lower level. This appearance
is real in so far as a crisis heralds the destruction of capital and hence capitalists while others survive in a stronger state; thus restructuring requires
the sacrifice of some capitalists in the interest of capital as a whole.

The problem of overproduction is in part alleviated by the devaluation of capital as this is passed on in the form of lower prices. However, from the viewpoint of not only realising the value necessary for simple reproduction, but also surplus value for future expanded production, then foreign trade, which involves selling in markets not penetrated by capitalist production, is more satisfactory and indeed necessary.

How has this theory of crisis been applied to the twentieth century? Most authors have tended to concentrate on the organic composition of capital aspect of the argument and neglected or underplayed the overproduction aspect. There are a number of exceptions, for example Mattick[30] and Yaffe.[31] Mattick considers the advent of inflation, linking it to the tendency for the rate of profit to fall, saying that it comes from two sources. First, the state increases the money supply to offset and service the debt necessary to stimulate expansion or lessen the effects of crisis for private capital. Second, capitalists put up their prices to maintain capital accumulation in the face of falling profit rates and the need of industrial capital to reassert its position against its financial and credit facilities, in other words to devalue money capital and weaken the power of loan capital.[32] He says, 'inflation is an expression of inadequate profits that must be offset by price and money policies'.[33] One aspect of state money policies and debt is that through expenditure new markets are formed, what Kalecki calls 'domestic exports', because they have a similar effect as non-capitalist markets.[34] These state policies, it is argued, lead to inflation, an argument which has been contested. The principal causes of inflation, supposedly, are high public spending and high wage demands, but these arguments suffer from the logical fallacy of competition: 'When everybody pursues the same policy (as when everybody gets up on their toes to improve or maintain their view of a passing parade), nobody finds their relative cost and export position (or vantage point) improved by their efforts; everybody ends up with lower wages (or comfort).'[35] If this statement is taken to be the case then inflation may primarily originate from the response to falling profit rates in production rather than and in spite of further exacerbation in circulation. Inflation can also be the result of the high cost of credit and state indebtedness, but both these phenomena are effects of a growing crisis as well as adding fuel to the problems. The political rhetoric is that fighting inflation involves lowering the value of labour power in order to restore profit rates. There has been an admission that Keynesian policies can no longer work, deflationary policies being adopted in their place. The analogy above remains true if everyone is adopting similar policies and thus some critics recognise that solutions to capitalist crises, and in this case the tendency for the rate of profit to fall, are not forthcoming.[36]

One restructuring advantage to inflation, regardless of its origins and precise links to the falling profit rates, is that it does devalue fixed capital and, therefore, cheapens commodities in this respect. It also devalues unrealised surplus value, contributing to the shake out and hence concentration of capital. Mattick makes a further point about devaluing capital. He states that the two world wars, apart from having imperialist implications, led to the destruction of values, both economically and physically, a process which provided the opportunity for the rapid expansion of capital, particularly United States capital, after the second world war.[37] War has, therefore, become an important means of restructuring.

A further characteristic this century has been the considerable increase in the organic composition of capital in the sphere of circulation, which has led to circulation costs disproportionately increasing compared to production. The result is a further acceleration of the tendency for the rate of profit to fall.[38] This increase in circulation is itself a symptom of overproduction, yet the sphere of circulation has not yet been subjected to the dramatic forms of restructuring being experienced in production.

Criticisms levelled at the tendency for the rate of profit to fall due to a rise in the organic composition of capital takes a number of forms. The first, and probably the most common, is that the empirical analysis of the theoretical explanation is very difficult, if not impossible, to examine. This is certainly true, but one of the main strengths of materialist analysis has been its penetration beneath the surface appearance of phenomena. If all that was needed was pure observation nothing would need to be explained. In other social sciences, such as psychoanalytic theories (and we may even include the 'hidden hand' of classical and neoclassical economics, which material analysis does explain) and the natural sciences, such as evolutionary theories or astrophysics, it is not possible to observe at first hand how empirical processes work their way through, but these theories remain generally accepted as legitimate even if everyone does not subscribe to them.[39] Nevertheless the evidence cannot be studied at first hand, so the criteria of evaluation must be whether the theory is internally consistent and whether it is appropriate to the balance of forces at work in the historical period under consideration.

Cutler, Hindess, Hirst and Hussain[40] have criticised Marx's analysis of capital, which includes a criticism of the tendency for the rate of profit to fall. Their concern is with the counteracting influences which can either be measures to postpone crisis or restore capital accumulation. Their argument is that if there are countertendencies, how can the fall in the rate of profit be seen as a universal tendency emanating from the relationship between capital and labour? Cutler *et al.*, however, conceive of counter-tendencies as processes which magically make the main tendency disappear, whereas they were conceived as processes adding successive layers to the main tendencies. The tendency does not disappear but is nullified. In other words countertendencies change the causal conditions necessary for a set of outcomes, in this case crisis–expansion–crisis, to take place. Cutler *et al.* conceive only of a linear causality, thus denying the dynamics of capital to be able to change to conditions of its own operation. Thus crises remain an inherent inevitability, but their precise timing, form and duration are subject to change because of the operation of the law of value and not in spite of it. The internal consistency of this theory is maintained.

Its appropriateness to the twentieth century is somewhat more dubious. It has of course been suggested that crises become progressively deeper and longer as the forces of production develop under capitalism; however, there does appear to have been a distinctive break at the beginning of this century. Whereas crises were periodic, although becoming worse prior to this century, in this century the norm has been crisis. Sustained crisis spanned two world wars with only a mini-boom after the first world war and the only period of sustained expansion occurring after the second world war. Can this drastic change about be explained in terms of the rate of profit falling? Mattick has tried to argue this,[41] yet it is hard to see why this disjuncture occurs. Certainly the means to restore the rate of profit has been applied in practice as avidly if not more vigorously than before, but to little or no avail. The conclusion from the effects is that the theory of crisis stating that a rise in the organic composition of capital produces a tendency for the rate of profit to fall cannot be dismissed as irrelevant or inappropriate, but it is not sufficient to explain the depth and length of crisis in this century.

The theory of overproduction

Luxemburg[42] takes up the many references of Marx to the overproduction of commodities for the size of the market. Instead of treating overproduction as an effect of the tendency of the rate of profit to fall, she considers it the cause of crises. The cause is located in the sphere of circulation although its conception cannot be divorced from the production of value, and hence surplus value, under capitalism. She states that capital cannot realistically reproduce itself on the same scale and must continually press for expanded reproduction. The initial thrust will come from the producers of the means of production, and their output is sold as constant capital to other producers, especially those producing the means of consumption, who in turn will increase output. The end result, however, will be simple reproduction and not expanded reproduction if the capitalists consume all the commodities not consumed by the workforce. This amounts to capitalists realising the surplus value at the expense of accumulation, thus producing the impossible situation of 'an expansion of production for its own sake'.[43] Under expanded reproduction capitalists must forgo their own consumption in order to expand production for the future, but this only leaves some commodities in their unrealised form. The core of the theory of overproduction is therefore that value, and hence surplus value, has been unrealised. There is an overproduction of commodities and of surplus value for the size of the market.

In one sense this theory of crisis is only the other side of the same coin as the underconsumption theory, but there is an important difference in Luxemburg's argument which makes it qualitatively different from that of Tugan-Baranovski and Hilferding to that of Kalecki and Baran and Sweezy. The significance of Luxemburg's argument is that she sees the way to overcome overproduction as selling the unrealised surplus value to foreign, non-capitalist markets. The net sales, exports minus imports, permit the crisis of overproduction to be removed under two conditions: '(1) Capitalist production supplies consumer goods over and above its own requirements, the demand of its workers and capitalists, which are bought by non-capitalist strata and countries ... (2) Conversely, capitalist production supplies means of production in excess of its own demand and finds buyers in non-capitalist countries.'[44]

The significance of Luxemburg's analysis is that once capitalism becomes a world-wide system in terms of production and consumption the crisis of overproduction becomes a phenomenon permanently on the capitalist agenda. External markets no longer exist and so the competition for internal markets becomes more and more intense, with the result that capital increasingly concentrates and centralises as weaker capitals are unable to realise the surplus value produced. This, however, does not restore capital accumulation, the source of overproduction still being present. Every attempt will be made to make new markets, but the end result will be competition, not just between individual capitals or sectors, but also between national capitals for access to markets because new markets cannot be created. This competition gives armaments production a high priority, itself an outlet for surplus value at the expense of state indebtedness. The competition culminates in imperialist wars, which redistribute markets at the expense of some national capitals and accumulation is renewed until overproduction re-emerges.

A large number of criticisms have been made of Luxemburg's thesis. Robinson[45] criticises her for forgetting that a crisis can promote further investment to reduce the value of commodities or the devaluation of capital leads to prices falling on the market. This will increase the turnover of sales and allow reproduction even if it is not on an ever extending scale. From this criticism we can conclude that the problem of overproduction may not be an independent cause by itself and can be overcome as an effect. Luxemburg states that once overproduction becomes apparent capitalists will withdraw investments. Kalecki counters this by saying that capitalists do not invest as a class but as individuals or by sector,[46] a process which leads to greater concentration at the expense of less competitive non-investing capitals which are shaken out, so renewing accumulation.

Kalecki further states that government expenditure should not be seen only in terms of consumption but also in terms of productive investment which simultaneously realises value and stimulates expanded reproduction.[47] Mattick accuses Luxemburg of divorcing her theory from the theory of accumulation derived from the laws of value. He says, 'it is therefore not the accumulation of capital that depends on the realization of surplus value, but the realization of surplus that depends on accumulation. To say this, however, is not to explain the mechanism of the realization process.'[48] Mattick of course explains the realisation process as a number of forces emanating from counteracting the tendency for the rate of profit to fall. Both Kalecki and Mattick are criticising Luxemburg not in terms of the overproduction theory itself but with the prior assumption of the validity of their theoretical standpoints. These criticisms all concern postponement by lifting the crisis on to a higher level and do not deny the existence of overproduction.

A more penetrating criticism of Luxemburg has been put forward by Rosdolsky and Mandel.[49] Rosdolsky and Mandel have respectively criticised Luxemburg for using the scheme of reproduction for the starting point of her analysis. They say that the two department model of simple and expanded reproduction used by Marx is only a scheme and not the real process of capitalist production and reproduction. The scheme was used to show that capitalism is theoretically possible as a system despite its contradictions. If it had been totally impossible of course it would not exist at all, but Marx needed to show that the system had a logical internal consistency and therefore confirm his analysis. It was only when he had shown that capitalism was a practical possibility and thus his theory of capitalism was a possibility that he could continue to demonstrate how the contradictions led to crisis under the process of expanded reproduction. The scheme is not, therefore, a theoretical point of departure or an explanation of crises and, indeed, Marx did not use it as such, developing his theory from the tendential processes at work.

This criticism of Luxemburg is entirely justified and therefore her explanation of crisis caused by overproduction must be rejected. Yet her most powerful point, which is simultaneously a theoretical and empirical one, still remains, and that is, once there is no external market for capitalism overproduction cannot as easily be overcome. In saying this, it must be remembered that overproduction is also an effect of the tendency for the rate of profit to fall. Critics of Luxemburg have tended to neglect this important contribution in their arguments, and none of the arguments invalidate this point.[50]

The synthesis

The analysis of crisis theories has not been exhaustive and nor have the criticisms of the theories, but the aim has been to provide an understanding of the main arguments and juxtapose these against some of the main criticisms. The analyses of the profits squeeze and underconsumption theories of crises have been found wanting, but the theory of the tendency for the rate of profit to fall has been considered as internally consistent and with relevance to the last century with a question mark concerning its current application. The overproduction theory of crisis was found to be methodologically unfounded but still relevant in terms of the need for external markets.

It is proposed to make a synthesis of these two aspects of crisis theory. It is quite possible to have one theory located in the sphere of production and one sited in the sphere of circulation, both acting to affect each other. It is not theoretically contradictory to propose that too little surplus value is appropriated in the sphere of production to maintain the rate of profit while too much surplus is produced to be realised in the sphere of circulation. Nor is it methodologically contradictory to take the theory of the tendency for the rate of profit to fall as the logical and chronological basis which leads to overproduction, which itself takes on a causal role once external markets have been incorporated into capitalism precisely because the means of production and consumption has been sold to these markets.

Prior to this century crises were periodic and although they became successively more severe, the crises of this century have been qualitatively different, being deeper and longer. This disjuncture between the periodic and sustained crises which occurred around the turn of the century was brought about because capitalism was becoming a world-wide system. Few external markets remained to absorb the overproduction of commodities arising from the tendency for the rate of profit to fall. As a result overproduction began to become a cause of crisis in its own right because the restructuring of the tendency of the rate of profit to fall could no longer be achieved. Devaluation of capital was now required on a massive scale over and above that achieved through concentration and the depreciation of fixed capital. The lowering of the value of labour power had no long term effect, because its success under the tendency for the rate of profit to fall is dependent on the lowering of value and hence prices of commodities through devaluation and subsequent investments in constant capital. The potential restoration of the rate of profit by pushing down wages could not be realised as the restructuring to eradicate overproduction had not been achieved, thus demand had not been restored, so capital accumulation could not be restored either.

Every effort was made to find new markets. The rise of Keynesian economics can be seen as a response to this problem. Policies of high employment levels would help increase effective demand, while state demand led management in investment and consumption terms helped create new markets ahead of accumulation. In other words the expansion of production was premised on the hope that surplus would be realised in future. The indebtedness of states led to inflation, a symptom of this postponement of overproduction, which was simultaneously being fuelled by individual capitalists increasing prices as their response to falling rates of profit. But eventually the analogy that everyone following the same policies leads to everyone standing on tiptoe, whereby no one is better off, but everyone is less comfortable, was fulfilled. Overproduction remains a world-wide crisis.

This crisis is experienced in all countries although in different ways. The leading western nations can control the rate of development of the third world countries to their needs because of their historical dominance in terms of capital accumulation. This exhibits the contradictions of capital. Leading western nations require market outlets, yet this third world consumption is historically limited while the third world consumption of the means of production could erode the dominance of the western nations if not economically and financially controlled. The eastern bloc was cut out of capitalist markets during the revolution and immediately afterwards with the result that it lagged behind the Western bloc following the counterrevolution.[51] This means the dominant eastern bloc states can only expand by maintaining an intensive rate of exploitation of satellites and their own working class. They have not historically accumulated the capital to invest in the means of production to move rapidly from the absolute to the relative production of surplus value. Their experience of overproduction is an inability to compete in the sphere of production, itself a symptom of overproduction.

The longer and deeper the crisis, the greater the causal significance of overproduction, although the tendency for the rate of profit to fall is the precondition. Following Luxemburg, the competition intensifies to reach a level of competition between nations which can only be resolved internationally. The result is twofold. On the one hand the conflict leads to a redistribution of markets between nations with a concentration of nation capital. On the other hand there is the mass devaluation of capital not simply through its destruction as value but through its physical destruction. The physical destruction gives rise to new markets during the reconstruction at the end of the conflict. The restructuring is complete and reconstruction takes place in the absence of overproduction until the tendency for the rate of profit to fall comes into play, which eventually will lead to overproduction, it again becoming the prime mover of crisis.

Those who support the tendency for the rate of profit to fall have disagreed whether this theory leads to an economic breakdown of capitalism. Luxemburg believed a breakdown would occur. In this synthesis it is proposed that a point is reached where an economic breakdown takes place, but this is usually coupled with the assumption that this inevitably leads to the succession of another mode of production. This assumption is rejected on the grounds that a political thrust has to follow an economic breakdown. If the working class can provide that thrust then succession is possible, if they do not capital is able to impose its solution, the political means being international conflict. However, the main economic conclusion, from the point of view of this analysis, is that the tasks of capital to develop the forces of production and develop the social cooperation of labour in the production process are complete and reach their limits once the tendency for the rate of profit to fall is succeeded logically and chronologically by a crisis of overproduction.

I have tried in this synthesis to take the theoretical strengths of the theory of the tendency for the rate of profit to fall, and, discarding the weaknesses of the overproduction theory, have used it to complement the tendency of falling profit rates. In so doing the shortcomings have been overcome.

Conclusion

This chapter completes the analysis of the economy as a whole. The task ahead is to show how this applies to the development and construction sectors in the British context. It needs to be stressed that in looking at particular sectors the picture is incomplete because individual capitals, sectors and nations do not exhibit the outline presented here in microcosm but contribute to and experience the effects of the whole process. Thus it has been essential first to analyse expansion and crisis in the whole economy.

2

Rents and property development

Property in general implies the right of ownership of a commodity to be used, unused or exchanged by the legal owner. In the context of the built environment it means something more specific, yet more complicated. Property is not the land, the freehold of which is owned by the landowner, nor is it just the building, which is owned like any other commodity, but in some way enshrines both. It is a truism that buildings are not physically cut off from the land and even if we had the technology to make them as mobile as, say, a washing machine, they are a precondition for other activities such as using a washing machine. There is, therefore, a physical relationship between land and buildings which is of importance in considering the social relationship between land and users. To understand this relationship, it is first necessary to consider land and ground rent.

Ground rent

The law of value and rent

The materialist analysis seeks the origin of ground rent in the production and appropriation of surplus value. This provides the means to pay rent, the landowner being able to charge rent because the capitalist needs the land to undertake production. This is the case whether the land is farmed or used in manufacture, although in the case of housing for the workforce ground rent is paid out of wages. The capitalist is not paying rent for the land as a factor of production but for its use value, that is, in the way it facilitates the production and appropriation of surplus value. It appears that ground rent is paid for the land *per se* because it is paid prior to the land being used. The quantity of ground rent, whether capitalised or paid periodically, is thus based upon the anticipated profitability of the production process undertaken on the land. The owner and the user will therefore estimate their required return on the investment and flow of profits respectively. Professional valuation techniques are trying to do this, and this is their contribution, but it is the land use which remains the crucial explanatory factor in the analysis.

To explain the origin of ground rent, its formation will be analysed. However, those familiar with the theory of ground rent may wish to proceed to the analysis of building rent.

The unlocking of this analysis requires a number of qualifications in order to clarify its basis in relation to the preceding outline.

The most crucial point is that rent is not a direct charge on surplus value. It is paid in the money form and, therefore, is located in the sphere of circulation. Rent is therefore paid out of profits. Surplus value has to be realised for rents to be paid, but, as stated, ground rent is paid prior to production. Just as capitalists are responsible for putting the labourforce to work and controlling the work process to ensure that the surplus value appropriated accords with their expectations, so too are rents agreed to accord with anticipated profit levels. Indeed, the ability to meet or even exceed these expectations is one measure of their success as capitalists, witnessed by their survival and expansion.

The quantity of rent paid is decided in the sphere of circulation during the formation and potential equalisation of the rate of profit. For ease of analysis it is assumed that the price of the commodities produced on the land remains stable except where certain conditions are relaxed to illustrate certain effects in respect of ground rent, but these conditions will be specified. It is also assumed that wages remain constant.

The formation of ground rent was considered by Marx, in answer to Ricardo, almost solely in terms of agricultural production. Ground rent is also paid with regard to industrial production, although this is more frequently capitalised, industrialists often being owner occupiers even though this trend has been decreasing.[1] Additionally, ground rent is paid with regard to shops, offices and warehousing which deal with the circulation process. Their profits are derived from a share of the surplus value from production by virtue of the specialist functions they perform, ground rent being derived from the efficiency and profitability of their operations.

The foregoing account has merely stated that ground rent is not an interest on capital invested in land but is a payment for its use[2] to which a number of qualifications have been added. The stage at which rent is paid and the stage at which the capitalist receives the amount of surplus value realised as profit, finally yielded as rent, has been stated, but no clue has been given as to the precise formation of ground rent. It is on this aspect the analysis now concentrates, which will show the formation of differential ground rents I and II plus the formation of absolute ground rent.

Differential ground rent 1

If we assume equal amounts of capital are invested on equal areas of land and surplus value produced is realised in the market place, average prices and average profits would be the anticipated result.[3] If certain land is more fertile or naturally productive than other land, profits would be greater with regard to the produce from these locations, due not to an extra effort and hence surplus value produced by the labourers, but by virtue of the natural advantages of the land, such as fertility or richness of seams. The capitalists using these lands will receive, therefore, surplus profits over and above the average profits in proportion to the advantages of the land. These differential advantages permit the landowners to charge ground rent, which is a tax on the surplus profits. This charge cannot exceed the total amount of surplus profits in the long run, otherwise the competitiveness of the users would be threatened and the reproduction of capital would be challenged, in turn removing the source of ground rent for the landowners. In order to determine the level of surplus profit on each piece of land it must be compared to the production on the worst soil where only average and no surplus profits are produced. All other soils which are more fertile will give rise to surplus profits, and hence rent, in proportion to the natural conditions. To distinguish the origin and formation of this rent it will be called differential ground rent 1, and for each location is the difference between the individual profit and the average profit.

If the demand for commodities rises, so will the price, permitting new and less naturally productive land to be brought under production. This land will become the new regulator and consequently differential rent 1 will be formed on the former worst land and will increase on all other land. If demand falls, production on the worst land will become uneconomic and the next least productive land will become the regulating land, thus inducing a decrease in differential rent 1.

Natural advantage is not the only criterion for the formation of differential ground rent 1. Location is important too. If the land is nearer to the market place, less labour time is required to take the produce to market, so forming a surplus profit, and hence potentially differential ground rent 1. Again the formation of the rent is regulated by the worst location, and so differential ground rent 1 is dependent on conditions at the physical and spatial margin. Whereas a fall in demand brings about a concentration of capital as the least advantageous locations go out of use, a fall also brings about a centralisation of capital as the most remote locations cease production.

The locational aspect is of crucial importance for industrial and commercial ground rent. Although in both cases there is no natural advantage because factories and offices are produced by people rather than being gifts of nature, labour time is saved due to favourable locations. Proximity is important in the sphere of circulation whether dealing with retailing or with management control functions and financial functions performed in offices, particularly where personal contact is emphasised. These two aspects tend to be mutually reinforcing as the latter provides a centralised market for manufactured commodities, while production can be extended if centralised locations help to speed up the circulation of capital for reinvestment.

If the demand for commodities increases, new locations to undertake production and facilitate circulation become economic and differential ground rent I increases, being highest where the greatest surplus profits are produced, realised and circulated. If demand falls, then activity becomes geographically more centralised. In both cases central business and retailing areas are where differential ground rent I remains highest. It must be remembered that only ground rent is being considered at this stage and buildings, therefore, are excluded in rent terms.

Differential ground rent II

The advantages land has are not only dependent on its nature. Its productivity can be increased by a further investment of capital. The assumption of equal amounts of capital invested in land will therefore be dropped and differential capital investments will be introduced on land located side by side and on land where there are successive investments on the same site. This potentially gives rise to the formation of another rent, differential ground rent II, the origin of which presupposes the existence of differential ground rent I. Successive investments of capital on the same or adjacent land provide the opportunity to increase productivity, thus making even greater use of the natural advantages of the land. This can give rise to surplus profits over and above average profits and surplus profits forming differential ground rent I, for which the landowners can charge differential ground rent II. This rent is, therefore, related to the differential output resulting from the additional capital investments. The capitalist land users still receive the average profit from the additional investments, although the ability to undertake this action from the users' point of view depends upon the availability of capital. From the landowners' point of view, the ability to charge differential ground rent II depends entirely on the actions of the users and not on any action by owners.

If demand increases, and assuming access to loan capital, then the users will have every incentive to invest successively more capital in the soil to

increase the output and meet the demand. With each successive investment, however, less produce will be yielded as full advantage is taken of
the natural conditions. This may not affect the average profits of the
capitalist users, but it will limit the formation of surplus profits and hence
differential ground rent II. Even though the surplus profits are decreasing
with each successive investment, these investments could put out of business other competitors operating in less advantageous conditions, the
result being that the price of production is lowered and the formation of
differential ground rent II is further limited. Paradoxically, surplus profits
are reduced yet the rent per hectare will still have increased because the
absolute surplus product will have increased, the condition necessary for
throwing other producers out of action. This is an important distin-
guishing feature of differential ground rent II. Whereas the rate of differential rent I remains the same per hectare, the rate of differential rent II
increases per hectare, though the surplus profits are falling.[4] Thus differential rent I operates relatively and differential rent II operates absolutely,
both being regulated by production under the worst conditions. Differential rent II, therefore, becomes increasingly more important as capitalism
develops. The worst land requires ever more capital investment to maintain output and hence capital tends to be concentrated on the most
favourable land in the most favourable locations. If demand is sufficiently
high the worst land and new land will be cultivated, thus maintaining and
increasing differential rent I respectively. This in turn will increase differential rent II as less capital will have been invested under the new
regulating conditions.

The tendency will be for differential rent I to be increasingly eclipsed by
differential rent II, which will be reinforced if demand falls. When
demand falls, competition is intensified, pushing down the price of
commodities, and thus the surplus profits become average profits. Production under the worst conditions ceases and a soil, site or location with
higher capital investment now becomes rentless in differential terms. The
result of the greater competition is an increased centralisation and concentration of capital, a process which paradoxically decreases the opportunity for landowners to extract differential rent II. Even though this rent
is eclipsing differential rent I, the higher investments which have historically occurred on the new regulating soil, site or location reduce the
surplus profits on other lands. If demand has fallen in relation to the
surplus product resulting from successive investments, then the total
differential rent II will remain higher than before; however, if demand
falls absolutely due to a crisis then differential rent II will fall absolutely.
This sets the scene for further opportunities for further investments on the
most favourable land to increase supply should demand increase again,

thus increasing differential rent II. Alternatively, competitors will be squeezed out if demand stays low, hence lifting the competitive cycle of centralisation and concentration to a higher level.[5]

The ability of landowners to take advantage of differential rent II depends upon the length of leases and rent review periods in relation to capital investment. Conversely, users may find conditions severe if demand drops yet differential rent II embodied in historically agreed rentals is not subject to renegotiation. Under these circumstances, surplus profits not yielded as rent may be cancelled out by rents subsequently eating into average profits. Subtractions from average profits could be handed on to the consumer as price increases only in periods of high demand, but under these conditions rent can additionally create its own existence as surplus profits increase.[6]

In the built environment where land is not used directly, in contrast to agriculture and mining, successive investments in plant, machinery, office equipment and so on permit the circulation of the surplus product to be speeded up, differential ground rent II being charged according to the labour time saved in each location. The favourable location of factories saves time in commodity distribution, that of retail outlets increases turnover and that of offices facilitates the coordination of management functions or speeds up the circulation of money capital, all giving rise to surplus profits in proportion to the locational advantages achieved compared to the least favourable location. The aspect of natural conditions, however, poses a problem. In the case of agriculture, fertility arises from natural conditions and from successive capital investments. In other spheres of production and circulation, a natural productivity does not exist, but successive capital investments do give rise to differential productivity and a speed up of circulation, but the condition and precondition for further investment require the construction of buildings. A differential ground rent II does arise because a surplus product and hence surplus profit arise, but not all the surplus profit is resolved into differential ground rent II. The complete explanation must therefore be reserved until buildings and development are considered in the context of rent.

The distinction between differential ground rents I and II becomes blurred in practice as capitalism develops, and the distinction between which part of the output arises from each successive investment cannot be empirically or analytically identified for differential rent II. Ricardo treated each investment separately, hence using a marginalist procedure, while Marx was interested in exploring the dynamics of capital accumulation and ground rent. The distinction was to show the origin and explain the formation of differential ground rent and not consider factors in isolation.[7]

Absolute ground rent

Ground rent is paid on all land which is used, even land used under the worst conditions. This is absolute ground rent, which is created by the right of freehold granted to landowners. The point of departure for absolute ground rent is differential ground rent. Capitals which have not invested heavily in tools, plant and machinery will require a higher proportion of labour power to produce the same commodities as capitals with an average or above average composition of capital. Capitals with a below average composition will produce commodities with a high value, and hence high surplus value, by virtue of the low productivity but the high amount of labour embodied in the commodities. These capitals will, therefore, produce a high rate of profit, higher than the average and general rate of profit, which means a surplus profit exists. In the outline of the law of value it was demonstrated how the equalisation of the general rate of profit was achieved by the ebb and flow of capital investment into spheres of production producing above average rates of profit. There would be a tendency for an average composition of capital, and hence average profits, to be produced amongst all capitals as a result of the ebb and flow. Landowners intervene in this equalisation process. The average profit plus the surplus profit are still produced, but instead of this stimulating the equalisation process the surplus profit is creamed off as absolute ground rent. This discourages investment and so capitals with low investment in plant and machinery are likely to remain backward in this respect.[8] Absolute ground rent is therefore a barrier to increasing capital investment and, thus, to increasing productivity by using more sophisticated methods. Absolute ground rent holds back the development of the forces of production.

Absolute ground rent does not take surplus profit out of circulation because landowners are themselves investors and consumers. Investment may be in more land or in other spheres of production and circulation. It is likely they will not invest in industrial sectors with low investment in plant and machinery, precisely because of the presence of absolute ground rent. This actually perpetuates the existence of their absolute ground rent and, indeed, investing in sectors with an above average composition of capital will increase the potential for absolute rent in other sectors. Landowners add demand for commodities through their own consumption and therefore spur on the expansion of production. Absolute ground rent, thus, should not be considered a complete brake on the development of capitalism, but as a barrier which changes the way in which it develops.

The starvation of investment in some spheres may stimulate a shortage of supply while additional consumption can increase demand for commodities, whether emanating from the investment and consumption of landowners or not. A high demand relative to supply will mean that commodities are sold at a market price above their market value. Where capital is highly concentrated and centralised a monopoly price may be charged. In both cases the price above the market value gives rise to a surplus profit above the average profit. This surplus profit can potentially be resolved into absolute rent.[9]

There are limits to the formation of absolute ground rent. Once all land is taken into use, which includes land under the worst conditions, landowners no longer form a barrier to the flow of capital, but new investments will still give rise to surplus profits forming the basis for differential ground rent II. Formerly unused land brought into use which immediately yields surplus profits may yield absolute rent if no investment, stimulated by high demand or competition, is made in the land.

It has been suggested that absolute ground rent is only appropriated for industries which directly use the land, such as agriculture, mining and extractive industries, forestry and fish farms.[10] While absolute ground rent may indeed be less for other production and circulation processes because of the capital investment in buildings and equipment, it should not be discarded completely because some spheres have not historically invested in more sophisticated means of production and circulation. This will be demonstrated in the next section.

Building rent

The landowner can be a different agent to the building owner and thus the rent accruing to the landowner, the ground rent, must be considered distinct from the remaining income flowing from the property. This would seem to leave us with the building as a commodity. The term 'development', however, implies something more than construction. Construction is a particular production process, which will be looked at in greater detail in the next chapter, and as with any other production process the commodity is exchanged for money to another agent who buys it for its use value. In the case of buildings the building user, building owner and landowner can be entirely different agents. The building producer or construction contractor is usually a different agent too. If the developer or property investor is the building owner, but neither the user, producer nor landowner, why do they undertake the action of development or property investment in a capitalist society? The notion that there must be some financial gain for the developer or property investor will be theoretically explained through the introduction of the concept which I shall call building rent.

Proposing building rent as a theoretical concept is a departure from previous analyses. There have been numerous attempts to apply the materialist conception of ground rent to the urban context, all of which have failed. Only Bruegel and Murray[11] have managed to maintain the link between the concept of value and rent derived from surplus profits in their analyses, most authors distorting the concept of rent[12] or lapsing into a Ricardian differential rent[13] when trying to apply the concept of ground rent to the sphere of the built environment. The reader is never really certain whether an urban rent is for the use of property but is paid as a rent for land, in other words as ground rent,[14] or whether the urban rent is for property and whether it is instead of or as well as the ground rent.[15]

The main problem arises from the failure to distinguish between the final use of the property, the land as a precondition for all activity and the intervening development process. This failure has led some authors to consider that construction is the source of any additional rent arising in the built environment.[16] There appears to be some logic to this if the author starts from the concept of ground rent; after all, grain is produced on farm land and buildings are produced on urban land. The final use value of the building is forgotten in this position. Grain was the commodity sold on the market, but in the built environment the building is not the final commodity, the building being rented or sold for its use value as a precondition for the carrying out of other department I or department II production and circulation processes.

Those authors who have started from the use value end of the analysis have said buildings are used in production, circulation and the reproduction of labour power and, therefore, urban land yields a rent derived in some way from its use value.[17] This ignores the qualitative difference between land used for the production and circulation of commodities which are exchanged and used elsewhere, and property in the form of land *and* buildings used in the production and circulation of commodities used elsewhere.

It is proposed, therefore, that it is impossible to conceive of an urban rent theory because of the intervention of the development process in the sphere of the built environment. It is only by breaking down the concept of property that we can analyse what is involved in the built environment concerning rent and construction. The analysis can neither start with ground rent nor with use values but must understand the physical and social relations of property in order to explain the different theoretical components. Property can be divided into three distinct components. Ground rent for the use of land has already been considered. The construction of buildings as a commodity will be considered in the next chapter. The third component is building rent which is charged for the use of the building.

Building rent is derived from surplus profit and is paid to the building owner by the building user. This will be the case whether the construction is in a rural or urban area, whether it is a building or a civil engineering construction, or whether it is a house, although in the case of housing it is paid out of wages rather than surplus profits.[18] I shall be using the concept of building rent in the same way that ground rent is used, but some important differences will emerge when this is done. In so doing I am not distorting the concept of rent. In the same way that land is a precondition of using the land in agricultural production, so too a building is a precondition for undertaking production and circulation in a capitalist society. It is a precondition because it is physically fixed in location and position as well as being fixed capital. It can, therefore, be the object of rent in the same way as land while simultaneously being an object of capital, in other words a commodity. Its use value is, therefore, something more than its value. The value embodies the labour time in its construction and while the use value reflects this it also reflects the fixed physical location of the building as a precondition of activity, and hence as a source of surplus profits in the same way that land is fixed by nature and is a precondition for other activity. Building rent is therefore socially derived whereas ground rent is both naturally and socially derived in capitalist society.

Building rent cannot be considered as an interest on an investment in buildings and thus the claims that property development and investment are purely a fraction of loan or finance capital[19] cannot be justified. Similarly the notion that the sector functions along the lines of commercial or merchant capital[20] is dubious, nor is there a distinct property capital,[21] but in the same way there are interests in the ownership of land[22] so there are interests in the development of and investment in buildings.

Differential building rent I

The analysis of differential ground rent I demonstrated that the rent was derived from two sources, the natural advantages of the land and the location of the land in relation to the market place. The more favourable the conditions the more labour time saved in comparison to production undertaken in the worst conditions. In the built environment the equivalent natural advantages do not exist because buildings are socially produced, but the locational factor does exist, although its significance diminishes in respect to differential building rent I as capitalism develops. Initial locational decisions may take advantage of natural features such as rivers for transportation or factories close to raw materials, but as capitalism develops advantages are derived from locations close to socially produced phenomena such as the central business district.[23]

Differential building rent II

The analysis of differential ground rent II demonstrated that if successive investments of capital are made on the same or adjacent land the enhanced fertility could give rise to surplus profits and hence differential ground rent II. This rent was very important in the development and concentration of capital. Differential rent II takes on even more significance in the built environment.

Successive investments of capital on adjacent locations or sites potentially give rise to surplus profits and hence differential building rent II. Differential building rent II can arise in industrial production because common services are supplied by the state or private utility companies or because the location of companies on the same estate or in the same area can give rise to industrial linkages. These and other benefits can save labour time compared to competitors operating under the worst conditions thus producing above average profits, in other words surplus profits which form the basis of differential building rent II. This assumes wages, salaries and other factors remain unchanged.

This rent will arise in the sphere of circulation where labour time is saved due to the proximity of location. Close or face to face contact may help in finance, management and retailing or between these sectors. Time saved will give rise to an acceleration of capital circulation which increases the turnover of surplus profits, being resolved into differential building rent II. The more capital invested in the built environment, the more this rent will grow. Users will still receive average profits from additional investments, but more surplus profits will be generated as capital centralises and concentrates, a process which the law of value promotes as capitalism develops and a process which differential building rent II accelerates.

In the case of differential ground rent II it was shown that if demand increases users will have every incentive to invest, but with each successive investment less produce will be yielded. This is also the case with differential building rent II. The intensity of use of density of the buildings can be increased but the benefits of investing more per square metre will reduce with each successive investment. It would be expected that the resultant drop in surplus profits would reduce the additional rent, although it will be remembered that the rent per square metre will still have increased because the absolute surplus profit will have increased. This was a condition necessary for shaking out competitors operating under worse conditions when demand fell. This also occurs in the context of differential building rent II, but, in the sphere of circulation under conditions of overproduction the process is accelerated. During the early phase of a crisis more investments will be made in the built environment in order to speed up circulation in the competition to realise surplus value, a proposition which will be investigated in the historical chapters. This increases capital concentration at the expense of weaker capitals. Two effects arise from this. Differential building rent II rises as a result of this additional round of investment in the built environment to accelerate the circulation of capital for which the buildings are used. Differential building rent II will fall once the effects of the investments have taken their toll. The least competitive capitals will have been shaken out and therefore a new regulating price of production will be established, and thus a higher average profit will be formed which will erode the surplus profits of other capitals cutting into differential building rent II. Again, this reduction in differential building rent II will not be absolute because the circulation of capital will have been speeded up in total and the rent per square metre will not have fallen.

This will hold true for only a short time. Once overproduction induces demand progressively to fall there comes a point whereby speed ups in circulation time cannot protect one capital at the expense of another and as surplus value remains unrealised surplus profits are eroded absolutely and differential building rent II must then fall absolutely. The failure of the rent to fall will eat into the average profits of users, thus adding to the threat of their reproduction.

The search by property investors, in particular institutions, for prime sites concerns the relation of the site to the remainder of the built environment. A site is prime if successive investments of capital in that area will give rise to surplus profits to the user to whom the property development will be let. This will yield the investor differential building rent II. A site can be made prime if sufficient capital is invested on that site so that it will draw other users into the area, making successive capital investments on neighbouring sites. Therefore investment on one site can induce investment on other sites giving rise to differential building rent II by successive investments in the area. Where developers concede or put forward planning gain similar results can be achieved to the benefit of the developer and the local authority.

The state contributes towards the provision of services and infrastructure. These successive investments give rise to differential building rent II. Indeed the failure of the state to make these investments, which frequently are unprofitable or yield below average rates of profit as commodities, can inhibit the growth or accelerate the decline of average and surplus profits and may induce a response of decentralisation rather than the centralisation and concentration of capital.[24] The state will receive a portion of this differential building rent II as rates. Rates form one basis of local expenditure which may give rise to surplus profits and so rates must be considered as the amount of differential building rent which does not accrue to the building owner.[25] Additional rent may be resolved as taxation for the provision of services and infrastructure on a regional and national scale.

Differential building rent II does not only arise where successive investments of capital are made in adjacent areas to a site, it also arises where successive investments are made on the same site. The act of development is itself an act of investment. This introduces the crucial difference between differential ground rent II and differential building rent II. In the case of the ground rent the landowner does not have to undertake any action to charge differential ground rent II. The decision to invest was entirely the province of the user, but this is not the case for building rent. The developer can to a very large extent determine the amount of differential building rent II to be received with respect to investment on the same site.

The amount of capital invested in development determines the size, density and quality of the development. This will influence to a large extent the range of functions that can be performed in the proposed development,[26] thus setting limits on the additional amounts of constant and variable capital employed in the use, whether for production or circulation. This in turn will decide to what extent the productivity or efficiency can be raised in the generation or realisation of further average and surplus profits. Surplus profits arising from investment in the building and the constant and variable capital accommodated in the building determine the potential for differential building rent II. The extent to which a developer can determine this portion of differential building rent II is dependent upon letting the completed development to an agent who can achieve these surplus profits. Professional valuation techniques provide a useful method for examining this problem assuming some information is available about the likely demand for premises.

Prestige buildings giving a status and image to the user are important in the capitalist economy. An international bank requires a luxurious image, inside if not always outside, to impress clients of their success in amassing average profits and, hence, coax them to place their investments in the bank's hands so it can continue to amass average profits and pay surplus profits as differential building rent II. Investments in prestige can therefore yield this rent.

Housing yields differential building rent II. Investments in housing plus services and infrastructure in neighbourhoods will determine the desirability of the residential area in terms of status in particular, plus the economy of labour time necessary to reproduce labour power. The journey to work, shops and leisure facilities are all important. Investment on the housing plot gives rise to the potential conditions under which labour power is reproduced in the home. The ease of living, in terms of cooking, cleaning, recreation and so on, contributes to the physical and mental well being of the occupants. The size, type and capacity of the house to incorporate labour saving consumption devices to ease reproduction further are all reflected in differential housing rent ii.

The difference with housing rent is that it is paid out of wages and salaries rather than directly out of surplus profits. Wages and salaries are differential and, as a generalisation, albeit oversimplified, these differentials reflect the varying degrees of dependence capital has on certain skills, abilities and ideologies. It is therefore these skills, abilities and ideologies that are given priority in reproduction. As users of housing, people representing these categories spend some of this differential in the form of housing rent in order to achieve this goal for capital and achieve their desire to increase their status and living standard. Differential housing rent ii is primarily formed on owner occupied and council housing and in the upper end of the rented sector.

Absolute building rent

Absolute building rent is formed by the interruption of the free flow of capital between sectors of production. Capitals with a low organic composition yield profits above the average rate of profit as absolute ground rent. Absolute building rent is less significant than its counterpart because the act of development increases the organic composition of capital, thus lowering the ratio of variable to constant capital. Sectors operating in the built environment in terms of production and circulation are those with a high organic composition of capital.

There are, however, differences in the organic composition of capitals in the built environment and to the extent to which these exist absolute building rent will intervene in the equalisation of the general rate of profit. Where demand is high for commodities the market price will rise above market value, or where capital is highly centralised and concentrated a monopoly price may be charged, again raising the market price above market value. In both cases this produces a surplus profit over and above average profits which can potentially be resolved into absolute building rent. In the built environment this is more significant than absolute building rent arising from a barrier being set up against the ebb and flow of capital between sectors in the equalisation of the general rate of profit.

The point of departure for absolute building rent is differential building rent II and, therefore, once overproduction first appears which gives a stimulation to investment in the sphere of circulation in the short term, this will be reflected in absolute building rent. It will hold back investment and thus prevent stronger capitals from temporarily alleviating the symptoms of overproduction and therefore will hold back the shake out of weaker capitals and stall the concentration of capital. Differential building rent II is more significant than its absolute counterpart and thus this process is not dominant.

There are limits to the formation of absolute building rent. Once all buildings are being used, including buildings which are in the worst condition and location, building owners will no longer form a barrier to the flow of capital, but new investments will still give rise to surplus profits forming the basis for differential building rent II. The barrier to the equalisation of the general rate of profit in the built environment, and hence to the formation of differential building rent II, is not absolute building rent but absolute ground rent on disused urban sites. This anticipates the discussion concerning the relationship of ground to building rent.

Absolute housing rent would appear to be an anomaly, but it does exist. Is there an equalisation of the general rate of wages? The answer to this question must be no, so how can wages and salaries be resolved into absolute housing rent? The answer lies not with wages for consumption but with wages as variable capital. Crises, absolute ground and building rent induce the unequal development of the forces of production and circulation, therefore wages and salaries will not average out between different sectors. Thus variable capital, as wages and salaries, will differ not because of competition between labourers to sell labour power as a commodity but because of the composition of capital. This variation permits the building owners or vendors to charge an absolute housing rent on houses rented or sold.

Absolute housing rent will be charged even under the worst housing conditions and thus act as a barrier to the free flow of capital into housing to improve the existing stock. It is a disincentive for building owners[27] to improve housing conditions. Why invest in housing to obtain differential housing rent II higher up the market if absolute housing rent can be charged at the lower end of the market with no expense? Thus, areas of poor housing can simultaneously have high rents even though housing conditions are deteriorating rather than improving. One way of considering council housing is that state intervention removes the obstacle of absolute housing rent which would otherwise threaten the reproduction of labour power. Absolute housing rent thus becomes differential housing rent II once the state improves housing conditions for the labourforce living under worse conditions.[28] Those living under the worst conditions in any tenure category may remain under these conditions as this section may represent the unessential labourforce to the reproduction of capital or the unemployed. Absolute rent is therefore more significant in the context of housing than in the remainder of the built environment.

Relating building and ground rents

The building owner receives the property rental from the user. This is divided into a part which contributes to the cost incurred by the owner paying for the value of the building, the other parts being building and ground rents. What, however, is the relationship between ground and building rents?

The division between these two rents depends upon the same processes which constitute the formation of rent. The building rent received by the building owner can be compared to average profits in the economy. The portion of building rent which yields an equivalent over and above average profits can be considered a surplus building rent which is resolved into ground rent. It can be seen that surplus differential and absolute building rent are therefore resolved into differential ground rent. Absolute building rent is not siphoned off as absolute ground rent.

This does not mean that absolute ground rent does not exist in the built environment. Indeed it plays a very important part. Absolute ground rent intervenes in the free flow of capital between sectors and prevents the equalisation of the general rate of profit. Absolute ground rent, therefore, intervenes in the free flow of capital in and out of development and hinders the potential formation of building rents equalling average profits. Absolute ground rent is a barrier to development and to some extent to redevelopment. This hinders the development of the forces of production in the economy and holds back the formation of differential building rent II.

Where ground rent exists the investment required to undertake development will make the development unprofitable. Using professional valuation techniques a negative land valuation represents the absolute ground rent acting as a barrier to the successive investments required to achieve average profits for the users and surplus profits yielding differential building rent II for the prospective building owner. Inner city sites exhibit the classic features of a high absolute ground rent, thus potentially minimal surplus profits for differential building rent II, a situation exacerbated by the high redevelopment costs to be passed on in the value of the building.

Successive attempts by the state to tax building rent because of its apparently speculative nature are in fact charging an absolute ground rent in the form of the betterment levy or development gains tax. These taxes merely slow or halt development activity as they prevent investment in development by in effect transferring potential differential building rent II to an absolute ground rent. The same is not true for development land tax, which has aimed in operation to make a charge on differential ground rent II arising from investment by the state or secured by the state through planning permission. If the land tax had been extended to the 100% level originally proposed it would have been taxing potential differential ground and building rent II, having the effect of setting up a barrier to investment in the form of absolute ground rent. In those cases the ground rent was accruing to the state rather than the landowner, therefore land would not appear on the market; hence the need for compulsory acquisition.

The halting or slowing of development was not the objective of policy but the failure to understand the rent relations in capitalist society led to the unintended effects. Planning on the other hand also facilitates the formation of rentals and hence building rent. Indeed the land use planning system can largely be seen as state intervention mediating between ground and building rent, particularly differential building rent II.

In order to maximise differential building rent II a degree of overall certainty is required for successive investments to be mutually reinforcing. Planning was largely conceived to be area based rather than site based, and therefore was originally more concerned with differential building rent II arising from successive investments of capital on adjacent sites or within the same area. The evolution of planning practice has seen intervention in the formation of the rent investment on the site requiring planning permission. Issues of design, layout, density and so on are seen by developers as too restrictive, although it should be borne in mind that these factors can affect the differential building rent II on surrounding sites. Successive investments side by side can mutually increase differential building rent II for all sites providing uses are compatible and preferably reinforcing through savings in labour time. Land use planning, particularly zoning, is a practice which provides some certainty concerning the potential formation and maintenance of differential building rent II with regard to successive investments in each area. Even the unintended effects of planning, such as the loophole in the third schedule of the 1947 Town and Country Planning Act, provide certainty from the developer's point of view.

Absolute ground and building rent inhibit the development of the forces of production preventing the equalisation of profit rates. In addition the interruption of capital accumulation due to crises affects sectors differently so that investment in production will vary across sectors yielding average rates of profit rather than average profits. The combined effect of these processes is that different rates of surplus profits are yielded, and hence investment in certain land and building uses will yield different rates of rent. The land and property markets reflect these differences in rents. For example, rents on office developments yield higher rents than industrial development because of the strategic position of circulation in the international operation of companies, banking and commerce in credit provision and profit realisation, a position which is enhanced under crises of overproduction.

Land uses will change if the landowner remains the same agent when the maximum rate of building rent achieved from, say, industrial property development is less than the rate of building rent received from property development for use as an office under the worst conditions. Using the net present value method of professional valuation techniques, if the answer is zero then average returns will be yielded. If the answer is positive, above average returns will be received. This in effect confirms that this office development will yield an average rate of return for that sector and yield an above average rate of return compared to the industrial property investment. If an above average rate is yielded on the office development then the ground rent could increase in sympathy.

Land used directly in production yields only a ground rent, but when developed this changes to a ground and building rent. For the landowner to want to change the land use the ground rent derived from the property rental must be higher than the ground rent from direct production. The relationship between absolute ground rent and differential building rent II is important in this respect. Invariably the ground rent will be higher in the built environment because the rent per hectare increases with successive investments of capital. Therefore, the ground rent from property development and investment is likely to be higher than ground rent for sectors which have a low differential ground rent II because of the high absolute ground rent acting as a barrier to the free flow of capital.

Absolute ground rent will act as a barrier to the formation of differential building rent II where the existing landowner sells the land to the prospective developer or user. If the landowner retains the land the ground rent need only rise after development to justify the change of land use. If the landowner sells the land then the anticipated flow of differential building rent II will be formed as absolute ground rent, which can act as a barrier to development. It will not act as a barrier if the anticipated flow of rent is estimated to be lower and this may be the case if the developer is able to obtain a more extensive and intensive use with planning permission. Alternatively the developer can hoard the land as a land bank assuming rents are rising until the historic cost of the land is reduced against costs or land prices. These arguments also hold true for housing development where rent is paid out of wages rather than surplus profits.

Planning intervenes in these processes. Designating land and areas to particular uses prevents the free transfer of property investment and development. This can ease the oversupply of buildings or the location of buildings which would reduce differential building rent II in periods of prosperity. The appearance may be that it acts as a barrier to capital. It in fact acts as a funnel which pours capital into areas to maximise differential building rent II and reduces the formation of absolute ground rent by restricting use and thus the monopoly power of landownership. If all land is used then absolute ground rent dissolves but is replaced by the potential for the formation of differential building rent II. Thus planning limits the formation of absolute ground rent promoting the formation of differential ground and building rent II in the built environment. Planning, however, does not determine rent but only influences it. It cannot operate in spite of rent, but can operate to modify rent relations and hence land and building uses over space. For example, the promotion of differential building rent II at the expense of absolute ground rent stimulates capital centralisation and concentration. Some operators will be shaken out, a new and higher level of average profits being formed and hence lower relative levels of surplus profits will be formed although at a higher absolute level. Planning, therefore, is dynamic, accelerating the inherent processes at work in capitalism but not replacing them. Indeed, it cannot go against the processes in capitalism even when more ambitious intentions are formulated.

The relationship between ground and building rent can take different forms. Long ground leases can exceed the life of a company and certainly the life of a building. The contract agreements frequently have not anticipated rental growth and certainly not inflation. This can mean that the building owner receives the building rent plus a large proportion of the ground rents despite not being the landowner where the two agents act independently.

In the historical period considered this anomaly has been reversed by the close cooperation of the landowner and the developer as the prospective building owner. Indeed the owner of land at the time of development who is usually a financial institution has usually raised the finance for the development and thus tries to take a share of the building rent. Complicated arrangements have emerged between the landowner and the building owner with the division between the rents cutting across the theoretical distinctions, being the subject of negotiation rather than strictly adhering to the underlying formation of an average rate of profit and an average profit. This distortion is possible because loan capital and absolute ground rent intervene in favour of the financial landowner as a ransom for the differential building rent II. The latter grows as capitalism develops and the anticipated flow of rent from a completed development is reflected in absolute ground rent acting as a barrier to development unless the landowner is willing and able to overcome this barrier. The landowner will be willing if it is a financial institution because capital investment in the built environment must be kept high to maintain the long term flow of ground and building rents from this and other property investments.

A number of arrangements between land and building owners can be identified which progressively complicate in practice the theoretical distinction between the two rents. The basic theoretical and empirical distinction is where the landowner leases the land to a developer, who under the lease can develop the site. The theoretical categories will be called *rents*, while the empirical prices will be called *rentals*. The arrangements which complicate the picture in practice are based on sale and leaseback arrangements.[29] The developer sells the freehold interest in a site to a financial institution, usually an insurance company or pension fund. The developer receives a capitalised ground rental plus finances for the construction of the building. On the completion of the building the developer leases back the building, a head lease, at a rental giving a fixed return to the institution on the capital invested. If the developer estimates the rate of rental to be 10% and the initial rental surplus would be 3%, the institution's equity or share is 7%. An interest on this 3% surplus would normally be conceded to the institution at, say, 25%. The estimated results are shown in the example below. If only 9% is received when letting the building in practice, the figures change. The institution still receives its fixed return and the smaller surplus is divided similarly; hence, the developer suffers disproportionately.

	Estimated income return	Actual income return
Institution	7 + 25% of 3 = 7.75	7 + 25% of 2 = 7.5
Developer	75% of 3 = 2.25	75% of 2 = 1.5
Total	10.00	9.0

However, the developer can benefit substantially from subsequent rental reviews. Assuming the original estimates of a 10% rate of rental were realised in practice and at the first five year rental review the rate of return increases by 6%, the breakdown would be as follows:

	Initial return	Rental review
Institution	7.75	+ 25% of 6 = 9.25
Developer	2.25	+ 75% of 6 = 6.75
Total	10.00	16.00

It can be seen from this that the developer primarily benefits from rental growth, particularly from increases in differential building rent II. The rental going to the institution increases by 60% while the developer's increases by 200%. This arrangement is called the geared leaseback.

The institutions realised they did well at first, but with rentals growing due to inflation and increased differential building rent II their investment in ground rent performed badly and so they began to demand ungeared leasebacks. The institution takes a share of the rental growth throughout, thus eroding the division between ground and building rent. The share or equity would be split with the institution receiving, say, 70% and the developer 30% in what is usually called the top slice or horizontal leaseback.

	Initial return		Rental review	
Institution	7.0	(70%)	11.2	(70%)
Developer	3.0	(30%)	4.8	(30%)
Total	10.0	(100%)	16.0	(100%)

The developer's position starts off stronger but is weakened with every rental review. An additional problem is that the institution is guaranteed its share, so if only a 7% rate of return is realised the developer would receive nothing. The developer takes the risks. Developers have resisted this method, arguing that the shares or equity should remain 7:3 throughout and for all income. This is the side by side slicing method or vertical leaseback.

Value of buildings

The value of a building is the same as for any other commodity, that is the labour time embodied in its construction. The value of the building is paid for as one component of rentals. This rule appears to be broken when the rental does not decrease when the original construction costs have been paid. The same is the case in the price of an owner occupied house. The construction costs are paid for over a long period, yet the price or capitalised rental does not decrease. The usual explanation put forward is that the house price embodies the current capitalised ground rent plus the replacement cost of the building. This is not the case and is obvious if the rental is not capitalised as in the case of, say, an industrial or commercial office investment. If the ground rent is discounted, the building rent does not fall regardless whether the value of the building or rebuilding has been discounted. Why is this?

A building is an item of constant capital, which is very durable, suffering little wear and tear. Compared to other items of fixed capital a very small portion will be yielded up as constant capital into the final commodities with each turnover of capital. It may be remembered from the theoretical outline[30] that constant capital can be yielded up into commodities directly, as in the case of raw materials, or indirectly, as in the case of materials consumed in the production process such as coal, electricity or wear and tear on machinery and buildings. Buildings as fixed capital will suffer a small amount of wear and tear in each turnover of capital, but over a number of turnovers this can amount to a large portion of constant capital. The use value of the building, therefore, is gradually consumed whether it is used in the sphere of production or circulation. It is worth labouring this point because it is the wear and tear which holds the key to the question although it is usually forgotten by academics in the case of buildings precisely because they are amongst the most durable items of fixed capital, whose consumption is hardly noticeable, and use value is not affected unduly by initial wear and tear. Accountants are, however, aware of depreciation.

The capitalist users and owners can either choose to pay off the value of the building or plan for the replacement at an early stage, in other words do not take profits until all debts or expenses are allowed for, or can choose to set up a sinking fund and pay for the value or replacement value of the building as the wear and tear occurs. The wear and tear is the destruction of fixed capital passing as constant capital into the final commodities. This wear and tear forms a part of the value of the commodities produced and, therefore, must enter into the price of production of these commodities. The price of production equals the cost price plus an average profit. The wear and tear enters into the cost price of the commodities, but the capitalists will be able to sell their commodities at the same price of production as competitors who may still be taking account of the wear and tear in their cost prices. The capitalists who have already paid for the wear and tear and allowed for the replacement value of their buildings have reduced their cost price but have not reduced their price of production. The wear and tear formerly entering into the equation as a cost price now enters in as an equivalent amount in the form of profit, but this produces a price of production with an above average profit while the actual wear and tear has not affected the use value of the building. The price of production becomes cost price plus average profit plus surplus profit. This surplus profit can be creamed off as building rent, mainly as differential building rent II. The equivalent of wear and tear can be charged as building rent because buildings are a precondition of production and circulation, which are physically and locationally fixed. Other components of fixed capital are theoretically movable, even if the practicalities of moving heavy plant and machinery pose problems. Plant and machinery are a condition for production, but are not a precondition in the way buildings are needed to accommodate fixed capital.

The argument concerning wear and tear is equally applicable to buildings used in circulation. Wear and tear enters into the cost of speeding up the circulation of capital whether this involves administration, distribution, retailing or banking functions. Buildings contribute towards the speeding up of circulation. The quicker capital circulates the quicker average and surplus profits can be reinvested to increase the mass of profits. The proportion of profits realised due to the acceleration of capital circulation which is over and above average profits can be resolved into building and ground rent in the sphere of circulation. A portion of the building rent can be attributed to the equivalent of wear and tear. In other words, some buildings due to their design, capacity and location permit average and surplus profits to circulate quicker and once the wear and tear of buildings has been accounted for the equivalent can form the basis of building rent.

Housing suffers wear and tear and, similarly, housing depending on its type and location facilitates the reproduction of labour power by saving the time required for reproduction compared to other housing, so even when the value of the house has been paid for the equivalent of wear and tear enters into the building or housing rent. This rent is a deduction from wages or salaries.

It appears that property rentals are either current ground rentals plus the replacement cost of the buildings or bear no relationship to the value of the buildings. This appearance is brought about because the rental, whether capitalised or not, does not diminish once the cost of the structure has been paid. Beneath this appearance the apparent anomaly is clarified once wear and tear on buildings is considered, showing how it can be resolved into building rent. The theoretically pure way of allowing for wear and tear would be to cost it as it occurs; therefore, it would enter into the cost price throughout the expected life of the building and a surplus profit would only arise should the building exceed its expected life. In practice the cost of the building is frequently written off as early as possible because it is a large debt for a company to accommodate. This is the case whether the building is owner occupied or owned by a property company. One benefit of doing this is that the value of the building improves the asset value of the company and may be used as collateral to raise finance in the future. This is particularly important in an era of inflation where the asset value or the capital investment keeps pace with inflation. Inflation has the effect of devaluing the historic value of wear and tear, but its equivalent in the form of building rent will be inflated. This is not a trick by building owners to squeeze more rent from the users. Their average and surplus profits are based on current market prices and the percentage of the surplus profits which accounts for wear and tear at current prices is resolved into building rent. This is a necessary requirement for the replacement of the building and thus for the future reproduction of capital. These practices do not of course undermine the theoretical argument, but they have the effect of adding layers of confusion which have helped to obscure the underlying processes at work.

Rent and crisis

There are two questions which need to be considered. What is the effect of rent on the users of buildings in crisis? And what is the effect of crisis on rent? The synthesis of crisis theory produced a theory whereby the tendency for the rate of profit to fall led to a crisis of overproduction. It is in this context that the question will be answered.

The initial form of crisis in this century is a fall in the rate of profit due to a rise in the organic composition of capital. Constant capital is increased at the expense of variable capital. Constant capital invested in buildings remains in the form of fixed capital for some considerable time, in other words is not yielded up as constant capital into the production and circulation process. This can pose serious problems for owner occupiers if capital is devalued, but in the case of tenants renting a building the fixed capital is paid for as it is used, that is, embodied in the rental as an element of the building value representing the wear and tear. Therefore investment in the built environment which enters into the property market does not immediately enter into the constant capital calculations of the users.

The potential use value of new buildings, and hence the way in which they are used, can permit the proportion of variable capital to be lowered immediately even if the constant capital is not increased in company accounts overnight. This still produces an increase in the organic composition of capital in the production process and can lead to a tendency for the rate of profit to fall. However in the circulation process, labour costs are reduced, which reduces variable capital used in circulation, but variable capital is a deduction from rather than a creator of surplus value in this sphere. There is therefore potentially a trade off between the benefits in circulation and drawbacks in production of investment in the built environment with respect to the tendency for the rate of profit to fall. In other words investment in buildings for production processes potentially leads to a fall in profit rates by reducing variable capital, whereas investment in buildings in circulation processes potentially leads to a restoration of profit rates in the related production process because variable capital is a cost rather than a creator of surplus value and hence profit in the sphere of circulation. Rates of profit will still fall but may be compensated initially by the acceleration in the circulation of capital at reduced cost. In the early stages of the tendency for the rate of profit to fall it would be expected to see ground and building rents rise in the sphere of circulation compared to the sphere of production. These propositions will be investigated in the historical chapters.

Once overproduction becomes causal the problem becomes one of realising value and surplus value. Again the sphere of production will be adversely affected. The demand for products will be reduced and production under the worst conditions will cease, for example in some inner cities and regions, so a higher average profit will be formed as a new location becomes the worst conditions under which production occurs, inducing surplus profits and differential building rent II to fall.

The sphere of circulation, however, gets a further boost of investment. Competition in and between sectors to realise surplus value will depend to a large extent on the speed of circulation enabling commodities to reach the market, be exchanged and the money capital handed to the producers, financiers and merchandisers. This competition will stimulate investment to improve the circulation process in the effort of companies to maintain their market standing and maybe improve it at the expense of others. Weaker productive capitals will be shaken out and some building sites therefore will fall into disuse, for example in the inner cities. This round of investment in circulation is an outcome of the first phase of overproduction and not a stimulus for growth. This will be investigated in the historical chapters.

The effect of this process will be to raise differential building rent II in the sphere of circulation. This, however, is the last opportunity for raising rent in a crisis. If surplus value is not being appropriated in the factory to maintain the rate of profit yet too much is in circulation for the size of the continually dwindling market then users of buildings, and hence land, will begin to question the rent levels they are paying. Ground and building rents will eat into average profits. This threatens the reproduction of capital.

Land and building owners are consumers and therefore constitute a market through their reinvestment and consumption of rent. This, however, is no consolation to capital because they are not adding any additional demand to the economy but merely redistributing surplus and maybe some average profits. The problem for capital is the creation and realisation of average profits.

As a crisis deepens the rental income will fall. This seriously challenges the notion that land and buildings as assets are secure in the long term. Once overproduction deepens rentals must drop and, therefore, so must the capitalised rental or capital investment of a property. Failure to do this further threatens the reproduction of capital and hence the very basis for rent. In the long term land and building owners are given no choice. In the short term, however, their beliefs in the safety of property as a long term investment are enhanced by the first phases of crisis stimulating investment in the built environment despite the symptoms of crisis.

It is the added stimulus property development receives in the initial phases of crisis that have led some authors, in particular Harvey,[31] to consider the way in which capital is supposedly switched into different circuits, investment in property being initiated by the overaccumulation of money capital. The switching of investments is a response to the economic conditions and is not therefore a structural framework for analysis. The useful point Harvey draws attention to is that investment for development in the built environment will have the effect of devaluing the existing buildings as use values. Productivity declines in relation to the productivity achieved in new developments with the result that the value of the buildings also declines. This will affect the rental which is paid for the wear and tear and thus minimise the potential building rent formed once the wear and tear is accounted for, although inflation will outstrip this process in rent terms because wear and tear will relate to current, albeit devalued, replacement costs.

The devaluation of buildings does take on a greater significance during crisis despite some contrary evidence in Britain during this century. The tendency will be to try to devalue capital during crisis, which at its deepest point can only be resolved through international conflict. The results are twofold. If a country is invaded with the aim of capturing new markets, property ownership can be redistributed and through this process fixed capital devalued and rents brought into line with the formation of average and surplus profits. The devaluation can be achieved through the physical destruction of fixed capital and hence building rent, a process which simultaneously opens up new long term markets for fixed capital. The physical destruction of capital will have the effect of reinstating differential building rent II on the remaining buildings, albeit at an absolute lower level as a large number of users have been destroyed. On the derelict sites absolute ground rent once again becomes a barrier to the formation of differential building rent II, thus protecting the existing rent on existing building uses until capital accumulation is renewed to a level to overcome the absolute ground rent, probably facilitated by state intervention.

It may be that one reason that rentals in Britain are amongst the highest in the world and certainly in Europe is that land and property ownership was redistributed and restructured through invasion in the rest of Europe during the second world war, at least in the built environment. The absence of this in Britain may have led to reinforcing the belief that property is a very secure long term investment.

The effects of a crisis at its deepest point on land and building rent are profound, and prior to the deepest point being reached land and building owners will experience the crisis in a number of ways. Undertaking development in a period of prosperity or crisis can lead to an overestimation of the demand in the market. This in turn will lead to an oversupply of floorspace. In a period of prosperity an oversupply is simply the result of misjudgement emphasised by the time lag between the decision to build and the letting of the building. During crisis oversupply is the developer's experience of overproduction. It has already been seen that initially the tendency for the rate of profit to fall and overproduction lead to further rounds of investment in the circulation process which can easily be misinterpreted as a renewed and sustained demand for floorspace. This will lead to an oversupply of space. If the developer has large uncompleted developments when the oversupply first appears in the market or confidence is lost in investment then the company may be overgeared. Overgearing is simply the commitment of too much borrowed finance for the rental income and asset backing of the company.

The experience of overproduction for the property investor rather than developer is overvaluation. The capitalised rental or capital investment or asset value of the portfolio will reflect anticipated rental growth. Failure to realise this growth in a crisis may lead to the downward valuation of a portfolio. The only test of a valuation is the open market, so that, if the particular portfolio is not up for sale or letting, comparison with other sales and rentals being achieved on similar properties will be used as a basis to revalue the portfolio in the books.

The property market is subdivided into development, investment and dealing markets, which are closely related. Similarly the experience of crisis, overvaluation, overgearing and oversupply are all closely related and ultimately return to the central question as to whether surplus profits derived from building and hence land use are being formed. This central question is regulated by production and circulation carried out under the worst conditions.

Conclusion

It has been argued that there is no urban rent theory. Rentals in the built environment can be divided into ground rent, the value of the building and building rent. The theory of building rent empirically relates to the property development, dealing and investment markets. It has been theoretically related to the value of the building and to ground rent. A further analysis has been given of the effect of building rent on building users in crisis and the effect of crisis on rent relations.

The weakness of this analysis is once again the problem of identifying the processes analysed empirically. This is a twofold problem, in that official data are not collected with the theoretical categories discussed in mind, and, second, many of these processes are the undercurrents beneath the surface. Although undercurrents are usually stronger than surface movements many of them would not be visible even if empirical data was based on these theoretical categories.

This weakness of the materialist analysis is simultaneously its strength, precisely because it does go beneath the surface appearance of phenomena. Therefore the strength of the theoretical analysis lies in its explanatory power. The problem is to fuse this with the empirical work. Before it can be seen whether this can be achieved in the historical work, it is first necessary to consider how construction and contracting can be theorised with regard to capital accumulation and crises.

3

Construction and contracting

Construction has posed problems theoretically and empirically. Like property investment and development it has not fitted into existing theoretical categories. In the case of property the problem was overcome by arguing that property had to be conceived with respect to ground and building rent plus the value of the building. The nature of the problem posed by construction is rather different. Construction is obviously a production process. Construction, therefore, is concerned with initially producing the value of the building, civil engineering works or other built forms. Like any other production process the value of the commodity is equivalent to the labour time embodied in the building or works and its price of production relates to the extent of the formation and equalisation of the general rate of profit. The construction sector empirically exhibits a rather different character to most, if not all, other production processes. It is this which has to be explained.

Virtually every text book or article on the construction industry spends a considerable amount of time describing the size and structure of the industry and endeavouring to define what construction is. These descriptions show the untypical character of this sector although they fail to explain why this is the case. It appears that the provision of the description of the different characteristics is either a justification or an explanation in itself. The most common description is that the construction sector is labour intensive with a relatively low level of capital investment. Mechanisation, flow line or mass production techniques are lacking. From this description it is generally concluded that the sector is backward; in other words, it has not made the same technological and organisational advances other industrial sectors have achieved.

This chapter will address these issues of the character of the construction industry and will examine the explanations of backwardness. It will be argued that the sector is not backward and indeed exhibits the flexibility and forwardness necessary for existence in contemporary capitalism. The character of the construction sector is explained by the way it experiences crises.

Characteristics and definitions

The industry's most conspicuous characteristic is contracting. Construction companies produce their commodities when they are awarded a contract. Two notable exceptions to this are private housebuilding for sale and construction companies acting as property developers. These exceptions, although important, do not negate the primacy of contracting as the dominant mode of operation. Construction companies or contractors[1] are responsible for the construction under the contracts they are awarded, but they are unlikely to undertake all the work, subcontracting many of the skilled and specialist jobs out to other companies. Indeed, most, if not all, of the work is subcontracted in many contracts. Subcontracting is a reflection of the dominance of the contracting system which is seen right through the spectrum of the sector. This is fine as far as it goes.

The conventional descriptive account of the construction sector usually concerns its definition. Civil engineering works, construction and building are frequently defined as different activities although the large construction companies undertake all these works and are prepared to switch their emphasis of operation according to circumstances. Certainly official statistics and classifications give no clear guide as to the definition of the sector. The Standard Industrial Classification (SIC) includes all these operations but also includes opencast coal mining and quarrying at one end and repairs, installing heating and painting at the other. Plant hire is also included. While all contractors and subcontractors are engaged in some of these activities it may be argued that not all those engaged in these activities are construction companies.

The size and structure of the industry are related to the definitional problem. At one end of the scale are very large companies operating nationally and internationally, most being engaged directly or indirectly in all the activities under the SIC definition. There are middle sized companies which concentrate on areas, regions or specialist markets. At the other end of the scale are a vast number of small firms, some only one or two people doing small works and repairs. Repairs and maintenance constitute one of the most important markets in construction and some reasonably sized companies as well as small companies operate in this area. However, some companies in other sectors have their own small works and maintenance divisions which would not statistically be classified under construction.

The academic text books usually detail the fragmented structure of the industry, cataloguing the size of the company by the number of people they employ. This shows a small group of large contractors employing large numbers and a multitude of small companies employing less than ten people. The size of output is also used as an indication of company size. How helpful are these definitions? Empirically employment is not very helpful and can be misleading. The size of the companies does not necessarily relate to the size of their workforce because of the widespread practice of subcontracting work. The size of the operations of companies is therefore underestimated by reference to the workforce size, while the number of contractors is overestimated due to the inclusion of subcontractors. The number, size and activities of subcontractors cannot be gauged from the data. In addition, labour-only subcontractors who are unregistered and usually referred to as the lump labour are not included in the statistics.[2] Output is a more useful guide but this can fluctuate substantially year to year according to the contracts on hand and the year in which they are accounted. The definition of activity, size and structure is therefore a statistical minefield.

Theoretically, the empirical evidence does not help to provide any explanation of the character of the sector operating in each definitional category. It shall not be attempted to provide a description of the sector, but should the reader wish to see how this is usually considered almost any book on construction and building will provide a detailed description. I shall be content to cast the net as wide as possible at this stage. The explanation of the construction sector's activities and organisation provided below will show it is no wonder that the sector cannot easily be defined or described, precisely because of the way in which the sector has historically evolved in relation to capital accumulation and crisis. Fragmentation, diversification and flexibility within the sector in its broadest sense, although not usually outside the sector,[3] are all important in these respects. The use of statistical data describing the industry is rejected in relation to an explanation of its character. It is not, however, a total rejection of data, which will be included to illustrate the argument. It is an explanation of the character of the industry which is sought in this chapter.

Productivity and backwardness

There are two ways of considering the notion of backwardness. The first is a technical conception whereby the sophisticated techniques employed in other industrial sectors are not applied in the sphere of construction. This, the conventional approach, will not be considered in this text, but the arguments and criticisms are documented elsewhere.[4] The second is the radical and materialist approaches which consider backwardness as a social as well as a technical relationship.

Definitions of backwardness and criticisms

The analysis of the development of capitalism provided by Marx[5] mirrors in certain respects the predominant view of conventional analyses.[6] The broad view is that capital advances through the development of the forces of production; in other words, the social and technical development of relations displaces variable capital with constant capital, so increasing productivity. More use values are produced with each commodity having a lower value because of the reduction of labour time. The increased productivity is broadly based upon the continual mechanisation of production. This is similar to the conventional analyses, but the important difference is that production is seen in social as well as technical terms.

The relations of capital were established socially prior to the technological advancement of the Industrial Revolution. Marx's conception of capitalist development started with pre-capitalist production involving simple cooperation and skills which gave way to a phase of manufacture under capitalist social relations which in turn gave rise to modern industry or 'machinofacture'. In this analysis the substitution of constant for variable capital was made possible by the establishment of capitalist social relations. The putting out of work by merchants to subsistence farmers was superseded by the merchants bringing the workforce under one roof where work could be coordinated and output controlled. Productivity was increased by intensifying the use of labour and by the division of labour in the factory to simpler repetitive tasks. This division later permitted the substitution of machines for simple tasks.[7] It was, therefore, the social relations which gave rise to new technical relations, the redefinition of labour processes and the reconstitution of the commodities produced. Craft skills were replaced by simple tasks, being in turn controlled by machinery which increasingly dictated the form, content and speed of work.

Braverman[8] and more recently Aglietta[9] have expanded these notions of the development of capitalism, drawing out the implications the analysis has for the labour process and accumulation. They have looked particularly at the application of the analysis to the twentieth century by stating that the increased division of labour and the substitution of labour for machinery give more control over the labour process to capital. On the one hand labour can be coordinated more effectively and on the other discipline imposed by the machinery intensifies the tasks performed. The subordination of labour to capital moves from a formal one based on the social relations in the main to a real subordination based on social and technical relations of capital to labour.

Braverman applies this analysis in the twentieth century by analysing how the control of the labour process has been increased through the introduction of scientific management of tasks associated with the ideas of Taylor, called Taylorism.[10] Aglietta has taken this analysis further by arguing that assembly line production with a high degree of automation, Fordism, brought in a new era of accumulation and hence capitalist development. If accumulation is to be renewed the almost complete mechanisation and automation of production, neo-Fordism, is required.

In these analyses labour is increasingly subordinated and even squeezed out of the labour process by the replacement of labour with machinery. The process is enhanced by the social character of capitalist production, militancy amongst the workforce frequently leading to a further substitution of labour for machinery. These analyses are premised upon the linear development of the forces of production and management in capitalism. There is a logical progression from one stage to another which can be summarised as: simple cooperation–manufacture–machinofacture–Taylorism–Fordism–neo-Fordism. This linear progression defines the advancement of capitalism socially and technically in production, and therefore, any sector which does not comply with this progression is considered backward.

Aglietta completely ignores the construction industry, referring to buildings purely in terms of housing for consumption.[11] Braverman pays scant attention to construction. Having harked back to the traditional analyses concerning the innate character of the commodity and work, he only offers the suggestion that components can be standardised in factory production and that the supposed trend towards mobile homes is the only indication of construction following the linear path of development.[12]

This linear path of development is clearly not applicable to the construction industry. Does this necessarily mean the industry is backward? There has been a consensus that the construction industry is indeed backward, although the explanations of backwardness differ. These explanations will be considered to prepare the way for challenging the notion of backwardness.

The construction industry has a low ratio of constant to variable capital, that is, a low organic composition of capital. The low composition implies that the value of the commodities produced has not fallen in proportion to the other sectors, and the sector therefore exhibits low productivity, which is equated with backwardness. In construction, capitalism has not fulfilled its prescribed task of revolutionising the forces of production, which advances production not only technically but socially, by inducing cooperation amongst the labourforce.

Various radical explanations of backwardness have been proposed, the most common being associated with rent and rent relations. The arguments concerning rent can be divided into two, focusing on absolute ground rent and differential building rent as the cause.[13]

The argument concerning absolute ground rent cites the presence of a low organic composition of capital as the cause of backwardness.[14] Absolute ground rent intervenes in the equalisation of the general rate of profit, that is, preventing capital being enticed into sectors with a low organic composition of capital in spite of the higher rate of profit. Had capital flowed freely the additional investment would have been invested in constant capital, thus increasing productivity and the mass of profits but reducing the variable capital and the rate of profit so that it is equalised across the economy. Absolute ground rent intervenes by creaming off the additional surplus value in the form of a surplus profit over and above the general rate of profit. This acts as a barrier to capital investment because the incentive to invest has been removed by absolute ground rent.

In the context of construction the argument is that the construction sector produces on land and has a low organic composition of capital, so it must yield a considerable amount of profits as absolute ground rent, thus explaining the backwardness of the sector. Ball[15] has pointed out correctly that the low organic composition of capital is a necessity for the presence of absolute ground rent but is not a cause. It is the ownership of land which permits the charging of rent, the effect of charging absolute ground rent being a low organic composition. Does, however, the low organic composition in construction result from the charging of absolute ground rent?

The act of development is itself an act of investment on land and thus must overcome the presence of absolute ground rent. It was argued in the previous chapter that it was the prospective building owner, frequently a developer, who has to overcome this barrier of absolute rent. This being the case the construction company would not pay an absolute rent unless the company is acting as a developer or private housebuilder. Absolute ground rent is ultimately paid by the user via the building owner. The argument ignores that construction is an intermediary production process prior to the final use of the built form on the land. The contractor only uses the land for a short period of time, probably between one and three years, while the final use will be considerably longer. Construction therefore is a means to an end, the built form being a precondition for undertaking another activity. Absolute ground rent is a barrier, but a barrier to the final use and not to construction.

Taking a hypothetical example of a developer in conjunction with a financial institution wanting to redevelop a town centre site, the developer and the institution are currently the landowners and the prospective building owners. Their objective is to minimise their costs and maximise their rental as far as possible. One of the most important elements in their costs is the price of constructing the building. They will not act as a barrier to their own objective of development. This they have overcome or taken into account in the land acquisition. They will not now charge an additional absolute ground rent to the contractor when undertaking construction; indeed, it is inconceivable how they could do this. They would only be once again paying the absolute ground rent. This would serve only to increase rentals making letting more difficult, which would either result in development being seriously impeded or building users having to generate further surplus profits to pay absolute ground rent to the landowner and absolute ground rent to the contractor via their rental payments to the building owner who has developed the hypothetical site.

The radical argument concerning differential rent is that it boosts the mass of profits in the construction sector to the extent that it acts as a substitute for the profits that would otherwise have been received from the sector investing in constant capital to increase productivity. Boosting the mass of profits from differential rent, in fact mainly differential building rent II, has the added advantage of maintaining an average rate of profit above the rates that would have existed by investing in constant capital because the tendency for the rate of profit to fall would be minimised.

This argument has primarily been put forward in the sphere of housing although it has a more general application. It is an argument which has roots in more conventional analyses,[16] but has recently received attention by Duncan.[17] He argues that when ground rent is removed as a source of profits for construction companies productivity increases. For example, in Sweden land is acquired by the state for housing and 50% of the construction finance is provided from the exchequer or National Pension Fund. Duncan states, 'The displacement of "non-capitalist" interests in Swedish housing provision since the 1940s has also been accompanied by a large increase in building productivity (c. 300% between 1950 and 1970; cf. UK 40–50%) and a change in the product so that the equipment of the dwelling has increased in value relative to the shell,'[18] whereas 'In contrast, housing provision in Britain is notorious as a vehicle for speculation where even house-building companies come to depend on land speculation for maintaining profit rates.'[19] The first point to make about Duncan's argument is that state intervention does not remove the possibility of obtaining differential building rent II because this is accrued by the housebuilder-developer when the houses are sold or rented. The state is intervening to remove absolute ground rent acting as a barrier to the formation of differential building or housing rent II. Here, then, absolute ground rent can act as a barrier to the construction industry, but only where houses and developments are built for sale or renting. Duncan's argument should be reversed. It is because the state intervenes that development takes place and it may be because profits comprise surplus value plus rents that construction is standardised and productivity can increase, rents being used to increase investment.

Productivity, however, has not increased that much even in the case of housing development. Indeed many construction companies include housing as one element of their activities. Where the state has intervened to remove absolute ground rent as a barrier to housing development an increase in productivity would be expected in line with other sectors. This has not happened. Conversely, if rent, especially differential building rent II, boosts profits in housing and property development then an increase in productivity would be expected with a spin off as new techniques are applied outside the sphere of development but within the construction sector. This has not happened. A low organic composition of capital exists despite rent and therefore either way Duncan's argument cannot be sustained with regard to backwardness.

Rent does not present a problem to the development of the forces of production in the construction sector. It does not provide an explanation of backwardness. Construction companies do not in fact pay any rent directly. They may pay rent indirectly. Rent arises from surplus profits over and above average profits or the average rate of profit for the sector. Differential ground rent I arises in part if labour time is saved as a result of locational advantages. The proximity of a construction site to materials, plant hire, labour supply and the head or regional office can all save time compared to construction projects located in the most remote areas. Labour time is also saved if natural conditions are favourable for construction. This will take account of climatic and ground conditions. This will give rise to differential ground rent I if conditions are favourable compared to those on the worst construction projects.

Differential ground rent II will arise if successive investments are made on the same site or sites in the same area. Investments on the same site would be found on a phased project where the contractor can make use of plant, labour and subcontractors in a continuous fashion. Investments on sites in the same area can occur where one contractor completes a project and another starts on a project nearby. The same labourforce could be used. These advantages are more likely to occur where the same contractor is operating in the same area and can plan the work between the two projects. Construction companies are not subject to absolute ground rent on contracts, even though they are working on the land and land is a precondition for construction. They are not subject to absolute ground rent because the dominant precondition becomes the building or civil engineering works, construction becoming the means to that end.

Construction companies acting as contractors do not pay rent because it is deducted from their tender prices through the process of competition for contracts between companies. The tender price is the price of production which the client, the building owner, agrees to pay in awarding each contract to the successful construction company. Rent, therefore, is a reduction rather than a sum creamed off as surplus profits. In periods of high demand when the capacity of the sector is fully utilised contractors will be able to retain some of the rent in their price of production and in these cases this will yield them a surplus profit which they retain for undertaking the work. It should be noted that the ground rent the contractor deducts from the tender price is in effect a payment not to the landowner but the prospective building owner. Once the development process is initiated the building or works becomes the dominant precondition.

A radical financial argument concerning the backwardness of the construction industry has been put forward by Ball.[20] He says that housebuilding requires additional finance: 'the statement that housing requires forms of finance over and above that derived from wages because housing is expensive to build is obviously a truism. But it is a truism which sites the reason for the necessity in the sphere of production and not in the sphere of circulation'.[21] Additional finance could increase productivity and hence lower the value of the commodity so that more use values can be produced at a lower value, which could facilitate the reproduction of labour power for capital. Additional forms of finance are not directly linked to increased productivity. The finance may lift the barrier imposed by absolute ground and building rent, thus having the indirect result of increasing investment in new and existing buildings to maximise differential housing rent II, and these returns could be reinvested to increase productivity in order to accelerate the circulation of capital, a process which has apparently occurred in Sweden.

It is difficult to see how Ball's argument would apply to the construction sector as a whole. Absolute ground rent has not provided a barrier to the flow of capital into the sector yet the organic composition of capital remains low, and it is not possible to explain the low organic composition of capital by the low productivity. As the low composition produces the low productivity this explanation would be tautological whereby the labour theory of value is inverted.[22] It is not even certain that finance has been restricted, and therefore any additional finance would not necessarily lead to a development of the forces of construction. Indeed attempts to develop industrialised and systems methods of construction have not revolutionised production even with state backing.[23]

It has also been argued that it is the dominance of the contracting system which is an impediment to increasing productivity, providing discontinuity of work which simultaneously has a detrimental effect on profitability and the security and conditions of work.[24] The contracting system developed out of the guilds, and using craft skills as the basis of the labour process the industry was well adapted to housebuilding and construction prior to this century. Subcontracting minimised risks in building for sale and contracting was used in building for clients.[25] The arguments focus mainly on the problems associated with the continuity of work for the labourforce, which it is argued cannot be achieved in private construction. State intervention or control could provide continuity and thus induce a change from the appropriation of absolute surplus value to relative surplus value without threatening profit rates. Implicit in these arguments, however, is the notion that if the construction sector increased its productivity then the relations of production would improve, in other words backwardness technically is also backwardness socially. The advancement is seen as necessary for capitalism to fulfil the task of developing the forces of production.

If the contracting and subcontracting system is the cause of backwardness, then the explanation of this cause either reverts back to the notion of the outmoded organisation of the industry, in this case of construction companies rather than professions, or to the nature of the commodity being produced. These are the same arguments advanced in the rejected conventional view.[26] The contracting and subcontracting system is the cause of the prevailing conditions within the sector, but this is not the same as saying that it is the cause of backwardness. The organisation of the industry may, therefore, be the result of the way in which the construction sector is related to the economy as a whole.

Conceiving and measuring backwardness

It is the place the construction sector occupies in the economy which explains the organisation of the industry, but this organisation does not necessarily mean the sector is backward despite the low organic composition of capital. Before putting forward this argument it is first necessary to challenge the notion of backwardness.

The argument concerning the linear development of the forces of production is based on high productivity as the key indicator of advancement. Virtually all commentators have adopted the linear notion of development, even though criticisms have been made of certain aspects. It is present in conventional analysis, is dominant in Marx, and total in Braverman and Aglietta. Braverman has been criticised for ignoring opposition from the workforce in the factory as a means for reconstituting the labour process[27] and for not appreciating the broader domain of political control and opposition.[28] This challenges the idea that the development of the forces of production is mechanistic, but it does not challenge the idea of the linear path.

The formal subordination of labour, it is argued, must be followed by the real subordination of labour to capital.[29] This linear progression has not occurred within construction. Mechanisation has not permitted this, and the organisation of the industry around contracting and subcontracting does not provide another means to that end. Construction, therefore, must still be craft based and hence backward. A problem arises with the use of the term 'craft', which Braverman equates with skill, arguing that the real subordination of labour induces a deskilling of the workforce. This is not the case. Mechanisation gives rise to new skills in new labour processes.[30] In construction crafts have not been superseded by complete mechanisation but this does not mean that skills have remained simple craft skills.[31] They have changed with the technical development of the forces of construction, such as they are, and with the changes in the requirements of the built commodities. These three processes are related, each affecting the other.

It can be concluded that the social and technical relations of production do not necessarily have to move from the formal to the real subordination of labour through the introduction of constant capital. Therefore, the linear path of simple cooperation–manufacture–machinofacture is not essential, even if this path has been dominant in other sectors. The implication is that construction does not move from the absolute production of surplus value because of the low organic composition of capital. Failure to follow this step does not mean that management techniques, such as Taylorism, cannot be applied to the absolute production of surplus value. It cannot be concluded, therefore, that failure to follow the linear path equals backwardness.

Critics, however, may say the productivity of the construction sector still falls short of other sectors, so that it is still backward even if it has followed a different path of development. Backwardness cannot be gauged by comparison between sectors, but only between time periods in each sector. If different paths of development exist there is no common way to measure productivity in relation to backwardness.[32] The concept of labour time can let us compare the relative productivity in different sectors, but the explanation of the productivity must be sought in the development of each sector and in its relation to accumulation in the economy as a whole. The explanation of the conditions and organisation of each sector must be historically based.

The erroneous notion that backwardness is determined by linear comparisons is being challenged.[33] Ball[34] and Tuckman[35] have argued that the industry is not backward. The labour process is different, which is the result of the contracting system. This permits, argues Tuckman, the sector to survive through the appropriation of absolute surplus value. Mechanisation takes place in the factory displacing more work off the site in materials and components manufacture, while work on site increasingly becomes a low wage assembly process. These characteristics are explained by reference to the contracting system, which allows the maximum use of labour in the appropriation of absolute surplus value because the period of employment is cut to a minimum. This is a dubious notion because it is always the province of the capitalist to put labour to work whether employed on an hourly, weekly or yearly basis. The fact that employment is temporary does not necessarily lead to an intensification of work on site. The contracting system is an expression and not an explanation of the experience of the industry. Tuckman, therefore, reverts to the notion of the nature of the commodity that it is the 'fetishism of site working' which gives rise to the technical and social relations of production.

The answer as to why the construction industry is different and not backward cannot be discovered by reference to the sector alone, but only by placing accumulation in the sector in the context of accumulation in the economy as a whole.

Construction and crisis

If accumulation in the construction sector is related to accumulation in the economy as a whole two things have to be clarified. First, the place of construction must be located in the economy and, second, the accumulation in construction has to be related to the theory of crisis. Having achieved this, it will be possible to explain the character of the construction industry in a capitalist economy. In this analysis it will be assumed that wages remain constant. In practice the sector has displayed a low degree of militancy this century, although the workforce has not always accepted attempts to push down wages during crisis.

The significance of construction and its experience of crisis

The construction industry is largely involved in the production of the means of production and circulation, department I, with the exception of housing and leisure facilities which is the production of the means of consumption, department II. Some facilities perform two functions simultaneously, such as roads and public utilities, and are frequently financed by the state. As already discussed, statistical data has limitations because of the basis on which it is collected, but as a guide to the contribution the sector makes to the built environment Ivc[36] has worked out the following estimation:

in 1977, the book value of 'stocks' (at 1975 prices) was some £34.5 billions, while the value of accumulated fixed capital was some £501 billions. Thus, over 90% of the total accumulated surplus appropriated by British capital (and held within the UK) comprises fixed capital assets, and over two-thirds (68%) of that fixed capital valuation is represented by built form – the product of construction and related industries.

Construction contributed around 6% to the gross domestic product (GDP) in the 1970s. On this basis the contribution of the sector to the economy is considerable, although this contribution is partly a reflection of the high value of the built commodities and a symptom of low productivity. However, the aim is to explain why the industry exhibits this characteristic, and so relate accumulation in the sector to the theory of crisis.

A crisis in the economy originating with the tendency for the rate of profit to fall would give way to sustained crises of overproduction once capitalism became a world system because the means to restructure the tendency for the rate of profit to fall could not be achieved. The theory of crisis concerns the whole economy and cannot be applied in microcosm to each sector or each company. Every company and hence sector does contribute to the whole process, and it is therefore possible to analyse their contribution to and experience of crises.

The construction sector produces considerable amounts of fixed capital which has the effect of raising the organic composition of capital in the economy as a whole. This contributes to the tendency for the rate of profit to fall, not only because constructions are a part of constant capital but also because they are a precondition for subsequent investments in constant capital.

The construction sector in its own right has not contributed to a significant rise in the organic composition of capital. It has already been extensively demonstrated that the sector has a low productivity, though there have been some improvements. Tables 3.1, 3.2 and 3.3 give an indication of some technical and social changes, and hence provide hints of the rise in the organic composition of capital within construction.

These improvements, and even falls in productivity, are not indicative of large scale mechanisation and, therefore, the sector cannot be considered to be contributing to the tendency for the rate of profit to fall within the economy.

Table 3.1. *Average rate of productivity increase in the UK, 1907–55*
(Percentage per annum)

	1907–24	1924–35	1935–49	1949–55
Building materials	1.9	2.1	2.3	2.5
Building and contracting	1.7	1.2	−3.6	3.6

Source: Lomax, 1959, table 8, quoted in Ball, 1978, p. 83.

Table 3.2. *Trends in output per employee, 1955–73*
(Percentage changes per annum)

	1955–60	1960–5	1966–71	1971–3
Bricks, pottery, etc.	n.a.	4.0	4.8	8.7
Construction	2.2	1.2	7.0	−2.2

Source: National Institute Economic Review (February, 1975), quoted in Ball, 1978, p. 83.

Table 3.3. *Replacement of labour by machines*

	Number of workers replaced
Excavator	20–160
Scraper	50–120
Dozer	70–90
Grader	30–50
Compactor	20–50
Building crane	30–40
Dumper	20–30
Mobile crane	10–20
Conveyor	3–5

Source: UN, 1970, quoted in McGhie, 1981.

Overproduction is not a phenomenon which can be seen in the construction sector except where construction companies are acting as builders of houses and developments for sale or renting. Overproduction is conditional on producing commodities prior to sale, whereas the contracting system guarantees the realisation of the value, and hence surplus value, embodied in the commodity prior to undertaking construction.

This does not mean the sector is immune from crises; indeed, it is frequently amongst the first sectors to feel the cold winds of recession. The construction sector does not experience crisis as one of overproduction but is affected by overproduction in the economy as a whole. Once overproduction becomes dominant one of the first items cut is investment in fixed capital. This is particularly the case in manufacturing, although it makes less than 20% of its investment in buildings,[37] and the state, which historically cuts fixed capital expenditure first. New buildings and works are more important in the sphere of circulation, accounting for around 40% of all new investment,[38] and this sphere receives two initial boosts of investment at the beginning of a crisis, one caused by the beginning of the tendency for the rate of profit to fall and the other at the first signs of overproduction becoming dominant.[39] As the crisis takes hold the contracts for construction projects will fall off and the sector is left with a lack of work. The experience of overproduction in the economy for the construction sector is underproduction.

Overproduction is the dominant cause and expression of crisis, which is characterised by too little surplus value being produced in the factory to maintain profit rates and too much being produced to be realised in the market. The construction sector experiences overproduction as underproduction, which is characterised by too little value and hence surplus value being produced to sustain capital accumulation. They are underproducers of value and surplus value. The surface appearance of underproduction is the same as the surface appearance of overproduction in the economy, that is, overcapacity.

Is this not the same as stating that the sector suffers from a low demand? Low demand, along with discontinuity of work, is certainly the empirical evidence of underproduction just as low demand and hence unrealised commodities are evidence of overproduction. Demand, however, is not an explanation of capital accumulation or an interruption of accumulation. A theoretical conception is, therefore, justified and necessary to explain the experience of the construction sector in a period of crisis and this is underproduction.

The work of others who have considered business cycles and long waves of accumulation and production of the built environment[40] has relied on descriptive accounts of demand, the demand always originating externally from the parameters of the study and therefore not in itself being explained. Underproduction in the case of contracting and overproduction in the case of building for sale are the theoretical explanations for the empirical identification of low demand. In periods of prosperity demand is high because capital accumulation requires buildings, the explanation being that capital is reproducing on an expanded scale despite its inherent contradictions. The construction sector is required to expand rapidly during these periods. In the 1960s, for example, it was estimated that if national output was to increase by 25% the construction sector would have to increase by 31%.[41] The sector, therefore, is required to be very flexible to adjust to high demand and also to low demand. Before this flexibility is elaborated it is first necessary to place the experience of underproduction into an historical context.

Construction's historical experience of crisis

Prior to this century it was argued that the tendency for the rate of profit to fall was the main engine of crisis, but it has already been stated that construction hardly experiences this tendency directly. If overproduction was not a cause of crisis in this ascendant era of capitalism, how did the construction industry experience crisis?

Prior to the establishment of the capitalist mode of production, construction had developed a number of sophisticated crafts with a high degree of cooperation, particularly on the massive construction projects for the church and the aristocracy.[42] Productivity was high. This method of simple cooperation was the form in which construction was taken into the capitalist mode of production. The sector was producing according to contract. At this stage capitalism had not developed any of the forces of production, unmechanised manufacture being the predominant method. Buildings were a precondition for manufacture, the first factories being converted houses and later ones being purposely built for manufacture and machinofacture. Buildings were physically fixed in location, and to this extent the nature of the commodity was significant in this period. Buildings were a precondition to the reconstitution of the labour process in the factory but were not themselves subject to reconstitution because the social and technical relations of production were not sufficiently developed at this time. The fact that buildings were locationally fixed and a precondition for other activities allowed the contracting system to change but not to be superseded by another method of production which could have reconstituted the labour process and commodity, and hence have increased productivity.

When crises occurred due to the tendency for the rate of profit to fall, which led to overproduction as an effect of crises, the unreleased value and hence surplus value were exported to non-capitalist markets. This was an essential component of restructuring the economy to renew capital accumulation. This could be applied to commodities produced in one place, but exchanged and consumed elsewhere. Buildings had at this stage to be consumed in the place of production. Construction commodities could not be exported. In addition contractors were operating locally and did not therefore have the ability to produce in non-capitalist markets.

From the very beginning of capitalism the sector experienced under-production. Had the sector increased constant capital at the expense of variable capital, the tendency for the rate of profit to fall would have pushed the sector out of existence because it would have been unable to restructure its own operations. For the survival of the sector and of capital it was, therefore, necessary to keep constant and variable capital as flexible as possible, in other words to minimise overheads should demand become discontinuous totally or locally. This led to the maintenance of subcontracting and the establishment of some subcontractors as contractors. Once the sector began to build for sale and renting, particularly the Georgian estates, the established form of organisation became adaptable to minimising risks[43] and, although standardisation developed at this time, the sector overall required the high degree of flexibility in terms of diversification and overheads[44] in order to maintain capital accumulation and survive crises.

In the twentieth century capitalism moved into an era of overproduction, construction being already adapted to these conditions able to respond to the needs of reconstruction or the depths of recession. The organisation of the sector had the necessary flexibility for the changing form of crises. The organisation of the industry can, therefore, be reconsidered in this context.

Flexibility and capital accumulation

The sector had not historically revolutionised its forces of construction. Construction companies do not have mechanised flow-line production, but this does not mean the industry has not changed its operations as much as other sectors. Work on site in this century has increasingly become an assembly process, resembling shipbuilding or aircraft manufacture more closely than its nineteenth century construction counterpart.[45] This is more characteristic of large projects, but in all spheres the standardisation of materials and components has taken more work off site into mechanised factories, thus reinforcing the site assembly operations.

The requirement for a sector, which experiences underproduction and historically has exhibited a different path of development, is flexibility. Reconstruction after crises places an initially strong demand on the construction industry which requires an ability to expand operations quickly. In recession the sector will wish to reduce overheads to a minimum. Sectors with a high organic composition of capital close down overcapacity and rationalise production. Contractors cannot close anything because they work to contract and construct in the location of use, and therefore reduce overcapacity by minimising overheads. This is achieved by employing directly as little constant and variable capital as possible so that when contracts are not forthcoming operations can be cut back with the minimum risk to the construction company.

Constant capital is kept flexible by hiring plant when and where it is needed rather than owning and transporting plant to any great extent. Plant hire is part of the construction sector under SIC and it is dependent on orders for the use of its services. It is closely tied into construction and related industries, and some contractors have their own hire subsidiaries. This is part of the diversification of larger companies, but their plant hire subsidiaries usually work with a high degree of independence, servicing other contractors as well as their own companies. Plant hire firms are vulnerable during crises because of the high fixed capital component, but subsidiaries are not reliant on parent companies for orders and will compete against other hire companies. The parent companies are not vulnerable should hire subsidiaries fail unless other company operations are failing. The local hiring of plant therefore minimises investment in constant capital and the location of work on site obviates the need for heavy investment in fixed building capital.

Variable capital is minimised by the subcontracting of labour or subcontracting work which involves both labour and machinery. This is crucial and means that construction companies employ directly few manual site workers. Labour is easily laid off when work becomes discontinuous and with the minimum of financial cost to the contractor. Contractors are, however, dependent on the appropriation of absolute surplus value as a result of this system. This can be achieved in part by piecework or a price for a subcontract, leaving the subcontractor to ensure that price is achieved in execution. These methods are essentially payments by results rather than by the hour or week.

The intensification of labour can also be increased by improving site operations. Gilbreth, a bricklayer in the last century who studied motion, tried to eliminate unnecessary effort in work. Gilbreth's work, combined with the work of Taylor, produced the time and motion study.[46]

Time is a crucial factor in the production of absolute surplus value. The quicker the turnover period of capital the quicker the money capital can be reinvested and renew the process, so increasing the mass of appropriated surplus value and hence profit. A large number of techniques have been applied to site and contract management to speed up the turnover of capital. The most well known and widely used method is critical path analysis, which details the estimated time taken for each operation and subcontract, the most critical series of operations in terms of the length of the contract being given the most attention. Contracts can be speeded up by crashing sections on the critical path of operations. If these sections are speeded up, so is the whole contract. Materials, plant and subcontractors are scheduled to meet the requirements of the programme. The average sized construction company has a rapid turnover in relation to capital employed compared to other manufacturing sectors.[47] The turnover is twice the turnover achieved in other sectors and underlines the different path construction has taken, yet explains how the sector has been able to increase profits despite its considerable reliance on the appropriation of absolute surplus value.

The most mature expression of minimising overheads, constant and variable capital, is the emergence of management contracting. The main contractor will not necessarily undertake any of the site work through the construction or subsidiary companies, the entire contract being subcontracted out to other agents. Subsidiaries may have to compete in the receipt of subcontracts with other companies. The management contract takes the construction company out of production *per se*, and indeed offers potential to take on the management of non-construction projects reliant on a high degree of central coordination or assembly, such as work in North Sea oil markets.

The minimising of constant and variable capital as components of overheads produces a flexibility with regard to demand, but the form of demand differs. The flexibility also allows companies to diversify their work in the long and short term by moving into and between markets. Most large contractors are very diverse in their construction work. It is a necessity to have a number of markets in order to reduce the risk on any one market. Construction companies, however, have been reluctant to diversify out of construction in its broadest definition. They have largely avoided diversification into building merchant operations, although they have diversified into raw material extraction and construction materials manufacturing. Management contracting has provided diversification opportunities outside the sector, but there has not been much diversification into sectors which produce for sale. Private housing and property development are two exceptions, but both are directly related to construction. Property development builds up the asset base of a company without threatening the minimisation of contracting overheads, while housing development is relatively independent of other contracting activity.[48]

The sector has not exhibited a marked degree of concentration; takeovers, however, can facilitate diversification. Takeovers are commonly used to diversify quickly and are prompted under two conditions. The growth of a market can result in takeovers to enter a strong market. They also take place at the end of a period of high demand because money capital reserves will have been accumulated and the policy to minimise overheads reinforces this. The loss of existing markets, therefore, prompts takeovers into new geographical and commodity markets.[49]

The policy of minimum overheads and maximum flexibility is aided by the reduction in the amount of working money capital required. Whereas the turnover of capital usually exceeds the period of production, in the case of construction the circulation of capital largely coincides with production with the exception of retention money held by the client at the end of a contract as insurance against poor work or default by the contractor. Stage payments are incorporated into almost every contract. This means the value of the commodity is realised into a money form as it is produced. This is necessary because the production process is long compared to many other industries and is possible because a contract is a guarantee of sale. Contractors are able to minimise their working capital by receiving credit from merchants and suppliers and from subcontractors, therefore payments for work during the contract can be phased to coincide with or take account of stage payments. This is in effect credit over and above facilities with financial institutions and is interest free.

There are different types of contract which have implications for the way projects are managed and profits are taken. The fixed price contract is awarded on an agreed price to undertake the basic contract. The agreement can be reached in a number of ways. Clients put the contract out to tender either in open competition or on a selective basis. Agreement can also be reached through negotiation. Under the fixed price contract the contractor has determined the price of production and is then required to manage the site so as to ensure that the appropriation of surplus value satisfies the profit margin.

The cost plus percentage contracts are based on a percentage profit for the contractor on all work undertaken. The work carried out is measured and returns are submitted for the work. There is every incentive for the contractor to increase costs to increase profits, and hence this contract is unusual and unpopular with clients. A variation, the cost plus a fixed fee, is more satisfactory to the client and costs saved can benefit the profit margins of the contractor. The contractor will increase the mass of profits by intensifying labour and reducing the turnover time of capital employed.

During periods of general prosperity with market expansion for contractors the negotiated forms of contracts, especially cost plus fixed fee, are popular. Contractors want to maximise turnover, and therefore do not wish to spend time on competitive tendering procedure. From the client's point of view a negotiated contract can often start earlier and the incentive for the contractor to complete quickly will minimise the client's interest costs and may facilitate market penetration ahead of competitors. A development of the negotiated contract is the design, build and supply contract, where the contractor coordinates the entire process by internalising or choosing their own professional consultants and arranges for the supply and installation of the plant, machinery and equipment to be used by the client on completion. This helps to accelerate completion times where one agent is coordinating the whole process. The most advanced form of this contract is the management contract, although these can be contracts obtained through selective tendering as well as cost plus fixed fee. Many contracts include agreements between contractors and unions to protect the client and contractor from unforeseen wage increases during a long contract.[50]

During periods of crisis the competitive fixed price contract is favoured. Clients are less concerned with speed of construction but are anxious to reduce fixed capital expenditure and competition in periods of low demand will depress profit margins and the price of construction will fall.

Conclusion

It has been argued that the construction sector exhibits distinctive characteristics and these are the result of the industry historically and currently working to contracts rather than production for sale. These characteristics are the result of the sector's experience of crises of accumulation as underproduction. Underproduction is empirically recognised by a lack of continuous work, a low demand and overcapacity. The sector is one of the initiators of reconstruction, buildings and civil engineering works being a precondition for renewed accumulation in the rest of the economy.

These features are characteristic of a sector that is different rather than backward and the flexibility of operation and management techniques employed are indications that the sector has advanced historically. Market diversification is a medium and longer term strategy to avoid dependence on any one market. Within each market, and the construction market as a whole, the greatest insulation from underproduction is achieved by ensuring overheads are kept flexible. Constant capital is kept to a minimum based on plant hire and subcontracting. Variable capital is minimised too through subcontracting work. The sector has developed a relationship to its labourforce based primarily on the appropriation of absolute surplus value, which is a powerful explanation of the characteristics it displays.

It has been stated that the agency of construction companies depends upon their ability to construct and compete within the sector and within the operation of the law of value.

4

Construction and the state during the second world war

Using theories of crisis, the second world war can be regarded as the result of growing international hostility at the depths of a recession. It was to transform national economies. The reconstruction period would provide great opportunities for renewed capital accumulation and prosperity, many industries restructuring their operations accordingly, while others emerged with new commodities based on technologies developed during the war.

One of the conditions for renewed economic activity was that the buildings and infrastructure were available, which was the responsibility of the construction sector. In order to undertake the massive projects of reconstruction such as power stations, steel and chemical works a sector with a larger capacity and different structure was necessary compared to the pre-war construction industry dominated by private housebuilding. The restructuring of the construction sector was therefore a *precondition* for reconstruction in the economy. This occurred during the course of the second world war, which resulted in a considerable concentration of capital among a number of large contractors, who either extended their existing capabilities or acquired new capabilities diversifying out of housebuilding into other building, civil engineering work and opencast coalmining. In other words, the construction sector's experience of crisis as underproduction had to be short lived, the end of the housebuilding boom leading rapidly to restructuring to increase construction profit rates. In so doing the sector was taken on to a higher level of activity as a precondition for reconstruction of the built environment, which was a vital component in the restructuring of the economy to restore rates of profit in industry.

This chapter analyses these twin processes of restructuring involving the concentration of capital and the diversification of work within the construction sector. The relationship between the sector and the state is of central importance to this relationship. The question is to what extent the intervention of the state into the operations of the construction sector was a hindrance, facilitative or necessary in the restructuring of the sector. To answer this question the timing and form of state intervention will be considered.

I shall argue that the intervention was necessary in order to meet the demands imposed by the war effort. These demands required changes in the structure of the industry which could not be achieved through competition alone, so the state had to take control of the construction market to meet its war aims and this restructured the sector in terms of diversification and capital concentration.

Rearmament, 1936–9

Private housebuilding had reached its peak by 1936, although it still dominated new works until the outbreak of war.[1] The growing market was government work, which rose from £11m to £66m between 1936 and 1939 (see table 4.1). The substantial proportion of this work was construction for the rearmament programme embarked upon because of the increase in international tensions. In 1936 the government outlined the rearmament programme,[2] which contained a net increase in expenditure in addition to the reallocation of existing expenditure from civil projects to defence works. The expenditure allocated for construction in this programme is detailed in table 4.2, although the programme was not completed before the outbreak of war.

Table 4.1. *Building activity in the UK: value of output in each year, 1924–39, in millions of pounds*

	1924	1927	1930	1933	1936	1939 (peace)
Dwellings	72.0	103.3	100.0	98.9	156.0	121.0
Factories	11.8	10.3	14.0	7.7	20.0	21.0
Government	6.0	6.0	4.0	4.0	11.0	66.0
Other	23.2	23.1	25.0	19.0	34.0	36.0

Source: Bowen, 1940.

A considerable amount of the work for the construction sector was for the Air Ministry. Early work involved the hard surfacing of runways on 9 airfields but later extensions and new airfields were ordered. Laing had carried out a large number of contracts for the Air Ministry during and after the first world war and was therefore well placed to receive a considerable number of contracts in the rearmament programme. Laing built 12 airfields prior to the war and a number of equipment depots.[3]

Table 4.2. *Estimated costs of the government programme in millions of pounds*

Date of estimate	Civil depts.	Service, defence & other depts.	Total	Programme completion date
June 1937	176	68	244[a]	1940
July 1938	317	150	467	1941
Sept. 1939	54	284[b]	338	1941

Notes: a. This figure includes £43m allocated for Scotland.
b. This figure includes £83.6m allocated for emergency building by civil departments.

Source: Kohan, 1952.

The programme did not involve any state intervention at this time because the government generally considered intervention would be objected to by the management of industry and might also induce political unrest.[4] For the large contractors in the construction industry the programme was a welcome tonic. Contract work had been in low demand and for those who had entered private housebuilding the market was showing signs of decline. The rearmament programme opened up new markets providing more certainty about workloads, particularly from Air Ministry work, although the War Office, Office of Works and Admiralty also had significant contract work. Construction companies could now compete in different markets taking some rearmament work, private contracts and completing housing estates, which undoubtedly led to an increase in their rates of profit. The competition between contractors was no longer aimed at obtaining shares of a decreasing market, but pivoted around obtaining shares of an increasing market. The experience of underproduction was shortlived at this stage.

The current leaders in the industry had no doubt that they could meet the growing demands, but in the long term interests of the contractors and the nation state they wished the government to announce the content of its construction programme well in advance and, furthermore, asked to be brought into consultation with the official agencies implementing the programme so that the flow of contracts could be regulated.[5] It was the private sector that was asking for indirect state intervention. This would have permitted contractors to have planned their workload and would have helped them to speed up the completion of contracts, but the government was reticent about taking this initiative or consulting with the industry's leaders. The reticence was not due to a general reluctance to intervene in industry. The state had directly and indirectly intervened in many sectors during the 1930s as the crisis deepened, but private house-building had rendered construction one of the few buoyant sectors, which government considered still required no assistance.

It was only after a memorandum from the National Federation of Building Trades Employers (NFBTE) in February 1937 that the government made the first attempt to coordinate the programme by setting up the Inter-Departmental Committee on the Building Programme of Government Departments. The committee was to ascertain which departments were responsible for implementing each part of the programme.[6] The industry had stressed that normal economic activity must continue because contractors could not rely on state contracts alone, but the regulation of the flow of these contracts was necessary if the industry was to meet the demands. The setting up of this committee did not lead to the regulation of workflow, but neither did the contractors supply the government or state agencies with information as to the respective workloads and capacity of the companies engaged in rearmament construction work. The onus appeared to be on the side of government, but the industry also failed to take the initiative in the face of government reticence. The programme began to fall behind schedule and the costs were escalating (see table 4.2). The seeds were therefore already being sown for the need to restructure the sector to meet the demands of wartime construction.

One reason for the substantial increase in costs was the extensive use of the cost plus contract, whereby there is no incentive for the contractor to keep costs down; indeed quite the reverse, the higher the costs are the higher the profit on each contract. Justification for the cost plus contract was that site work started earlier, avoiding delays in the preparation of designs, bills of quantities and tendering, but it was soon realised by the state that these forms of contract were not efficient in cost terms and in many cases were not speeding up completions. Costs had increased considerably above the estimated costs. As an indication, Admiralty expenditure on construction rose from £0.79m to £7.2m between 1935 and 1939 while Air Ministry expenditure rose from £0.9m in 1934–5 to £20.57m by 1938.[7]

One of the problems of the cost plus system was that contractors had a tendency to take on more work than they could meet and this led to fears amongst some of the industry spokesmen, such as Sir Jonah Walker-Smith of the NFBTE, that this would lead to direct government control. Accordingly a number of leading men in the industry, including Sir John Laing and Frank Taylor, lobbied for an end to the cost plus contract in favour of the target cost contract which incorporated incentives whereby the contractor retained 25% of any savings made,[8] an aim which was not achieved until the first year of war, although the War Office had adopted the target cost contract for militia camp construction by 1939 while the Admiralty had generally used the lump sum contract.

There had been a tendency for contractors to concentrate their labour on cost plus contracts at the expense of target cost and lump sum contracts in order to maximise profits. There were also accusations of contractors using underhand practices to secure labour and materials for their sites, but the nature of these practices means that they have not been disclosed. The tendency to take on too much work and to concentrate on the most profitable contracts was disruptive to the speedy completion of the programme. Although these and other underhand practices undoubtedly occurred, they should not be exaggerated. Profit margins were high at this time, regardless of underhand practices, but competition was strong for contracts put out to tender. For example, the Royal Ordnance Factory at Bridgend had been put out to tender to John Mowlem, Balfour Beatty, Topham Jones and Railton, and Sir John Jackson. Sir Robert McAlpine was on the provisional list but was not invited because it was thought '[they] were unlikely to be prepared to submit a tender except on their own terms'.[9] McAlpine had laid down terms due to cost increases experienced on other lump sum contracts, but asked to submit for this contract in competition despite possible cost increases[10] and received the contract.[11] The construction market, therefore, was still competitive in 1937.

The shortage of skilled labour, and to some extent materials, was becoming an increasing problem adding to contract costs, in particular the cost plus contracts. This was due to many contracts being located in rural areas away from the supplies of skilled construction labour. Contracts were increasingly awarded on the basis of continuity of labour supply and continuity of work for contractors in the same area. This feature was not only confined to cost plus contracts. Gee, Walker and Slater had won the service installation contract at Bridgend, but all agreed McAlpine should take over the £5,000 contract because it was further ahead with the ordnance factory contract than Gee, Walker and Slater was with their local Brackla Hill contract.[12] McAlpine also received the £580,000 contract for the filling factory no. 11 at Bridgend because it could provide continuity and hence an early completion of work even though the contract did eventually extend into the war.[13] Work was becoming more urgent and contractors were being allocated contracts rather than competing for work. For example, 14 initial emergency sites for protective balloon barrages were equally divided between Laing and Wimpey in 1938.[14] Informal arrangements were made between contractors and the state agencies implementing the programme, but no formal intervention took place at this stage.

The Inter-Departmental Committee on the Building Programme of Government Departments had considered the possibility of restricting private building, giving priority to certain contracts and finding a new source of labour supply. These questions had been deferred because direct intervention was considered unacceptable politically, but it was decided to set up formal liaison between industry and government in the form of the Joint Consultative Committee on the Building Programme of Government Departments in 1937. However, while liaison became formal, the allocation and control of work were increasingly undertaken on the basis of informal mutual agreements between the industry and the state agencies, which did not always have the desired effect of speeding up the rearmament construction programme at the minimum increase in cost.

The rearmament period saw an upturn for the major contractors, such as Laing and Sir Robert McAlpine, and provided a springboard for the others to diversify out of private housebuilding into building and civil engineering work on a national scale. Taylor Woodrow had decided to go into contracting in 1937 with the formation of Taylor Woodrow Construction, although it was not very successful in obtaining contracts in this period. However, it formed a joint company with Wimpey, who had too much work, called Western Engineering, work being shared equally.[15] Costain also began to diversify, although in the cases of both Taylor Woodrow and Costain the transition was not immediate and pre-tax profits fell as housebuilding declined and government work grew.[16]

The period was undoubtedly a favourable one for contractors with 'about half the value of all annual investment in fixed capital goods' going into construction work.[17] The outbreak of war, however, was to cause substantial changes which would transform the construction sector. Underproduction had been overcome but the restructuring of the sector through concentration and diversification had only begun in the drive to lift construction capital on to a higher level of activity.

First year of war, 1939–40

It was during this period that the government directly intervened in the operations of the construction sector, but the evolution of controls became very complex, subject to frequent reassessment and change. Figure 4.1 provides a calendar of principal programmes prior to and during the war, and it is against this background that the direct controls developed. Table 4.3 provides details of the estimated construction costs during the period between 1940 and 1945. Unfortunately the costs are

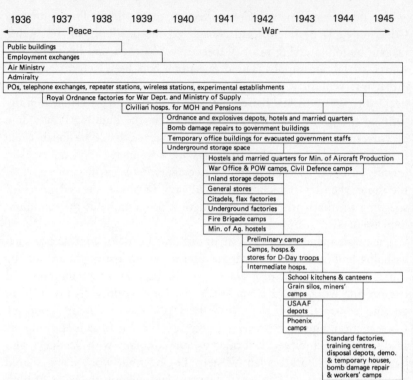

Figure 4.1. Calendar of principal programmes: new works, 1936–45
Source: adapted from Kohan, 1952.

not disaggregated on the same basis as the principal programmes, though they do provide an illustration of costs. Table 4.4 does, however, break down the costs by department for 1940.

Although the costs of the total programme increased during the war compared to the rearmament programme,[18] this cost increase did not reflect the full increase in construction activity during the first years of war. One reason was the abolition of the expensive cost plus contract in 1939. This pre-empted to a large extent the excess profits tax, which was introduced in May 1940 at a rate of 100%.[19] Not only were profits controlled but also loans were restricted by the Capital Issues Committee from the outbreak of war. The banks were erratic in their implementation of these loan controls, but the aim was to channel loans to companies engaged in defence, export, coalmining and agricultural activities. This included making loans available to contractors, but the Governor of the Bank of England in particular asked banks to increase loans to expanding subcontractors who did not receive stage payments for work done, which main contractors benefited from in maintaining their working capital and

Table 4.3. *Estimated cost of construction output*[a] *in millions of pounds*

	1940	1941	1942	1943	1944	1945
Military construction Airfields, camps and training establishments, defence works, storage depots, wireless telegraphy, etc.	140	120	125	122	49	12
Industrial facilities Factories, storage, docks and harbour works	80	76	65	46	29	25
Civil defence Air raid precautions, public shelters, etc.		42	23	12	9	[b]
Residential buildings New hostels and new housing		22	16	6	13	30
Roads and streets		2	3	3	3	2
Public buildings Hospitals, schools, etc.	88·	6	6	9	6	5
Public utilities Electricity, ports, waterways, tramways, etc.		19	16	12	8	12
Mining		13	18	16	23	26
Air raid damage	6	63	61	50	58	113
All other work	111	107	92	74	92	65
Total	425	470	425	350	290	290

Notes: a. Building and civil engineering. Firms of working principals which employed no operatives are excluded; the estimated cost of their output being £16m in 1946.

  b. For the purposes of this table it has been assumed that demolition work only was carried out under this heading in 1945.

Source: Ministry of Works and Building.

liquidity. Interest rates for loans were kept at the artificially low level of 3%.[20]

The main interventions which affected construction were those aimed primarily at the sector. To understand the evolution of controls an appreciation of the complexity of the programmes and the involvement of some

Table 4.4. *Summary by department of estimates of expenditure on building works in 1940*

	£m
Admiralty	25.048
War Office	40.599
Air Ministry	70.635
Air Ministry (factories and extensions to contractors' works)	22.712
Office of Works	25.595
Ministry of Supply	18.820
Home Office (approved schools and prisons)	2.286
Home Office (air raid precautions)	57.845
Board of Education	12.808
Ministry of Health	
Ordinary housing and hospitals	6.050
Emergency housing	17.025
Essential buildings	8.800
Children's camps	0.710
Water supply, sewerage and public buildings	15.000
Ministry of Agriculture and Fisheries	0.200
Miners' Welfare Committee	1.011
Scottish Office	
Department of Health	7.898
Education Department	3.100
Special Areas Industrial Estate	0.965
Other departments	0.552
Total	337.659

Source: Kohan, 1952.

of the main contractors in these programmes will be outlined before an analysis of the controls is possible.

One of the early war programmes was the shelter building programme which cost £57.8m between 1939 and 1940. The Admiralty had a programme costed at £7.2m in 1939 and £16.8m in 1940. Most of its work was concentrated in the south, south west Scotland and the Orkneys. The War Office's programme totalling £10m was largely controlled by the Office of Works and the Ministry of Supply. It was geographically diffuse, involving the construction of barracks, camps and ordnance or munitions factories.[21] The Air Ministry programme amounted to over £70.5m for airfield stations, 69 new stations being completed between 1939 and 1940[22] costing £200m, for which 136 different contractors were used. However, for contracts over £25,000, of which there were more than 800, only 6 contractors were used. The Air Ministry provided the largest single market for contractors, but was very selective in the use of contractors, concentrating the work into a few hands. Hudson comments about these arrangements: 'The Air Ministry were fortunate or perhaps far-sighted enough, in the early stages of the war programme, to select and encourage several contractors of repute, with national spirit, sound organisation, and resources for large-scale airfield work. It was on the foundation of those few contractors that the airfield construction programme was based.'[23] The work was specialised, particularly in plant requirements. Laing undertook the construction of 54 airfields for the Royal Air Force (RAF) and 3 air stations for the Admiralty,[24] 14 of which were built in 1940.[25] Sir Robert McAlpine undertook 20 major airfield projects which included the construction of hangars and accommodation.[26] Wimpey also had a large number of airfield contracts, its selection perhaps being due to its experience of road surfacing.[27]

The majority of the Air Ministry contracts were located in Scotland, the north, north west and Midlands,[28] while factories were being located in the north, north west, Midlands and Greater London.[29] Defence strategy demanded that these and many other construction projects were decentralised.[30] Contractors had been working predominantly in the south and south east prior to the rearmament period and war. Operations were not on a national scale and decentralised, and so companies began to develop new forms of organisation. Corporate strategies were adopted with head offices controlling a growing number of regional branches. The geographical diversification was an important component of restructuring the construction sector, expanding operations nationally from a predominantly regional basis.

The decentralisation of construction created a shortage of skilled labour. This had been the case during rearmament, but with programmes increasing and the signing up of people for the forces at the outbreak of war the problem was exacerbated. Contractors tried to keep the same gangs of workmen. The formation and maintenance of gangs obviously favoured those contractors who had built up their workforce and acted as a powerful inducement to concentrating further contracts in their hands.[31] In the case of Air Ministry work, the situation was reversed, as the contractors had already been selected and they then needed to maintain gangs in order to fulfil contracts. Accusations of hoarding and poaching labour were made between competing companies,[32] a situation which only tended to exacerbate delays caused by labour shortages. Some contractors tried to ease the labour supply by recruiting additional labour directly from Eire: for example, Wimpey had recruited 3,000 by August 1941[33] and 1,000 were recruited by Taylor Woodrow.[34]

Although there was competition to attract labour and even though the problems were eased by recruiting from Eire, contractors did not wish to enter into cut throat wage competition and so in June 1940 a Uniformity Agreement was reached between the building and civil engineering sub-sections of the sector on wages, hours and conditions of work.[35] This was important in maintaining the appropriation of absolute surplus value.

While there was competition between contractors, as well as the informal allocation of contracts to particular contractors at the outbreak of war, there was also intense competition for being considered eligible for government work. Intense undercutting occurred to receive the first contract and hence get on to the list for unlimited work. The *Manchester Guardian*[36] objected to the War Office awarding the initial militia camp contracts to a limited number of contractors, and *The Times*[37] more generally complained that the allocation of 'war contracts with an extremely small group of firms "selected on no clear principles"' could not be justified.

There was a basis, however, upon which contractors were selected. The larger contractors with experience of particular types of work were in the best position to receive contracts in competition or to be allocated work through informal channels. These contractors were unable to meet all the demands and hence the medium sized housebuilders and contractors, who could adapt the most quickly, diversifying both geographically and into new types of work, were well placed to receive the vast majority of the remaining work. Contractors who were unsuccessful in the competition for government work experienced severe underproduction resulting in an increase in bankruptcies due to price cutting in the residual and dwindling market.[38] The process of capital concentration in the sector was under way as the large and flexible middle sized firms restructured.

The larger and expanding contractors had shown considerable flexibility in responding to the increased demand, but the programmes were not being completed within the desired time. The shortage of labour, some materials and the acceptance of too many contracts by some contractors led to the programmes being delayed. The acceptance of an overload of work was an ironical situation at a time when other medium sized contractors were unable to obtain sufficient work. In this respect government intervention came too late to meet the demands of the programmes; it was, however, the growing problems of implementing and completing the programmes that led to a series of direct government interventions to control the construction market.

The Inter-Departmental Committee on the Building Programme of Government Departments had not achieved its objectives of coordinating the programmes and flow of contracts as each department closely guarded its autonomy and the committee had neither the power nor the staff to circumvent the problem.[39] Indeed, the rivalry between departments had helped to exacerbate some contractors receiving work over and above their capacity. The Control of Employment Act, 1939, did not improve the supply or competition for labour in construction. In the autumn of 1939, shortly after the outbreak of war, the Inter-Departmental Committee was reconstituted as the Works and Building Priority (Sub-)Committee[40] with the aim of giving an order of priority to contracts. This new committee came under the jurisdiction of the Ministerial Priority Committee, chaired by a Cabinet Minister without portfolio, drawing its membership from the Ministers of the service and supply departments, the President of the Board of Trade and the Minister of Labour. The Ministerial Priority Committee was replaced in May 1940 by the Production Council, which in turn became the Production Executive in December 1940 in an effort to streamline the administration, which had caused a deterioration of relations between departments.[41] The Works and Building Priority Committee remained after the dissolution of the Ministerial Priority Committee; however, the priorities for construction contracts were guidance measures and these changes had little effect on the speeding up of programmes.

It was realised that direct intervention would be required, particularly regarding the control of private civil building and the control of the labour supply, if the overall demands of the war economy were to be met. Kohan summarises the situation in the following way: 'Not until autumn of 1940 was it found practical to call a halt to the manifest waste of labour and materials on "luxury" building ... and while it was doubtless true that in the pre-war period, and later, shortages of materials did not here and there seriously retard the building programme, its effect on private enterprise building was not conspicuous.'[42] The problems were not simply private versus public works, but were more and more concerned with the implementation of the defence programme on its own terms. The contractors, however, feared that intervention might lead to the nationalisation of the sector. They argued, 'the more private enterprise is allowed to function profitably, the greater will be the financial resources upon which the Government will be able to draw for war purposes'.[43]

In fact the profitability and the private ownership of the construction industry were not in question. The government interventions were always aimed to control the market rather than replace it. Bevin, who was the Minister of Labour, proposed that a new Ministry be set up to take direct control of the construction programme. This was the Ministry of Works and Buildings (MOWB), established in October 1940, which absorbed the former Office of Works.[44] Lord Reith became the first Minister of the

MOWB, inheriting a programme about which the government knew little in terms of labour and materials requirements or even work in progress as accurate records had not been kept. Reith acidly wrote: 'About twenty departments were involved; all fighting for priority; all competing for labour and materials. A great number of private firms were at work on their own, or under the *aegis* of some department or several departments. Quite chaotic.'[45] Reith was criticised for his attitude and bluntness which made him very unpopular with Churchill, eventually leading to his dismissal in 1942.[46] Despite his political naivety, he did make an important contribution towards coordinating the programmes, which perhaps could most easily be achieved by someone formerly outside the centre of politics. The Ministries of Service and Supply did retain control of their respective construction programmes, but the MOWB had an overview of all construction, even that outside its control, because Reith was a member of the Production Council.[47] A system of priorities had been established by the Production Council in June 1940 to coordinate the programmes. The War Cabinet had the power to designate contracts 'super-priority' while the remainder were designated: WBA – high priority; Neutral; WBZ – low priority. Although labour and materials could be withdrawn from WBZ contracts, in practice few contracts were designated Neutral or WBZ.[48] The failure by government to improve its implementation of the programme led the MOWB, shortly after its formation, to restrict private civil building. New works exceeding £500 in cost required a licence. The costs were lowered to £100 and to £10 in the London area. The effect of these measures was not felt until 1941 and so improvement in the implementation and completion of programmes did not occur in the first years of the war.

The powers for the Minister of Labour to control the employment of all labour came into being under Regulation 58A of the Defence (General) Regulations Act, 1940. All labour was required to register through the employment exchange when seeking employment and employers were not supposed to advertise posts. The Minister did not, however, use these powers immediately, but these measures and the restriction of private building were the foundations for the control of construction in 1941.

In summary, the government had been slow to recognise the need for direct intervention to control the flow and allocation of contracts and labour. Political considerations had led to a reticence to take direct measures during rearmament or make contingency plans in the event of war, and a lack of knowledge in the state agencies plus the rivalry between the agencies prevented a central coordination of the programme prior to the formation of the MOWB and the passing of the Defence (General)

Regulations Act in 1940. Large contracts were placed in the hands of a relatively few number of contractors compared to the size of the programmes, especially in the case of the Air Ministry's programme. This occurred through both tendering and the informal allocation of contracts. The result was that a large number of medium sized and small companies were squeezed out of the market, some of whom were shaken out of business.

The sharing out of the market into a relatively small number of hands resulted in a concentration of capital in the construction sector which did not meet the immediate requirements of the state agencies to speed up the completion rate of the construction programmes. However, in terms of the requirements of the construction programmes at the end of the war and during reconstruction this concentration of capital was advantageous. For individual companies engaged in the programmes turnover had increased dramatically, even if this was not always reflected in profits immediately, and work had diversified in nature and geographical distribution.

1941

The priority system for contracts began to break down, with few contracts being designated Neutral or WBZ. This problem was seriously exacerbated by the blitz, which caused the War Cabinet increasingly to resort to designating air raid damage repairs, proposals to disperse factory locations and special airfield work as super-priority between September 1940 and May 1941. The result was the failure of the priority system.[49] An overhaul was necessary which was announced by the Parliamentary Secretary of the MOWB, George Hicks, in Parliament:

We have, therefore, instituted a new system which is just coming into operation, whereby we first estimate the total quantity of building of which the resources of the country is capable in each given period. We measure this by value and, in accordance with the instructions of the Production Executive, we allocate it between Departments so that each Department knows what share of the building capacity of the country it will have at its disposal for a given period ... It is the job of the Departments to arrange with their own allocation which jobs are to be speeded up, which to be stopped, and so on. We are limiting the programme so that the amount of construction work to be undertaken will be as closely as possible related to the labour and materials available, and, as far as possible, only those works which will be effective before or by the end of the summer are being proceeded with. Works requiring a longer period for their completion or new works are only being permitted if they are of great strategic importance.[50]

In March 1941 the Ministry of Supply's work was also brought under the jurisdiction of the MOWB.[51] Control was centralised within central government, whereas the implementation of the programme was coordinated by the appropriate state agencies, the operation and construction of the programme being handled at a national, regional and district level depending on the nature of the project.

The centralisation of control within government was dependent upon the control of labour as this was more crucial than the supply of materials. The powers of the Ministry of Labour under Regulation 58A of the Defence (General) Regulations Act, 1940, were used to control the labour supply. Labour could only be engaged through employment exchanges, and using the Essential Works Order could be allocated to specific contracts. This required a greater knowledge of the supply of labour and contract requirements in order to coordinate the programmes. This information was unavailable due to the shortcomings of previous attempts at coordination, so a Director of the Building Programme[52] was appointed who took command over the labour supply.

Ironically the industry had a high level of unemployment during the first year of war, but it was reduced from 354,028 to 78,334 by autumn 1940[53] as labour transferred from former private to current public work, as labour no longer could play the field to increase wages after the Uniformity Agreement was introduced, and as labour was enticed to contracts in rural areas. The situation was changing dramatically, 64% of the labourforce being absorbed into the armed forces during the war,[54] which was exacerbated in 1941–2 as Eire commenced a large building programme, thus curtailing the supply of Irish labour.[55]

The MOWB received the monthly labour returns from the contractors. This was possible because the construction companies were required to register with the MOWB under Defence Regulation 56AB. It not only permitted labour to be allocated to contracts but also enabled the contractors to be coordinated in relation to the programme requirements. The state had now taken control of the construction market. The flow of contracts, the registration of contractors and labour were under the direct control of the government, but the market had not been replaced. Construction remained in private hands. The appropriation of surplus value and the realisation of profits were never in question.

The registration involved organising contractors along national, regional and district lines. Around 150 contractors were permitted to operate on a national basis, the medium sized contractors organised into 12 regions through the Building Emergency Organisations set up in December 1941, being allowed to tender for contracts estimated not to exceed £25,000. Each region had advisory committees to advise a regional director. Smaller companies operated on a district level and came under the jurisdiction of the Building Emergency Organisation for each region.

Contractors made objections to the measures enacted in 1941. Contractors considered that the allocation of labour by the Director of the Building Programme would have a detrimental effect on the productivity achieved on contracts. Gangs who were used to working with each other and who had developed particular skills would be broken up. The adverse effect on productivity would be felt not only by the contractors but by the industry as a whole. While there was some truth in this, contractors were receiving continuity of work in the type of work and frequently in the same area and, therefore, continuity in the size and composition of the workforce was also achieved in many cases. Indeed labour productivity was enhanced by the National Arbitration Tribunal's decision to introduce payment by results,[56] which is essentially a piecework means of payment, replacing payment on a time work basis and reflecting the adoption of pricing work on a schedule of rates basis. The quicker the labourers worked, the more money they earned, the more profit the contractors made and the quicker the work was completed. The measure also helped induce rivalry between gangs,[57] although the increases in productivity were more than cancelled out by many of the younger and skilled operatives being drafted into the armed forces. The unions initially resisted the proposal on the basis that payment by results was potentially very exploitative, but accepted it as a wartime measure,[58] although the practice continued after the war. Payment by results intensified the production and therefore appropriation of absolute surplus value. Pushing down the value of labour power is one essential feature of restructuring each sector in order to overcome the crisis in the economy.

The unions, who were party to this intensification of labour, worked closely with both contractors and government. Although a large number of unions existed, their national and regional organisations reflected the national and regional organisations of contractors. Union representatives were on all the major government advisory panels and committees.[59] They were, therefore, able to play a full part in the development of government policy in the same way as the contractors.[60] The unions were also party to the Uniformity Agreement, which for the first time regulated wages between the building and civil engineering sub-sections of the sector. This was achieved through representatives of the two sides of industry, the National Federation of Building Trades Operatives (NFBTO) and the NFBTE meeting as the National Joint Council for the Building Industry. The Secretary of the NFBTE, C. G. Rowlands, stated that the National Joint Council 'regulates wages and conditions of employment and provides the machinery for the prevention of labour disputes'.[61] The National Joint Council came into being in 1921 and since 1924 no serious and generalised strike or disturbance occurred in the industry. This record was sustained during the war, although the number of policy changes by government and changes in conditions and wages, such as the introduction of payment by results, put a strain on it. This record was enhanced by support from leftist organisations which traditionally opposed many practices. For example, the Communist Party contradictorily stated: 'The problem confronting building workers is twofold: to adapt their forms of organisation and struggle to the changes in the industry, and to secure the mobilisation of every resource of the industry for the struggle against fascism.'[62] More important in maintaining the record was the cooperation achieved at site level. Contractors were not always sympathetic to production committees being formed on site, but stewards and site officers were established in joint production committees on the large contractors' sites; indeed the Ministry of Supply made these committees virtually compulsory on many projects and set up a special Works Relations Department.[63] These channels helped to maintain and increase productivity by filtering minor complaints and preventing stoppages of work.[64] Although labour was allocated to contracts the subcontracting system and casual nature of employment in the industry were maintained. Bevin as Minister of Labour had resisted intervening in the docks, which set the precedent for construction and influenced employment patterns for the period after the war.[65] Flexibility for construction capital was therefore maintained.

The effect of these direct controls on the construction sector was to divide formally a market which had hitherto been informally divided. In considering the way the market was divided it is necessary to distinguish between the large and small companies. The large and expanding had established their market share through competition and the allocation of contracts. This position was institutionalised with the introduction of controls. Their market share was guaranteed within limits through registration and selection to operate on a national basis. Indeed, the market was growing at this time. The Air Ministry commissioned more airfields, expenditure rising from £50m to £125m in 1941,[66] and the Admiralty programme increased by over £2m to £18.9m. The number of male operatives[67] employed reached a peak at 560,900 in October 1941, although employment on Air Ministry contracts, which constituted the largest single construction market, increased until January 1943 when 130,200 were employed.[68] The total work carried out in 1941 was estimated at a total of £470m (see table 4.3).

The large contractors experienced few problems in maintaining or expanding workloads at this time. Indeed, those which had initially taken on too much work in terms of the demands to complete the programmes as quickly as possible could use these additional contracts as a reason and means to expand operations by securing labour, plant and finance from the appropriate agencies. This enhanced the process of capital concentration in the sector.

Some contractors were very successful at sustaining their market share and increasing market penetration in the regions. Wimpey is a case in point. The firm was so successful in receiving contracts in Scotland that accusations were made that the company and government were acting improperly, which led to an inquiry conducted by J. L. Clyde, KC.[69] Table 4.5 shows the number of contractors used in Scotland and table 4.6 shows the breakdown of the contracts received by Wimpey. Certainly Wimpey

Table 4.5. *Number of contractors employed in Scotland by the main departments between the outbreak of war and December 1941*

Department	Scottish companies	English companies
Admiralty	36	10
War Office	348	12
MOWB	171	19
Ministry of Supply	15	3
Air Ministry	95	14
Total cost of contracts	£22.7m	£18.8m

Source: HMSO, 1942.

Table 4.6. *Schedule of contracts in Scotland between the outbreak of war and April 1942*

Department	Total number of contracts	Number of contracts placed with Wimpey	Cost of Wimpey's contracts as a percentage of total
Post Office	460	2	1.10
Admiralty	54[a]	1	0.02
Min. of Transport	33	1	1.80
War Office	4,300[b]	8[b]	3.00
MOWB	686[c]	3[c]	28.00
Min. of Supply	37	2	28.00
Air Ministry	1,010	53	22.00

Notes: a. Excludes contracts of less than £10,000.
　　b. Excludes contracts of less than £50.
　　c. Excludes contracts of less than £250 and contracts placed before the war but were completed after the outbreak of war.

Source: HMSO, 1942.

received a considerable amount of work in Scotland, but as Clyde argues[70] the company had built up a workforce, available plant and local experience of conditions and types of contracts to the extent that it was able to take on work on a more competitive basis than many other contractors when they had sufficient flexibility to meet the additional demand.

Wimpey opened a branch office in Scotland in 1931, employing 3,000 people by 1937 and 7,000 by June 1940. Out of a total workload estimated at £46.9m, 15% or £7m of these contracts were located in Scotland. Wimpey won two out of four contracts in competitive tender and was allocated two further contracts, plus a further very large contract won in competition in a joint venture with the Scottish contractor Leggats. Wimpey and Leggats received a further £2m of work when government negotiations with another company broke down. The allocated projects were carried out on a lump sum basis. Wimpey tendered for airfield contracts of which it received six, but decided it could undertake only four, one of which was in Scotland.

Later contracts on this airfield were put out to tender on a target cost basis plus fee, Wimpey submitting prices at nil fee, in other words based on a schedule of rates rather than at target cost.[71] Wimpey had achieved sufficient continuity of work and gained sufficient experience to be able to realise a profit margin within the schedule of rates which placed competitors in an impossible position. The retention of staff and gangs, increasing productivity through bonus schemes and the use of joint production committees to deal with problems helped increase productivity, while pension, superannuation and annual bonus schemes were inducements for the workforce to stay before direct controls were imposed by government. Against this background it is not surprising that the market was increasingly concentrated into the hands of the large contractors.

The smaller contractors were in a less favourable position. They were confined to the regional and district markets and were not able to compete with the 150 national contractors for the work over £250,000. Regional contractors found that insufficient work was available, and consequently a large number of regional contractors became subcontractors to the main national contractors on large contracts.[72] This process undermined their status as contractors. However, many other companies suspended operations or went out of business. There was, therefore, a shake out of some of the medium sized and smaller contractors as the large and expanding contractors grew, a process of restructuring through capital concentration which was recognised by the Director-General of the MOWB,[73] who wrote: 'I think, therefore, that Government must take responsibility for stating now openly that its policy is to see a balanced industry is preserved in all its grades and divisions as far as possible. Many firms must inevitably close down, permanently or temporarily, but we must keep as many of the efficient alive as possible.' The implementation of government policy was therefore central to accelerating capital concentration.

However, the construction programme overall had reached its peak and there were signs that the programmes would be curtailed after 1941. The programme of the Ministry of Supply was declining, ordnance factories were being completed and the Production Executive was cancelling new factories in August 1941. The Admiralty and War Office programmes were also showing signs of curtailment by the reduction of labour being employed.[74]

This decline was in part deliberate. The Prime Minister, Winston Churchill, requested in a personal minute to the Production Executive in August 1941 that the programmes should be cut. It was realised by the Production Executive that the programme demands exceeded labour availability, but additional curtailments were agreed. However, Churchill issued a second directive in November requesting that the labourforce should be reduced from 920,000 to 792,000 by April 1942 and to 770,000 by June 1942. As projects were completed it was hoped to reduce the figure further to 500,000.[75] These reductions were considered necessary in the context of financing and manning the war effort as a whole.

There were now signs that the output of the construction industry could be substantially reduced without other programmes dependent on infrastructure and buildings being too adversely affected. What had been achieved, however, was that the state had taken control of the construction market, which was coordinated through the Director of the Building Programme at the MOWB. The detailed carrying out of the programme was the responsibility of the various state agencies and contractors concerned. The government had shown initial reticence in taking direct control and the evolution of controls left something to be desired in the coordination of the programmes, proceeding out of trial and error rather than determination to implement controls effectively.

The result was that the position of dominance achieved by the large and expanding contractors in the first years of war was now institutionalised. Construction capital had been concentrated, the larger contractors expanding turnover, diversifying geographically and by the nature of work undertaken. Smaller construction companies were being shaken out or confined to regional and district locations, many acting as subcontractors on large projects. While the process by which this concentration of capital occurred was not the most efficient in terms of speeding up and completing the programmes for the needs of war, in retrospect it will be seen that the process was probably advantageous for the construction sector as the workload declined in the last years of war and expanded again during the reconstruction period. The declining market was shared amongst fewer contractors, hence avoiding a shake out of large contractors, and the process induced fewer but larger contractors who gained the capacity and diversity to undertake the largest contracts during reconstruction.

1942–3

The priority system was used to respond to Churchill's demands to cut back construction programmes, but the response was short lived because the entry of the United States into the war in December 1941 required extensive construction for the American troops arriving in Britain. The name given to this new programme was Bolero, which was a British responsibility under the supervision of the War Office. The Bolero programme was the beginning of reciprocal aid to the United States amounting to £92m by July 1943, £100.9m in the next year, £19.6m in the following year and finally £6.4m between July 1945 and September 1949, a total of £218.9m.[76]

Bolero involved the provision of camps, hospitals and storage depots costing a total of £49.9m, the first phase providing accommodation for a million people, the second phase beginning in July 1942 increasing the accommodation to cater for 1.14 million, reaching a total of 1.44 million at the end of the fourth and final phase in April 1944. The problem of labour supply was overcome by using American military labour supervised and paid by the contractors at the civilian rate.[77]

The American air force, the USAAF, required 50 airfields, 36 of which were constructed under the jurisdiction of the Air Ministry, adding to the construction market for contractors. One feature of the construction carried out by the United States was the introduction of heavy plant, particularly for earth works and concrete mixing, which had not been used in Britain.[78] The use of heavy plant was to become common among British contractors during the following years.

Coinciding with the arrival of American troops in Britain a number of administrative changes occurred which had implications for the control of the construction market, although no fundamental changes were made. Reith was succeeded at the MOWB by Lord Portal in February 1942. Lord Portal used the official committees and agencies to obtain advice and control the programmes, but personally consulted John Laing and Godfrey Mitchell, chairmen of Laing and Wimpey respectively.[79] The

Minister of Production assumed control of the Production Executive's function also in February 1942 and in March Lord Beaverbrook was succeeded as the Minister of Production by Oliver Lyttleton. Government control was becoming more centralised, and policies reflected these changes. The labour allocation system was changed at this time. Labour had been allocated to programmes and state agencies had been responsible for the allocation of labour within their programmes. The Minister of Labour took complete control of the labour supply, not only allocating labour to programmes, but also allocating it directly to contracts. This centralised the control of the construction programmes at government level, with, in particular, the MOWB and Ministry of Labour.

By 1943 the MOWB had changed its name to the Ministry of Works and Planning and in March 1943 also took control of the Directorate General of Aircraft Production Factories of the Ministry of Aircraft Production,[80] all of which concentrated further powers into the hands of this Ministry both in terms of the construction programmes and planning for reconstruction.

The MOWB began to act as an agent to the Ministry of Fuel and Power in December 1942 for opencast coalmining,[81] which opened up another potential market for contractors who had or were expanding their earth moving plant and equipment. Sir Robert McAlpine began opencast mining in 1942 and mined 1.97m tonnes (2m tons),[82] Taylor Woodrow mined in the Midlands and Wales,[83] while Holloway Bros. mined in the Nottinghamshire and Newcastle areas.[84] Laing,[85] Costain,[86] Sir Lindsay Parkinson and other contractors also entered this market. Hand in hand with the centralisation of power and the concentration of construction capital came the diversification of activities amongst the major contractors.

A decision to undertake another major project was taken in October 1943.[87] Operation Overlord was the plan to invade Europe, which had as one of its main components the construction of a series of floating harbours which could be taken across the Channel to France as an alternative to trying to capture an existing port. They were called the Mulberry harbours and consisted of 98 concrete caissons measuring 62m by 17m by 18m (204 ft by 56 ft by 60 ft). The caissons were code named Phoenix and were constructed at Middlesbrough, Goole, Southampton, Portsmouth, Tilbury, East India Docks, South Docks and on 12 basins excavated along the banks of the Thames.[88] The Phoenix project employed 20,000 operatives,[89] some of whom were withdrawn from Air Ministry contracts,[90] and an embargo was put on all new works within 30 miles of the Phoenix sites, which included the whole of London. Although the project used

payment by results with additional bonuses, this was insufficient to increase productivity to meet the deadlines, so some skilled operatives were
released from the army and the unions agreed to a further relaxation of
skill and job definitions.[91] Shifts were up to 36 hours long in some cases
and work continued in the dark during air raids.[92]

The preparations of some of the London docks for Phoenix were
carried out by Sir Robert McAlpine and Mowlem.[93] The construction of
the caissons involved 23 main contractors.[94] Contractors were allowed to
use their own construction methods, 20% of Phoenix being built by Laing
and McAlpine, each constructing 10 caissons.[95] In addition to the
Phoenix caissons, a number of other components went into the Mulberry
harbours, the pierheads which were code named Whale being one of the
other important elements. Holloway Bros. acted as the coordinating contractor, using a number of other contractors and assembling military
labour.[96] The concrete pier and pierhead pontoons were constructed by
Wates, Monk, Trussed Concrete Steel and Laing.[97] The Mulberry harbours were completed in April 1944 and were assembled at Selsey in
Sussex before being towed across the Channel.

Another project at this time was the Fog Investigation Dispersal Opera-
tions (FIDO) which involved the installation of petrol burners on airfields
around the country. The main manufacturers and contractors were
Babcock and Wilcox, J. L. Eve Construction, Kinnear Moodie and Co.,
Monk and Co., William Press and Son, George Wimpey, and Taylor
Woodrow.[98]

The Pipe Lines Under the Ocean project (PLUTO) involved the laying
of oil pipelines across England, the Channel and the northern part of the
main European continent to provide a constant flow of oil supplies. A
number of contractors were engaged in pipe laying and the construction
of pumping stations in England, including Mowlem and Taylor
Woodrow.[99]

Despite the directives to curtail building programmes Bolero, USAAF
airfield construction, the Mulberry harbours, FIDO and PLUTO maintained higher levels of construction activity than had been anticipated.
Opencast coalmining had become an additional market for contractors.
Departments engaged in these projects had increased their labour allocations. The War Office reached a peak with 78,300 operatives and the
Air Ministry peaked at 130,200 operatives in January 1943.[100] Efforts to
reduce the Admiralty programme by nearly £4m to £15m in total were
dashed as the programme reached £18m in 1943. The Air Ministry programme increased from £125m in 1941 to £145m in 1942, although it
was reduced to £126m in 1943 when airfield construction had passed its
peak, but a considerable number of contracts were still in progress.[101] The

total estimated construction output was falling. Output fell by £45m to £425m in 1942 and again to £350m by 1943 (see table 4.3).

The restructuring of the construction sector had to a great extent taken place. The large and expanding contractors had increased their workload and diversified activities into large civil and other engineering projects, undertaken opencast coalmining as well as the more conventional construction work. The boost to construction as a result of Bolero, Mulberry, FIDO and PLUTO produced work which could only be undertaken by the large and expanded contractors. The size of the work and the specialisms required or acquired were only in the capabilities of these established companies. Although the programmes were beginning to decline, they were better placed to maintain their workload due to the nature of the work.

Smaller regional contractors were unable to compete in the national market, and therefore were more adversely affected by underproduction, which resulted in their continued shake out and subordination to the main contractors. National contractors were, however, able to compete at the regional level with regional contractors for work, thus further affecting the regional companies. Companies were permitted to undertake a workload up to 60% of their annual turnover at any one time. If this figure was exceeded the company would be suspended from taking on new work until the figure dropped to 40% of the turnover. This measure had been aimed to prevent companies exceeding their potential capacity. National contractors were permitted to choose whether their regional branches were treated as independent units competing for contracts not exceeding £25,000.[102] National contractors could therefore compete on an equal footing with regional contractors in areas where they no longer had substantial national contracts but had a regional office. The system was also used in another way by national contractors. When their national workload became excessive a contractor could ask for regions with considerable portions of this work to be considered as independent units and be suspended from taking on more contracts. For example, the Newmarket branch of Costain had contracts of £270,000 in hand in March 1943 with an annual turnover of £71,000 for that regional office. The company asked for the regional branch to be discounted from the national operations. The Newmarket branch was suspended,[103] but the result was that the company had made a net market gain to the contract value of nearly £200,000 without affecting national operations and the Newmarket branch would be increasing its turnover against which contracts could be allocated in subsequent years. Market penetration was increased both nationally and regionally, and therefore state control of the construction market not only formally concentrated construction capital, but allowed further concentration through the informal use of the controls by the large national contractors in their favour.

The construction programme was in decline and it became important for each national contractor to try to increase market penetration. This could be most easily achieved at the expense of the regional contractors. The number of construction companies fell by 2,503 or 5.8% between November 1942 and October 1943,[104] and this figure obscures the falling workloads of regional contractors and the extent to which companies had become subcontractors.

The last years of the war

The Mulberry harbours were completed in April 1944, but at the beginning of 1944 attacks on London by V1 flying bombs and V2 rockets caused extensive damage. Many smaller contractors were called in to undertake repairs, but some of the major contractors were given responsibility for coordinating repairs in each borough under the jurisdiction of the London Repairs Executive. This increased work for the large and small contractors.

Government controls continued essentially as before, although regional officers were given more responsibility for the allocation of contracts and labour[105] and so control was decentralised to a small extent. Labour supply was becoming less critical, but materials were increasingly in short supply, a problem which the flying bomb attacks brought into focus and a problem which was to remain during the reconstruction period.

The construction market was diminishing in size rapidly (see figure 4.2). The major programmes and projects were completed or nearing completion. The Admiralty programme was reduced to less than £9m and the Air Ministry spent £40m on construction in 1944 at home and abroad, which was 30% of the programme of 1943. The pre-tax profits of the contractors were sustained at a high level because less capital was reinvested or required as working capital for contracts. Contractors began to undertake more work which would contribute towards reconstruction. Taylor Woodrow undertook the construction of a penicillin factory and the provision of temporary houses, for example.[106] Sir Robert McAlpine was engaged in the construction of a factory for ICI and power station work,[107] and other contractors also began this transition. New markets were therefore being sought.

Government contracts were allocated to a small number of contractors. Out of 881 companies 579 were receiving contracts up to 10% of their

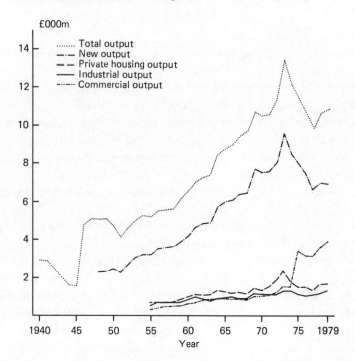

£000m

Figure 4.2. Total, new and private construction output at 1975 prices
Sources: Ministry of Works, Ministry of the Public Board of Works, Department of the
Environment.

annual turnover and carried out 65.7% of all work done, while 7 companies were receiving 50–60% of their turnover and carried out 0.8% of
all work done, and 11 companies received contracts over 60% of their
turnover and carried out 1.2% of all work done.[108] Although the number
of contractors operating nationally had increased, a high degree of
selectivity was shown, so the fall in the total construction output was
not at the expense of the dominant national contractors, who received a
large proportion of government construction contracts and were already
looking forward to reconstruction markets to maintain turnover and
maintain their dominance in the post-war period.

The effects of government controls were to reinforce capital concentration during the last years of war. The controls did not restrict the size
of the market because the short supply of labour and materials would
have had the same effect even in the absence of controls. The controls,
however, still had the same effects on the division of the market, the
dominant national contractors receiving a large proportion of the
market.

Conclusion

The construction industry was transformed during the course of the war. Prior to rearmament existing contractors were experiencing under-production, while those who had entered or were expanding through private housebuilding were not experiencing overproduction.

Rearmament and the war induced a series of large construction pro-grammes and large projects, from which the existing large contractors considerably expanded. Former housebuilders, which were most success-ful at divesting their land banks to release tied up capital and at diversifying into becoming building and civil engineering contractors, emerged at the end of the war as very large contractors. Looking ahead to 1970, it is interesting to note the five largest British contractors measured in terms of annual turnover were Wimpey, Laing, Sir Robert McAlpine, Costain and Taylor Woodrow,[109] all of which were amongst the most prominent contractors during the second world war. Laing estimated that they were responsible for 5% of the total wartime construction pro-gramme, having a turnover of £45m and directly employing over 10,000 people.[110]

The war presented the opportunity for contractors to diversify their activities by the nature of the work undertaken and the geographical spread of the work, in so doing requiring the development of corporate management structures and efficient site management and union cooperation.

The development and emergence of these large contractors, which were to dominate post-war construction, were the result of capital concentra-tion at the top of the industry and the reduction and subordination of medium and smaller contractors at the lower end of the sector. The concentration was achieved through competition during rearmament and the first years of war, but concentration was institutionalised through the direct intervention of the state to control the market from 1941 onwards. This intervention accelerated and reinforced the process of concentra-tion. It was necessary in terms of the requirements of war and the restruc-turing of the sector prior to the end of the war. The sector needed to be amongst the first industries to restructure in order to undertake its tasks of reconstruction so that the entire economy could be restructured, and the restructuring required within construction was too extensive to be carried out at the level of the company alone.

State intervention could have taken a number of forms. The evolution of controls proceeded by trial and error prior to 1941 and was not always carried out with a high degree of efficiency. In terms of the construction needs of war, intervention could have occurred and become effective earlier; although this would not have achieved such a high degree of concentration in the sector which might have caused more serious problems in the last years of war when work was in decline and might not have produced adequate concentration for the needs of the economy during reconstruction. The forms that controls took were to control the construction and labour market, the private ownership of the industry not being in question. Further intervention was unnecessary to achieve the aims of war and restructure the sector for the needs of reconstruction.

One of the ironies of the restructuring of the sector was that the construction of use values were of a temporary nature, such as the Mulberry harbours, or were inappropriate for a peacetime economy. Although few new technologies were introduced during the war,[111] contractors gained experience in techniques which had not been used extensively and gained a greater knowledge of materials, especially the use of concrete. The introduction of heavier plant from the United States was, however, an innovation for British construction.

Labour productivity fell during the war. Tasks took 31–47% longer in 1946 than they had done in 1937[112] despite the use of new plant, payment by results and the development of site management methods. The labourforce had diminished in size during the war from 560,900 operatives in October 1941 to 242,500 operatives by July 1945.[113] It was an ageing labourforce which would require reconstitution for the tasks of reconstruction.

The completion of the wartime construction programmes and the restructuring of the sector could not have been achieved without the cooperation of the workforce. A leading union official, who had been a member of many government and state construction companies, summarises the situation: 'No industry has ever been faced with such a variety of tasks as has the building industry during the war. Our men responded to every change of practice within the industry.'[114]

The world economic crisis had reached its deepest point, the culmination of which was world war. The war provided the conditions under which the value of labour power could be reduced, constant capital could be substituted for variable capital and the overproduction in terms of the labour market reversed. Additionally, and most significantly for the crisis theory, international markets were redefined, capital was devalued and physically destroyed, hence opening up new markets during reconstruction.

A precondition for reconstruction was the prior restructuring of construction capital. This was achieved during the war through capital concentration and both geographical and market diversification in the absence of any significant labour unrest. In the case of construction measures were taken to intensify labour although productivity continually declined. The appropriation of absolute surplus value remained dominant rather than changing to the appropriation of relative surplus value. Constant capital was not increased to threaten the flexibility of contractors and the contracting and subcontracting system was reinforced. The war created new markets both for the war effort and during reconstruction through the destruction of the built environment and new capital requirements as other sectors began or completed their restructuring to overcome the economic crisis of overproduction.

5

The reconstruction period

The second world war provided the opportunity and need for reconstruction, not only in the physical reconstruction of the built environment but in the reconstruction of the world economy. Reconstruction would be the prelude to renewed and sustained capital accumulation, but the path of reconstruction was neither easy nor straightforward. The war had cost nation states considerably in terms of debts to finance the war economies, the devaluation of money capital and the destruction of the means to produce raw materials and primary industrial commodities used in other manufacturing processes. Additionally, the labourforce had been depleted, had aged, and many were neither healthy nor adequately housed.

Britain was severely affected by the war and consequently lost much of its economic power as a national capital, particularly to the United States, a situation which was subsequently reinforced by the Marshall Aid Plan. Reconstruction in Britain, therefore, took place in less favourable conditions than in many other countries. Although plans for reconstruction were conceived early during the war, few were ever enacted. Many proposals were rejected on the grounds that centralised state control was considered inappropriate and politically unacceptable in peacetime, while many other proposals were diluted during the course of war. Indeed planning in its broadest sense was largely a misnomer as reconstruction was mainly steered by the adoption and adaptation of wartime measures. These controls were now mostly negative rather than positive in nature, and many were overtaken by national and international events rendering them redundant or irrelevant as the threats of renewed economic crisis appeared in a variety of forms. Additional problems were created for the speed of Britain's reconstruction by the growth of state agencies whose developing bureaucracies neither had the experience of steering an economy in peacetime nor the means of implementation.

The reconstruction period can broadly be divided into two phases. From the end of the war to 1948 controls were an important feature although they were gradually eased in the second phase between 1948 and 1955 to a level of state intervention which would remain for the next 25 years. Between 1945 and 1948 controls remained important, being steered towards the financing and production of the means of production and exports. It will be argued that this took precedence over welfare orientated reconstruction. Housing construction, therefore, was important, but the construction of power stations and steelworks, for example, was considered to be of greater strategic importance. It will also be argued, however, that the control of building and development through building licences was largely unsuccessful, especially in the case of housing. The continual economic problems and other indirect government controls proved to be a far greater constraint on building and development than licensing. In addition, sufficient capital had not been accumulated in industry and commerce to justify expenditure on construction or high rentals. Similarly wages and salaries could not stimulate the housing market. Demand would not be present until the 1950s except where the physical destruction of the built environment had been so considerable that construction and development became economic through war damage finance.

Controls began to be eased in 1948 and were gradually lifted over the following years, most having been erased by 1954. Despite continual economic problems reconstruction had largely been achieved by the mid-1950s. The economy was showing signs of sustained growth as existing sectors completed their restructuring and new sectors emerged. The construction industry was one sector which had largely been restructured during the war, but reconstruction brought a number of changes. The property sector emerged as a new sector distinct from the 'landed' property interests, the war providing the opportunity and momentum to reconstruct dramatically the built environment beyond the extent of war damage and on a scale not previously seen in this century.

Construction, 1945–8

The growth of the welfare state was dramatic in the reconstruction period and ushered in new construction demands, for example, housebuilding. However, in many commentaries and thinking this growth has eclipsed the broader reconstruction of the economy. Housing together with health and education were important to the population and in providing a workforce for production and circulation to operate at capacity, but it is easy to overemphasise the new rather than the renewal of the old. The reconstruction of the economy took precedence not only as a matter of political and economic necessity but also to finance or even deficit finance welfare benefits.

In many people's minds planning was synonymous with the welfare state.[1] Plans, however, were conceived for industrial and commercial as well as welfare construction. Planning was also seen as being synonymous with the philosophy of the Labour Party.[2] Although the Conservative Party did not always embrace the broader and more sweeping conceptions of restructuring Britain, beneath the rhetoric a large measure of common ground emerged during the wartime coalition government,[3] which was reinforced as the post-war Labour Government proceeded primarily on the basis of negative controls rather than positive planning.

The housing markets

Keynesian economics and the recommendations of Beveridge were very influential and contributed to the growth of welfare provision. Housing provision was one of the most important welfare needs and was transferred to the Ministry of Health under the jurisdiction of Bevan in the Labour Government, thus reflecting the welfare status the government wished to emphasise. However, the significance of housing in the context of the economic reconstruction has been overemphasised in the past and certainly for the construction market was not the most significant market, particularly for the major contractors.

Few of the main national contractors returned to housebuilding in a big way after the war, although many retained an interest. The housing market had changed. Private housebuilding for owner occupancy was no longer the main market, public housing, especially council housing, being the main market. Only two major contractors substantially entered into public housebuilding: Wimpey and Laing. Godfrey Mitchell and John Laing, the respective chairmen of the companies, had been close advisers to Lord Portal, the Minister of Works, in particular contributing advice on cost yardsticks and minimum standards for housing.[4] This gave these companies an intimate knowledge of requirements and emerging government policy, which may have contributed to the decisions to enter this market.[5] Wimpey and Laing used non-traditional concrete construction, although they changed to brick construction as cost or material shortages dictated.[6] The Wimpey method used 'no fines' concrete[7] and a similar system, Easiform, had been used successfully in the interwar period by Laing. A large number of non-traditional designs had initially emerged for public housing. The British Iron and Steel Federation had developed a design which was used during the war and was extensively used immediately after the war. A total of 31,076 houses was erected by Costain, Bovis, Henry Boot, Gee Walker and Slater, Laing, Lovatt, Mowlem and Pauling prior to October 1950, although less than 500 were subsequently erected, their steel construction proving unsuitable in use.

William Airy and Sons built 20,920 of their system before October 1950 but less than 5,000 afterwards. Other contractors experienced similar market declines, although from lower output thresholds. Local authorities had considered speed the most important criterion at first, but as problems in use became apparent to the authorities and the more conventional appearance of the rendered *in situ* concrete houses of Wimpey and Laing were preferred by the users, the local authorities concentrated on a small number of contractors. Wimpey had built 6,488 'no fines' houses prior to October 1950, which was 5.5% of the market, but had built 46,883 between October 1950 and April 1955, which was 30.9% of the market. Laing built 14,690 Easiform houses prior to October 1950, which was 12.5% of the market, and built 28,516, 18.8% of the market, between October 1950 and April 1955. Wates also developed a favoured system, increasing its market share from 4.5% to nearly 8.9%.[8]

The total housing market was expanding but the use of government licensing controls inherited from the war did not achieve the stated aims of policy. In 1945, 901 private houses were completed under licence compared to 229 public houses. The situation was not reversed until 1947 when 83,615 public houses were completed exceeding private house completions by over 53,000.[9] This was in part due to expenditure on public housing being £22m in 1945–6 but rising to £107m in 1946–7 and £210m in 1947–8.[10] It is commonly believed it was the control of the housing market, particularly the private housebuilding market through the use of licences, which hampered builders. In fact there is little evidence to support this. In 1945–6, 279,936 tenders were approved for public housing yet only 23,923 completions were achieved, and although 70,994 licences were issued for private housebuilding only 28,175 were completed. In terms of the total and private housebuilding market approvals far exceeded output.

Looking more closely at public housing, Rosenberg[11] has commented that the government claimed to be planning the public housing programme but was in fact allocating finance, tender approvals and licences to start contracts. It was therefore concerned primarily with demand rather than supply or output. Rosenberg states that the industry was blamed by the Ministry of Health for the disparity between policy aims and actual output,[12] but the inadequate planning or, more cynically, the concern of the government with giving the political appearance that something was being done are more adequate explanations.

Having initially used the controls inadequately, it would have been difficult to redress the disparity, and the position was exacerbated by a shortage of labour, particularly skilled labour. Although the workforce increased by 300,000 between June 1945 and April 1946 an insufficient number went into housing, at one time there being a national workforce of one person per house. Locally conditions were made worse as local authorities did not know which licences had been granted for other public and private projects in the area which would be competing for labour.[13] Many operatives entered the small repairs market and black market.

The shortage of materials posed a further and longer term problem. In April 1946 the government attempted to control the distribution of materials according to the priorities of reconstruction. Contracts designated WBA received priority which included local authority and other government work. Other designations, WBB and WBO, were referred to the Regional Director for work less than £20,000 and to the Regional Building Committee for work exceeding £20,000. If materials supply posed no problem then the designation would become WBA/MAT for the contract.[14] In practice the diffuse implementation between agencies and departments failed to allocate adequately materials to contracts. It was this aspect which limited the public housing programme.

Public housing was cut back in 1947 as austerity measures were introduced by the Treasury. Fuel shortages had reduced the manufacturing of materials and timber imports had fallen to 30% of pre-war levels.[15] Although the control of timber and other materials was integrated into the licensing procedure between May and June,[16] the demand and output disparity were not balanced as approvals and starts exceeded the capacity of both the industry and economy. Local authorities had already begun to reduce their commitments. The disparity between approvals and starts fell from 101,000 in April 1947 to 42,000 by April 1948 and completions rose by nearly 100,000 for local authority housing. Expenditure on public housing fell in 1948–9 to £221m.[17] The government's financial deficit was increasing and stimulating inflation, the government having committed £728m largely to public housing and war damage compensation.[18] Cuts became necessary and the Federation of British Industry had lobbied successfully for the curtailment of capital expenditure on welfare capital projects such as housing, schools and hospitals.[19] The housing programme was cut, being justified on the basis that the supply and demand for housing had to be more realistically balanced. The balance was achieved, but the cuts were absolute rather than adjustment, the growth of welfare provision being curtailed having been overtaken by national and international economic events. The reconstruction of the economy and hence also the built environment is dependent upon renewed capital accumulation. The national economy was not able to sustain a large housing programme at the current level of accumulation in relation to government deficits and balance of payments.

The large contractors with the notable exception of Wimpey and Laing had not substantially entered the public housing market. A number of contractors had tried to keep or kept a small interest in the market but found profit higher on other work. Costain, for example, had used local authority work as a stop-gap.[20] The large contractors did not move back into the private housebuilding market. Contractors had wished to in many cases, but blamed the licensing system. In fact, as we have seen, this provided little obstacle apart from the bureaucratic procedures. The supply of materials, development charges and the lack of finance amongst potential buyers were the main barriers. Private housebuilding did not become sufficiently profitable again until 1955.[21] Output increased threefold between 1952 and 1955. While this coincided with the easing of controls the overlicensing suggests controls do not provide an explanation, although their easing may have contributed psychologically, housebuilders believing the removal of bureaucratic procedures released a market perceived as heavily constrained. The financial ability of consumers to buy housing constitutes a more satisfactory explanation.

Housing construction permitted a large number of small and medium sized companies to re-establish themselves and gave an opportunity for many small contractors to start up, entry into the industry not being difficult because of the low capital requirements at this level with performance bonds being obtained from banks, therefore providing greater security for the clients. They could compete against the larger contractors in this market because of their low overhead and administrative costs. The repair, maintenance and black market work encouraged the proliferation of small building concerns. The war had squeezed many operators out of business or curtailed and subordinated their activities. The renewed proliferation diluted the concentration and increased the fragmentation of capital in the whole sector, but the dilution had no effect on the major contractors, which were operating on a different scale. The opportunities of reconstruction stimulated construction output, so the major contractors, having begun to suffer signs of underproduction at the end of the war, were experiencing an increase in demand and renewed competition to consolidate and strengthen their market standing.

Building and civil engineering markets

In order to appreciate the relative strategic importance of building and civil engineering over and above housing construction, the broader economic context needs to be outlined. In doing so it is also necessary to distinguish between policy and economics in government strategy. While the intentions were a fusion of the two, national and international events dislocated the two strategic elements, the broader economic events affecting the economics of the strategy and preventing the implementation of policy.

At the end of the war the external debts of the UK had grown to £3,355m compared to the pre-war debt of £476m. Exports had fallen from £440m to £272m, while net gold and dollar reserves had fallen from £864m to £453m over the same period. In addition, the physical destruction of buildings and infrastructure seriously reduced the capacity to expand output. Industrial plants and factories had been seriously bombed, but maintenance and repairs had been postponed to an estimated amount of £885m.[22] The total value of construction output had fallen to £290m (£1,629m at 1975 prices, see figure 4.2).

The primary aim of the government was to reconstruct industry, but the only means to achieve this lay in wartime controls, applying them indirectly, or informal and voluntary agreements. The Finance Corporation for Industry was set up in 1945 as a public company with the Bank of England as a minority shareholder in an effort to reconstruct and hence restructure medium and large sized companies. It set up the National Investment Council which laid down guidelines for investment and savings. It was largely ineffective although potentially could have adopted a direct role to facilitate industrial reconstruction.[23] Bank advances to industry were low, but did modestly increase in 1947. There was a reluctance in the financial markets to invest in industry to restore its depleted stocks and fixed capital, because this type of investment would not immediately generate high rates of profit[24] and interest rates were currently artificially low and therefore would not yield an average rate of return on the investments for the financial institutions. However, these features were simultaneously necessary for, yet held back, industrial reconstruction. This initial reticence of the financial markets did not conform to the Keynesian-type policies being adopted by the Chancellor, Hugh Dalton, who kept bank and interest rates low.[25] The government controlled only the recently nationalised Bank of England and therefore could not directly control investment. The risk was that industrial reconstruction would be slowed by a lack of investment, while cheap money policies would lead to inflation.[26] Paradoxically both occurred and contributed to a growing economic crisis.

A number of problems had culminated in 1946 and 1947 to produce a severe economic crisis. Fuel shortages, particularly coal, which constituted 93% of primary fuel, held back industrial reconstruction. Coal output was low, the mines having been starved of investment since the end of the first world war.[27] The banks were using the increased money supply to invest abroad while dollar reserves were low and other investors converted investments to gold.[28] The result was that the strategic policy aims of reconstruction were not being achieved and a balance of payments problem was precipitated, placing Britain in a considerably weakened position against other national capitals.

The new Chancellor at the Treasury, Sir Stafford Cripps, introduced a budget which was designed to reduce expenditure and increase taxes at home while placing exports as the first priority in order to overcome the balance of payments deficit.[29] Ironically the modest increase in financial investment at home in 1947 was criticised in 1948 when the banks were accused of failing to aid the Chancellor's deflationary budget.[30]

The controls used were largely those inherited from the war. The principal ones were consumer rationing, the informal investment allocation, import controls, price controls, building licences and materials allocation. In addition there was a continued ban on strikes.[31] While these controls did not always have the desired effect, as we have seen in the case of housing and will see for construction generally, they necessitated close liaison between the state and private agencies. State intervention into private interests was also accompanied by the greater participation of private intervention in state interests. Although the controls were not long lasting the liaison that had built up during the war was to be largely sustained during the post-war period under consideration. While the controls did last, their failure in economic and policy terms should not therefore be seen as simply the inadequacy of government or the reticence of private interests, but a more reflexive relation between the two operating in a national and international economic context. This reflexive relation was essential to reconstruction, and hence to capital accumulation. The state and private interests are inextricably linked.

In the case of construction, controls were aimed to channel investment and construction activity into industrial reconstruction. The Capital Issues Committee affirmed its intention to support government policies with regard to physical investment.[32] The WBA, WBB and WBO designations were given to contracts with approvals. The lowest priority, WBO, was in practice seldom used. This did not pose problems for the large building and civil engineering projects in terms of materials. Large contractors experienced few problems regarding materials. Prefabricated techniques and material substitution were used to overcome shortages. Many of the techniques subsequently used in indigenous industrialised and systems building of the 1960s were developed in this period.[33] The use of prestressed and reinforced concrete became increasingly popular in Britain, although the techniques had been in existence prior to the war. Contractors with their own material supply companies, such as Taylor Woodrow, were strongly placed. The priority and flexibility acquired by major contractors with regard to material supply date back to their re-structuring during the second world war.

Labour supply posed some problems, particularly as people returned from the forces. Many went into repairs and maintenance, but most of this was probably at the expense of the housing programmes rather than industrial reconstruction. The largest labour demands were for the Ministry of Works and the Ministry of Fuel and Power. Repairs to existing factories constituted a large market, but the supply of factories was increased by the government selling many of its wartime factories while keeping closer control of large contracts for new plants and factories.[34]

If labour and materials supply was not a very serious problem on major contracts, the bureaucracy in obtaining licences on civil projects was a source of complaint.[35] The procedure involved contact with the Capital Issues Committee, the regional controller of the department responsible for that region's production, usually the Board of Trade, for a development certificate which indicated that the scheme was consistent with overall UK location of industry policy. Next, application for Town and Country Planning approval was made to the local authority. Ministry of Health standards were considered. Application for assessment of development charges was referred to the Central Land Board. Application was made for materials and submitted to the regional office of the Board of Trade. An application under £10,000 was dealt with regionally and referred to the regional office of the Ministry of Works, Ministry of Labour and any other interested departments. If approved the Ministry of Works would issue the licence and authorise acquisition of controlled materials.[36]

Despite the complexity of procedures more licences were granted than could be met by the existing finances of companies, contractors and the capacity of contractors. Under these circumstances the procedures themselves cannot have been considered a deterrent for industrial applications. The complexity of the procedures may have contributed to more approvals being granted than the economy could accommodate due to an inability to monitor and control these procedures, thus echoing the problems faced in the housing programme; however, the policy aims were to achieve a speedy reconstruction and the problems of 1947 were not anticipated. Above all, the government was very concerned at maintaining 'full employment' after the war and it is this factor which led to the political expediency of granting more licences than the economy

Table 5.1. *Estimated construction investment in the UK in millions of pounds*

	1947	1948
Fuel and power	40	60
Transport, shipping and communications	105	115
Agriculture, forestry and fishing	25	25
Manufacturing industries	95	100
All housing work	460	475
Other social services	40	65
Defence and administration	45	55
Northern Ireland	15	20
Total	825	915

Source: HMSO, 1949.

Table 5.2. *Building licences issued*

	1945 (peace)	1946	1947
War damage repairs (non-housing)	4,524	17,667	17,356
Factories, etc.	21,957	132,420	147,163
Hospitals and schools	558	4,962	6,504
Farms	1,353	8,118	9,868
Miscellaneous	2,973	30,129	17,347
Total	31,365	193,296	198,238

Source: adapted from Rosenberg, 1960.

could accommodate. The government could not politically afford the accusation that it might be preventing the maintenance of full employment.[37] The granting of licences exceeding the capacity of the economy continued until 1948.[38]

The estimated construction investment in the principal programmes is given in table 5.1 and table 5.2 shows the number of licences issued. The value of the licences issued for factories by the Ministry of Works was estimated at £146m in 1947 and at £140m in 1948 while other non-housing work was valued at £240m and £209m for the same years.[39] Combining the estimated construction investment on government contracts and all housing work (see table 5.1) with the licences granted for other work, a total potential output of £1,175m for 1947 and a total potential output of £1,264m for 1948 can be estimated. Comparing this potential output with the official output of total work of £1,047m[40] for 1947, a large disparity exists, especially when this actual output figure includes repairs and maintenance. A more accurate assessment can be made of the disparity for 1948. The potential output of £1,264m compares with the actual official output for new work of £545m, thus indicating an overlicensing in the region of £700m for the year. The licensed market was considerably larger than the actual market and even these figures underestimate the disparity because work valued at less than £1,000 did not require a licence yet comprises an unknown proportion of the actual output and output of new work. Even a five-month ban on issuing licences up to April 1948 only provided a short term reduction with a rush of industrial approvals once the ban was lifted (see table 5.3).

Table 5.3. *Approved new factory buildings*

	In DAs		Outside DAs		Total	
	No.	£m	No.	£m	No.	£m
Dec. 1944–Apr. 1947	908	0.06	1,838	0.06	2,746	0.12
Apr. 1947–Feb. 1948	312	0.03	388	0.02	700	0.05
Feb. 1948–June 1948	−37	0.00	45	0.00	8	0.00
June 1948–Dec. 1948	84	0.00	896	0.05	980	0.05

Source: Board of Trade, quoted in Morgan, 1979.

The government's fear of the return of high unemployment is reflected initially in the granting of licences by area and region. The Distribution of Industry Act, 1945, identified Development Areas (DAs) which were almost the same as the pre-war Special Areas,[41] where unemployment had been high, for special attention. Towns and areas which had received particularly severe damage from bombing were identified as Red Areas, such as Bristol, Southampton, Hull, London and some military areas in Surrey and Hampshire,[42] in order to rebuild an otherwise active local economy rather than generate formerly declining local or regional economies as in the case of Development Areas. Table 5.3 demonstrates the higher levels of activity in the 'regions' prior to 1948. This provided a broad geographical spread of contracts during reconstruction, which permitted the large contractors, who had developed strong regional market penetration during the war, to maintain the spread of national operations.

Contractors had a diversity of work at the end of the war. Of the 19 registered contractors who employed more than 1,000 operatives, more than 8,000 operatives were employed on housing and related infrastructure, over 8,500 were employed on other new construction work and more than 5,500 were employed on war damage and repairs out of their total employed workforce which exceeded 37,000 operatives.[43] Although 36% of the employed operatives of these largest contractors were involved in housing and repair work at the end of 1945, this is a relatively small proportion as housing and repairs comprised 70% of the total construction in 1947 and 69% in 1948[44] and the major contractors were at this stage increasingly concentrating on the large scale contracting and civil engineering projects. These contractors had developed the capability of undertaking the large and complex projects and pursued these markets rather than the small scale projects and fragmented housing market.

The major contractors were involved in factory construction but one of the largest markets was power station construction under the programme of the Ministry of Fuel and Power. Most major contractors were simultaneously constructing a number of thermal power stations at this time. Investment had reached £40m in 1947, increasing to £60m in 1948 (see table 5.1). Taylor Woodrow, Laing and Sir Robert McAlpine were involved in this market. McAlpine, who had built stations before the war, had contracts from seven private companies.[45] An advantage of power station work was that there was political continuity and so once the first contract had been received construction companies were reasonably assured of continuity of work.[46] McAlpine usually had at least eight power station contracts at any time during reconstruction.

McAlpine concentrated on heavy and large construction and civil engineering contracts during the period, operating through a series of regional subsidiaries which proved to be very successful.[47] A new subsidiary was set up in South Wales in 1946 leading to the construction of plants at Pontypool for British Nylon Spinners and the Margam steelworks for the Steel Company of Wales, for example. McAlpine was also responsible for the reconstruction of one area in South London, and also undertook harbour contracts and hospital work. Approximately 50% was new work and 50% was repair and war damage work.[48]

Other contractors, such as Laing, operated on a more centralised basis. Laing built up its workforce at a rate of 100–150 people per week and in particular adopted a policy of recruiting and training school leavers.[49] Work included, apart from power station contracts, the Paton and Baldwins knitting wool factory at Darlington in 1946 which included a power station, a 4.5m litre (1m gallon) reservoir and a water treatment plant.[50] Other work included further defence contracts on aerodromes, the Abbey steelworks, also at Margam, a cement works at Shoreham for

British Portland Cement, local authority housing and housing contracts.[51]

McAlpine, Laing, Taylor Woodrow and other major contractors were
engaged in opencast coalmining. The opportunities for contractors to
undertake opencast mining dated back to December 1942 when the
MOWB began to act as agent to the Ministry of Fuel and Power.
McAlpine, for example, was mining around 1m tonnes (1m tons) each
year.[52] Opencast coalmining had one of the largest labour allocations
after the war.[53]

Despite the increased annual turnover as the construction markets expanded as a result of reconstruction, the increases were not always reflected in increased profits for the major contractors. The harsh winter and
the fuel crisis, while providing a stimulus to opencast coalmining, added
to the economic problems of 1947. Difficulties were experienced in some
aspects of contractors' operations. Plant and materials subsidiaries faced
intense competition in a market constrained by controls, shortage of
suitable contracts and materials supplies. Taylor Woodrow, for example,
invested in the latest equipment to maintain market penetration, export-
ing the old, reconditioned plant to third world countries.[54] The increase in
turnover again permitted the most competitive major contractors to consolidate the advantages they had gained in the war, so being in a position
to take higher profit rates when the economy and construction market
permitted.

It has been seen that economic reconstruction took precedence over
welfare provision, although the policy aims exceeded the capacity of the
economy. There was a lack of control in coordination and implementation, particularly due to the political expediency of showing 'concern' for
full employment policies. The capital concentration and diversification
resulting from the restructuring of the construction sector during the war
enabled the major contractors to undertake the major reconstruction
projects.

Construction, 1948–55

The housing markets

Public housing programmes had been cut back following the problems of
1947. This had the effect of bringing approvals and starts into line with
output. A fresh commitment to housing was introduced by the new Conservative Government in 1951. It proposed that 300,000 houses would be
built each year, but the undertaking should be primarily met by private
housebuilding for the owner occupied market.

On the one hand this was facilitated by the progressive relaxation of licensing, Defence Regulation 56A finally being withdrawn in November 1954. Development charges were withdrawn in 1953 so that the increased capitalised rental or a 'development value' would not be taxed.[55] In effect this was the removal of a tax on differential housing rent II which indirectly strengthened the barrier absolute ground rent put up to private sales and hence private housebuilding. The response from private housebuilders was not immediate. Apart from the expected time lag between the decision to build and completion, local authorities had requisitioned some of the land banks of a number of housebuilders and new land had to be sought.[56]

On the other hand expenditure on local authority housing rose by only 18% despite inflation rising 37.5% between 1948 and 1955. Coupled with this, loans obtained for public housing from the Public Works Loans Board by local authorities became subject to interest rates at market levels in 1951.[57] The change in policy had the effect of squeezing out some of the smaller operators who built public houses but could not raise the capital to obtain land banks for private building. It raised the profit for housebuilders who could take profits not only from the construction process but also from the capitalised housing rent. Some major contractors re-entered the private housebuilding market, but not to a large extent, their operations being more diverse with reconstruction contracts still being undertaken.

The switch from public to private housebuilding was not a very surprising outcome[58] because of the cutbacks in government capital expenditure following the problems of 1947, the failure of government controls in relation to policy and the greater commitment of the Conservative Party to support private interests overtly. Party ideologies, however, were not the most influential forces. The Labour Government in practice had supported rather than undermined the vast majority of private interests and the Conservatives adopted an interventionist role. Indeed, there was a high degree of continuity between the Labour and Conservative Governments.

Building and civil engineering markets

The building and civil engineering markets were set against a background whereby the economy appeared to be recovering between 1948 and 1950. A four year plan was outlined for the economic recovery in 1948, which included 33% of investment going towards industrial reconstruction.[59] Like previous plans, it was not implemented and the actual levels of capital investment were subject to dispute.[60] Industrial reconstruction, however, was still the priority as the Chancellor, Sir Stafford Cripps, made clear in a speech in 1949: 'You will see, then, that as long as we are in this impoverished state, the result of our tremendous efforts in two world wars, our own consumption requirements have to be last in the list of priorities. First are exports ...; second is capital investment in industry; and last are the needs, comforts and amenities of the family.'[61] The 1948 budget marked time, but many of the controls were lifted in what has been called the 'bonfire of controls'.[62] On the one hand this can be seen as an admission by the Labour Government of its failure to implement its policies, hence yielding to pressure from private industry to reduce restrictions and allow the market, determined by the rates of profit that could be achieved in different spheres of productive activity, to achieve reconstruction. On the other hand it could also be seen as a lost opportunity to steer the economy now that a greater balance had been achieved between the demands of policy and actual output.

In retrospect, given the form of the controls, such a course of action would have failed, being overtaken by national and international events, which are the most powerful forces as informed by the theory. Economic problems resurfaced in 1949 when the pound was devalued, which necessitated a further curtailment of capital expenditure, general construction and housebuilding suffering in particular.[63] The cuts proposed were £140m, of which £93m would be attributed to construction.[64] The Labour Government was losing its momentum by this time. The *Economic Survey for 1950*[65] was notable for the absence of Labour ideology or measures to sustain the reconstruction of the economy. *The Economist* commented, 'the perplexing thing about the *Survey* for 1950 is its lack of plan'.[66] Controls were further eased following the 'bonfire' of 1948, but the pressure for complete decontrol was strong.[67] Although the Labour Government was narrowly re-elected in 1950, it paved the way for, and was defeated by, the Conservatives in 1951.

The problems of devaluation over, the new government inherited the effects of world political and economic problems generated by the Korean war. The inheritance was a renewed raw materials shortage, depleted gold and dollar reserves, a renewed balance of payments problem and a surge in inflation of around 20%,[68] which finally led to the admission that inflation was not a temporary phenomenon but structural, as is war. The new government also inherited an economic expansion, albeit inflationary.[69] Defence expenditure increased as America demanded rearmament, which in turn expanded the British defence construction market. In 1950–1 defence spending was £830m of which £82m was spent on construction, which increased to £145m in 1951–2 and to £475m in 1952–4, remaining around 10% of total defence expenditure. Essential repair work still constituted a major problem, but construction activities were drawn away from repairs and into defence construction and private housebuilding. Restrictions on industrial and commercial building were therefore tightened.[70]

Despite these problems industry was beginning to recover through increase in productivity and exports, capital being accumulated as an indirect result of previous investments in war damage and repairs, the modernisation of fuel and power supplies, steel, chemical, engineering and agricultural production.[71] However, the Conservative Government was not very popular with its supporters. The government had been forced to maintain many controls or only partially relax controls due to the balance of payments problem and defence expenditure in 1951. This meant that the government withdrew its election pledges, weakening links between government and industry and reinforcing a trend which had begun with industry's disaffection with the Labour Government in its last years of office.[72]

The Korean war had threatened wider international conflict and posed economic problems, but it also stimulated the economy. As the threat of war receded, the economic recovery was sustained, partly because of the drive to build a total of 300,000 houses each year, but mainly because rearmament stimulated production and individual consumption increased. The rise in consumption was to produce further balance of payments problems as the expansion drew in imports leading to a trade deficit again in 1955.[73]

The construction market suffered as a result of cutbacks in capital expenditure despite the increase in defence spending on construction. Although the value of output increased between 1948 and 1955, discounting inflation the market shrank in real terms between 1948 and 1954, reaching a trough in 1951 (see figure 4.2). Even though construction suffered from reduced expenditure its significance in the British economy was growing. The percentage of the gross domestic fixed capital formation to the gross national product increased from 14.7% in 1949 to 17.0% in 1955 (see table 5.4), which gives an indication of the growth because most fixed capital formation which is not construction in itself requires buildings and infrastructure as a precondition of the investment. Gross trading profits for the industry increased from £47m in 1949 to £70m in 1955 with profit margins on total output ranging between 10.0% and 12.9% between 1950 and 1955 (see table 5.5), although the margin was 15.6% in 1949 (the first year for which margins can be calculated), thus suggesting, combined with the real reduction in output, that competition had intensified as reduced government expenditure and private investment

Table 5.4. *Gross domestic fixed capital formation as percentage of gross
national product at factor cost*

1949	14.7	1959	17.4	1969	17.3
1950	15.3	1960	18.0	1970	17.3
1951	15.2	1961	18.9	1971	17.1
1952	15.4	1962	18.5	1972	16.8
1953	16.2	1963	18.1	1973	17.1
1954	16.4	1964	20.0	1974	16.6
1955	17.0	1965	20.1	1975	16.6
1956	17.4	1966	20.3	1976	15.9
1957	17.8	1967	20.8	1977	15.3
1958	17.7	1968	21.4	1978	15.6
				1979	15.6

Source: Central Statistical Office.

worked their way through to the market. This shows the strategic importance of construction in the reconstruction and hence restructuring of the
economy in the aftermath of crisis, and shows the effect on capital
accumulation in the sector even though the problems of financing reconstruction induced mild symptoms of underproduction.

The Labour Government had given up attempts to redirect construction labour and influence the allocation of materials prior to the 'bonfire
of controls'.[74] Labour subcontracting, which was an essential feature of
construction during economic uncertainty, permitted labour to move
from site to site to find employment[75] and allowed labour to move into
repair work if new work was not available.[76] The Korean war drew labour
away from repair work and labour was concentrated on other construction projects resulting in higher productivity, but the desire in 1948 to
induce labour into export related industries was not achieved.[77]

The government finance of factory building in Development Areas was
reduced in part to reduce expenditure, partly to alleviate the overlicensing, but also to stimulate optimum industrial location and production in
the Midlands and south east so as to improve exports, and thus overcome
the balance of payments problems. The Board of Trade had assumed full
control of industrial approvals. Industrial building approvals in DAs had
been 46% in 1945, 44% at the beginning of 1948, but around 10% from
the end of 1948 onwards.[78] The aim of pursuing full employment policies
in the DAs took a lower priority in the face of national and international
economic events.

The construction market declined in real terms due to the cutbacks and
became increasingly centralised in the Midlands and south east. It gave a

Table 5.5. *Gross trading profits of the construction sector at 1975 prices and profit margins*

	Gross trading profits in £m	Profit margins as a percentage of total output
1949	194	15.6
1950	167	12.7
1951	158	11.2
1952	159	10.0
1953	203	11.6
1954	227	12.3
1955	241	12.9
1956	271	13.1
1957	287	13.4
1958	293	13.4
1959	300	12.5
1960	344	13.1
1961	342	12.0
1962	369	12.2
1963	433	13.9
1964	547	15.1
1965	526	13.7
1966	475	11.8
1967	436	9.7
1968	439	9.6
1969	601	11.6
1970	627	11.4
1971	700	11.4
1972	856	12.3
1973	916	10.3
1974	625	6.2
1975	742	6.5
1976	758	5.5
1977	691	5.0
1978	697	4.3

Source: Central Statistical Office.

stimulus to contractors to look for further work abroad. Costain decided in the early 1950s to seek more work abroad. It was to be the first company to achieve continuity of work in overseas markets on a large scale and from this time the combined turnover in overseas markets has been at least 40% of the group turnover.[79] The decline in the home market was not severe enough to stimulate capital concentration. This was in contrast to many other sectors in the economy, the 1940s and 1950s being a period of takeovers and mergers.[80] Construction, however, had already restructured its operations during the war and the increased competition was reflected in lower profit margins. The number of small firms began to fall as repair and maintenance work was completed or postponed,[81] but this had little effect on the top end of the construction market.

Major contractors did, however, develop and extend their corporate structure at this time,[82] a process which had begun during the war, with the result that a number of subsidiaries and regional offices were set up to reflect the growing diversity of operations, hence devolving the centralised control.[83] Laing, for example, adopted a regional basis of operation in 1948, having had highly centralised control after the war, and this was followed in 1952 by the company going public[84] with the property and contracting company being brought together under the ambit of John Laing and Son (Holdings) Ltd.

Laing illustrates many of the main trends and diversifications. It continued to undertake council housebuilding, having completed the 30,000th Easiform house by 1953 and the 50,000th by 1955. Industrial work had begun to decrease at the end of the 1940s and in the early 1950s, but increased again in 1953–4 particularly due to major contracts for oil companies, for example, work for Shell at Stanlow and Shell Haven and for Esso at Fawley. Other work included contracts for the government, the Air Ministry, power station contracts, chemical works and flood prevention work following the floods along the east coast in 1953. The company followed a conservative financial policy in the face of increased competition, keeping £3.6m as a general reserve in the accounts.[85]

Laing strengthened its current market position and looked towards the future through diversification. In addition to building and civil engineering work, heavy civil engineering work was pursued with contracts for pipelines, hydro-electric schemes and nuclear power contracts for the Windscale plutonium factory in 1948 and the Berkeley nuclear power station in 1955. Laing opened its first Thermalite building block plant in 1950, which was to open up an important market for the company when lightweight building blocks with a high thermal value or 'u-value' were demanded, and started a research and development centre at Elstree. The construction of offices began to show signs of constituting an important market, the company undertaking a number of schemes in London and anticipating future work through the formation of a joint development and construction company with Grosvenor Estates called Grosvenor –Laing, which would undertake developments in Britain and Canada.[86] This anticipated the drive to accelerate the circulation and realisation of surplus value in the economy as a whole and the growing demands from state agency office users.

Overseas work was growing, especially in South Africa, some of which was undertaken with Marley, Crittal–Hope and Glaxo. Laing, Wimpey and Holloway Bros. also had a maintenance contract for the Suez Canal base,[87] but work overseas was very sporadic a great deal of the time.

The heavy industrial construction and civil engineering projects were the mainstay of Laing at this time, leaving the company in a strong position by 1955. Pre-tax profits stabilised[88] but the company had consolidated its financial position despite the devaluation of the pound and inflation, and increased its asset backing through incorporating the property company into the main holding company.

In summary, total construction output increased dramatically after the war, and, although it fell due to problems facing the world economy between 1948 and 1951, it expanded subsequently in what was to begin an unprecedented growth in construction output (see figure 4.2). Wartime controls on development and construction had been removed by 1954 and therefore provided no future obstacles to the industry, not that they had posed any serious problems to the expansion of construction output during reconstruction.

The sector had already been restructured during the war, but its reconstruction activities aided other sectors to restructure, particularly steel, oil and chemical production, laying the basis for sustained capital accumulation in the economy. At the beginning of the reconstruction period only about 3% of the registered construction companies accounted for new construction work[89] and although some of the medium sized companies were beginning to re-establish themselves they did not pose severe competition for the large contractors, and many of the small companies and concerns which had proliferated immediately after the war and were engaged on repair work were declining in the 1950s. The main thrust of post-war reconstruction was therefore economic rather than welfare construction work for the main contractors as a precondition for a period of sustained capital accumulation in the economy as a whole.

Property, 1945–8

The context

Prior to the war the property and particularly the land markets were depressed.[90] Income from property fell by 15% during the war,[91] although property prices began to rise in the last 18 months of war when victory was in sight.[92]

The war damage was extensive although centralised in a number of areas. Bristol, Southampton, Hull, parts of Coventry and Plymouth had suffered severe damage. Nearly one third of all houses were damaged in the war,[93] but worst hit was London. About one third of the City was totally destroyed, the most damage being caused in the blitz between the winter of 1940 and spring of 1941.[94] The destruction extended from St Paul's and the Guildhall to the Whitbread Brewery in particular, with other pockets of destruction in other areas in the City.[95] The destruction was not so extensive as to reorientate spatially the economic activities of London, but 0.882 million m² (9.5m sq. ft) were destroyed throughout London.[96] The potential for redevelopment was therefore considerable. This potential was reinforced by the age of the remaining built environment, much of which was neither built for, nor could accommodate, the future and expanding circulation functions in the City of London (see table 5.6).

Table 5.6. *The age of offices in the City of London*

	Office units %[b]	Office floorspace %[b]
Pre-1880	20	11
1881–1909	28	16
1910–1945	22	23
1946–1965	19	33
1965–[a]	2	6

Notes: a. This information was compiled prior to 1974 and therefore includes the effects of the Brown Ban, but probably excludes the second postwar boom that followed.

b. Offices of mixed ages or without an age classification are excluded; therefore the columns do not add up to 100%.

Source: Corporation Land Use Survey, 1974, adapted from Barras, 1979a.

A number of individuals saw the short term opportunities opened up by war damage, if not the long term development potential. Had Britain lost the war they would have lost little, but victory secured them considerable gain. They were mainly individuals with an intimate knowledge of London, therefore not surprisingly 40% of the founders of development companies were estate agents and 10% were solicitors. They bought up bombed sites when the market was depressed and hence paid low prices.[97]

The plans and proposals for reconstruction dated back to 1941, but the main concerns to the future developers were the proposals on land use planning. Land use planning became a paradox for developers, some aspects acting as restraints, others enhancing their activities. Reith had envisaged reconstruction to be planned nationally, regionally and locally embodying social, economic and physical criteria, but over the course of the war the aims Reith had supported and the conceptions of how this might be achieved were gradually diluted. The council of Ministers first blocked the national–regional component of reconstruction, while the removal of Reith as Minister of Works and Planning with responsibility for reconstruction ensured that land use planning was disembodied from the other aims, being seen as a technical and physical matter.[98] The Uthwatt Committee, which had been concerned with compensation and 'betterment', had proposed land nationalisation, although in consequence only the charging of a 'betterment' levy on development and compensation for the loss of development rights were considered. The former was a deterrent to activity as betterment was a tax on differential building rent II, in effect enhancing the barrier posed by absolute ground rent. In retrospect it may seem strange that the radical proposals of land nationalisation should come from the conservative members of the Uthwatt Committee and that these proposals gained a degree of support amongst other members of the establishment. However, private interests, particularly industrialists, were concerned that agencies, such as the individuals who were to become developers and the financial institutions, would actually inhibit reconstruction by charging excessive rentals.[99] They had not appreciated that rents can only be charged on surplus profits over and above average profits which result from using that building and location compared to activities carried out under the worst conditions; hence rents can only undermine overall profitability when rates of profit fall in a recession and rentals are not reduced accordingly. There had also been an overestimation in some corners of the establishment of the political legitimation of increased direct state control at this time.

Land or bombed sites, however, which had not been bought at low wartime prices could pose a serious problem to future development during reconstruction if landowners held out for high land prices based on long term potential building rent levels. Land nationalisation could have overcome this problem, but land use planning as it emerged was sufficiently facilitative to overcome this obstacle by not only protecting but enhancing differential building rent II, although the betterment levy in contradiction did the reverse. What emerged at the end of the war was therefore a land use planning system which in essence was facilitative for the reconstruction and expansion of the economy, which developers could use to their advantage although it also had a constraining content.

Structuralists, however, have argued that this state intervention was necessary to buy off or overcome opposition from the working class,[100] although there is little evidence to suggest that this was the aim of planning rather than the reconstruction of the economy.[101] The population were more concerned with their day to day living at this time than with the rhetoric of politicians or the content of implemented policies,[102] while capital had been concerned with resolving the competition and conflicts over the form the reconstruction of the economy would take. Newman's criticism[103] that 'structuralists' ignore the actual processes in favour of focusing on the possible functional effects is therefore vindicated. Planning was and is therefore primarily facilitative, the most powerful contribution it makes to the development of capitalism being the surmounting of absolute ground rent as a barrier to investment and, thus, the formation of differential building rent II.

The property markets

The post-war property companies had three main origins. The public property companies emerged in the 1860s, such as the City of London Real Property Company.[104] They had primarily been investors although some were to enter into the development market after the second world war. The large estate landowners mainly retained their ground rents, but a few entered into property development. The remainder had largely stagnant ground rents and many of the buildings they did own were damaged in the war. A number of families were severely affected by death duties,[105] the result being that few could compete in the emerging development market. Additionally they did not have the foresight to buy low priced land during the war which would have risen in price, but were forced into sales after the war to meet commitments. The main origins of the developers were the small scale interwar high street and suburban shop and residential developers and the individuals who had bought land during and immediately after the war. They were concerned with development for sale and investment, whereas prior to the war investment had been considered an end in itself.

When the war did end development did not take off immediately. There were a number of reasons for this. The first and least significant was the 100% betterment levy which potentially acted as a deterrent to development, although in practice settlements of the levy had not been reached by the time it was abolished by the Conservative Government in 1951. Planning offered constraints in certain locations and on certain sites and building licences presented some constraint. But the most important constraint on development despite the licences was the insufficient accumulation of capital to justify expenditure on new offices and retailing outlets. The primary policy aim and function were to reconstruct the economic base of the nation state, which concentrated on restructuring in the sphere of production. It was only when this task was achieved that rates of profit were being received in industry to justify companies in the sphere of production and circulation investing in the built environment to speed up the functions of administration and the realisation of profit. This was not possible between 1945 and 1948 except for some companies concerned with exports which were a priority during reconstruction in the effort to re-establish capital accumulation and hence stave off renewed overproduction.

Property developers were primarily concerned with office developments, almost exclusively in London, and were not concerned with industrial development especially in Development Areas where nearly 50% of industrial development was being undertaken at this time.[106] During this period the government had an easy task controlling the number of licences issued for office development, but developers were able to obtain licences under two circumstances which were sufficient for them to establish themselves initially.

The first means was to develop offices which would be leased to the government. The state was expanding rapidly during this period as its welfare and economic functions multiplied. Marriott[107] criticised the government for renting from private developers rather than using its compulsory purchasing powers to obtain land and construct its own offices. However, the government's relative economic position was seriously weakened by the war and for its policies to be pursued finance had to be carefully allocated. After 1947, cutbacks in capital expenditure would certainly have curtailed this activity even if it had at first been pursued. From the government's point of view preferential terms were received, the Ministry of Works limiting developers to an 8% rate of return on their capital investment. Although this rate was small, particularly compared to later rentals, the market was certain from the developers' viewpoint, with no problems obtaining licences or raising finance for the construction as the proposed tenant was considered by the banks as safe and secure.[108]

The second way to obtain a licence for an office development was to let it in advance of construction to a company engaged in exports. A demand existed, but it was not substantial at this stage, government lessor schemes being the main market. Housing, although a priority in policy terms, was not a development market because housing rentals were frozen until 1950 due to the Rent Act of 1939, and thus rentals on potential developments would be uncompetitive in comparison with existing rentals if set at levels to justify an average rate of profit.

A further restriction faced by developers was the Capital Issues Committee limit on borrowing which was £10,000 per annum until 1947 when it was raised to £50,000. Developers overcame this problem by setting up separate subsidiary companies for every development, each of which would borrow the maximum amount.

Although this period permitted the developers to establish themselves initially, reconstruction in the sphere of circulation had hardly commenced. The provision of mortgages by members of the British Insurance Association represented only 6.2% of their funds in 1947[109] and is an indication of this. Profit rates had to be restored in production before capital investment could accelerate and intensify the competition to circulate and realise surplus value in the economy.

Land Securities was a small company which owned three houses and had assets of £19,321 in government securities in 1935 when Harold Samuel, a former estate agent, bought the company in 1944.[110] It was destined to become the sector leader. Harold Samuel is often considered the founding father of the post-war property company. Land Securities certainly introduced a large number of innovations. They introduced the full repairing lease, which made the building users responsible for maintenance. This reduced the management and administrative overheads of property companies. The company initially grew by the skilful use of borrowed finance. Expansion was primarily obtained through property investment, although a government lessor scheme was undertaken by the company. Property investments bought with borrowed money could in part be mortgaged, the properties acting as collateral for further borrowing as the capitalised rental or the book asset value of the property grew at the end of the war. The devaluation of property had ceased at the end of the crisis, reconstruction bearing the potential to increase capital accumulation in the economy as a whole with some property investments potentially yielding surplus profits for their user in the future. This potential for creaming off the surplus profits as rent was being capitalised in the asset value of these investments.

Some of the investments Land Securities undertook were blocks of flats which had been requisitioned as offices during the war. It was generally believed that these properties would be subject to the betterment levy once derequisitioning took effect unless they reverted to their former use. This was not the case and Samuel, recognising this aspect of the Town and Country Planning Act, 1947, acquired a number of these investment properties.

Industrial property development was an active market, but property developers were not very active. The government had built its own factories during the war or had requisitioned factories, and so new development had not been undertaken during the war. Slough Estates was an established leading company. The estate at Slough had not suffered from war damage and therefore a need for redevelopment did not arise during reconstruction.[111] There was an initial demand for new factories on the estate after the war, but the company was constrained by a shortage of materials, by problems of obtaining licences because of the supply of labour and housing in Slough in relation to employment and in relation to national employment policy, and finally by constraints on borrowing due to the advice of the Capital Issues Committee. Therefore development was restricted to constructing factories and extensions for existing tenants.

However the company began to expand outside Slough. The Board of Trade asked the company to develop a government sponsored estate in Swansea in 1945. It also acquired a site five miles south of Birmingham town centre. A further acquisition was made in 1948 at Greenford, Middlesex. The 8.9 hectare (22 acre) site was formerly an ordnance depot already containing 21 units let to the War Department on a lease which would expire in 1959.[112] Although rentals only increased from £151,000 in 1945 to £180,000 by 1948, the asset value of the investments was calculated in the books to have increased from £2.3m to £3.0m over the same period.[113] This rise reflected the future development and hence rental potential of the company.

The tenants on this type of industrial estate were predominantly engaged in light manufacturing, many of the commodities being produced for consumption rather than other production processes. The impetus behind industrial reconstruction particularly focused on the production of the means of production, in other words raw materials and primary commodities such as steel, oil and chemicals.

In summary, the property sector was not very active in development, although during the first phase of reconstruction the preconditions were present and the conditions were emerging for future expansion as the theoretical arguments anticipate. It was not therefore government controls which were the main constraint but the lack of demand in the economy for commercial and light industrial buildings.

Property, 1948–55

The commencement of the restructuring of the sphere of circulation began at the end of this period. Although Marriott[114] states that it was the lifting of the licences in November 1954 which was the 'starting gun', development had been gathering momentum in advance, and while licensing had created some pent up demand in the last years the amount of unsatisfied demand has been exaggerated in the past. The recovery of the economy was the undoubted cause of growing actual and future demand for offices, and the licences were a secondary factor to the gathering momentum for office development. The drive to increase export penetration and the restructuring of the sphere of capital circulation in efforts to sustain capital accumulation and offset the tendency for the rate of profit to fall were emerging.

What did emerge in this period were the conditions for the expansion to come. Industry was completing its restructuring and the new property sector was emerging in order to meet the demands which the economy would make. The war had created the preconditions for the emergence of the sector, and during this second phase of reconstruction the conditions for large scale development, particularly office development and particularly in London, matured.

Finance for the property markets

Prior to building licences being lifted in 1954 approximately £50m of building work was in the pipeline[115] and therefore developers had been anticipating a considerable increase in demand regardless of whether licences were lifted. One of the major problems for developers was financing schemes. Initially this had been overcome through the setting up of subsidiaries for each development to circumvent the restrictions of the Treasury's Capital Issues Committee, but with property investors and developers wishing to expand in a period of inflation new means of finance were required. Links with the financial institutions, particularly insurance companies, dated back to the interwar period, but new formal links were to be forged in this period although their widespread use and acceptance occurred in the late 1950s.

Insurance companies had high liquidity with investments rising by 73% from £2,561m in 1947 to £2,816m in 1953 and to £4,440m in 1955.[116] The insurance companies were looking for long term investments, which would maintain their money value in an economy that was considered inflationary in the long term since the advent of the Korean war.[117] Equities or shares were yielding 3.8% in 1945 increasing to 6.1% in 1953 but falling to 4.4% in 1955.[118] However, it is the fluctuations of the share markets which make it primarily for short term investors and indeed the British Insurance Association members only increased their investments in equities from 10.5% of their annual investments in 1947 to 15.4% in 1955.[119] Government gilt edged securities have traditionally been considered a long term investment but yields ranged between 3% and 4% whereas prime shop and office yields were around 5.5% and

6–7% respectively.[120] The notion that everything was safe in bricks and mortar was becoming generally accepted at this time, property appearing to be a very appropriate investment for the insurance companies and later for pension funds once they were permitted to invest in property from 1955. Insurance companies increased their mortgage provision from £153m in 1947 to £531m in 1955 and their investment in property and ground rentals increased from £148m to £360m over the same period.[121] This represents an increase of 247% and 143% respectively compared to the 73% increase in equity investments. Indeed the Norwich Union had been the first institutional investor to undertake direct development in 1949.[122]

Prior to referring to the case studies a few introductory remarks concerning the financial structure of property companies will be helpful.

Property companies are traditionally highly geared, unlike industrial sectors. This is because their earnings are relatively stable and therefore less subject to short term fluctuations in the economy. In terms of their financial gearing, property companies try to maximise their borrowings and minimise their share or equity capital, although the ratios become more closely related as insurance companies and pension funds provide loans for schemes in return for equity in the schemes or in companies through convertible share loan stocks. Asset gearing is intimately related. The principal asset of a property company will be its property investments and land bank, which it can mortgage or use as collateral to raise borrowings. In other words the growth of assets leads to the growth in borrowing thus increasing the potential to expand development or investment activity. Asset gearing is also high in property companies and expansion can become a self-generating process provided the market remains buoyant, thus not threatening the capital asset values of property companies. This process is reinforced by the belief that investments in bricks and mortar are always safe. The fall in property prices preceding and during the war in Britain was being forgotten at this time and the large scale restructuring of land and property ownership through invasion was not experienced in Britain in either world war. This new perception, coupled with institutions looking for long term investments, was not surprisingly leading to the growth and reinforcement of this belief. It is also worth noting that investment trusts tend to be highly geared, thus making them an appropriate vehicle for property entrepreneurs, like Harold Samuel and Lew Hammerson, to take over to pursue their investment and development activities.

The institutional links were reinforced after the lifting of the licences in 1954. The government was faced with inflationary trends and a deteriorating balance of payments due to increasing consumption drawing imports into the economy. The response was to reintroduce lending restrictions and raise the bank rate, hence pushing up interest rates. Simultaneously the Capital Issues Committee began to refuse company applications to raise finance through rights issues[123] and so property companies turned away from higher interest rates on bank loans and new share issues towards the fixed low interest rates on loans offered by the insurance companies. Conditions in the world market therefore affected the financing of the property market.

The insurance companies required equity participation in order to enter into these arrangements. The sale and leaseback was used to satisfy those requirements. The arrangement simply involves the property developer selling the completed development to an institutional investor and then leasing the development back from the institution, paying it a ground rent which may also involve a portion of the building rent. The developer could then repay all the loans required for the assembly of the land and construction. If these loans initially were obtained from an insurance company, as was increasingly the case at this time, the loans may have been made for a long period of time, so that they would be rolled over to finance future developments as each sale and leaseback was undertaken. These loans frequently took the form of convertible loan stocks which are fixed interest loans that can be converted into ordinary shares of the property company at specified rates and at specified times.[124] These borrowing and financing arrangements meant that the links between the financial institutions and the property developers soon became long term formal links deriving from short term financial necessity. The institutions were therefore taking equity in individual schemes, which was to become a central feature of the property market.

The sale and leaseback, although agreed prior to construction, takes effect on completion of the development and therefore the developer may require short term finance to bridge between the commencement and completion of the development. In many cases loans from the banks or institutions would provide the bridging finance, although raising loans was difficult in the 1950s, the links with the institutions not having matured at this stage. Many contractors were looking for new markets during the early 1950s as workloads declined. A number of contractors were willing to finance the construction for developers to prevent underproduction. There were reasons for this. First, they anticipated this as an important new market which would yield above average profit margins. Second, their low overheads, the use of subcontractors and credit from materials suppliers meant that they could undertake the financing of their own work without threatening their liquidity. Sir Robert McAlpine, for example, undertook a number of these arrangements, although not on all developments.[125] Other financing contractors included Costain, Cubitts, Laing and Taylor Woodrow.

The property markets

Developers had to obtain planning permission for development proposals. It is obviously to the advantage of the developer to maximise the floorspace within the planning densities. The Third Schedule of the Town and Country Planning Act, 1947, provided a loophole which allowed 10% to be added on to pre-war buildings in terms of volume rather than floorspace. When the Conservative Government came to power the Minister of Housing and Local Government, Harold Macmillan, allowed this to include post-war buildings. This had two effects. First, the redevelopment of an old Victorian building permitted a greater amount of floorspace within the same volume with modern lower ceiling heights and, second, 10% could immediately be added on to the total volume of the building once planning permission was obtained. The original aim of this schedule was to permit the expansion of an existing building without betterment having to be paid.[126] Betterment was abolished but the schedule remained, providing the means to rebuild the built environment on a large scale once the main vacant war damage sites had been developed. Local authorities could oppose the Third Schedule in principle, but in practice were unable to as they became liable to compensate the developer for the loss of development potential.[127]

The City was designated by the Holden–Holford plan[128] a single commercial use zone with no distinction between office and other business premises. The result was that there was a net transference of industrial and warehousing uses to office uses in the course of redevelopment. Office space increased by 11.2% between 1939 and 1949 and by 3.9% between 1949 and 1959, while warehousing fell by 6.3% and 3% and industrial floorspace fell by 1.6% and 0.5% over the same period.[129] This process was facilitated by the fact that over 50% of the industrial and warehousing stock had suffered war damage.[130]

The way had been paved for the first property boom in the late 1950s and early 1960s, but the market was already expanding. The increase in interest rates which had stimulated developers to look for new funding arrangements also helped increase the market for renting.[131] The finance required for reconstructing industry, the restrictions on raising capital plus the capital expenditure and interest on borrowed money rendered owner occupancy uneconomical for industrial companies. However, industrial companies were requiring more office space, not only to 'impress themselves and their clients'[132] but also to increase their efficiency in the administration of their corporations and realising their profits. The strategic importance of offices economically and geographically in the circulation of capital and the realisation of surplus value into profits in the competition to realise above average rates of profit in the short term and stave off overproduction in the longer term for each user was beginning to become an important force in the property market.

The City development market was also growing. The first major postwar development in the City was along the south side of Cheapside, EC2, undertaken by the Bank of England. The land price in the area was about £107.6 per m² (£10 per sq. ft). Once Barrington House and Garrard House in Gresham Street, EC3, were let to City tenants, other developments were undertaken. The City of London Real Property Company had begun to develop bombed areas south of Fenchurch Street, EC3.[133]

The development market for central London was showing the signs of expansion. Planning permissions between mid-1948 and 1955 totalled 2,557,000 m² whereas completions during the period amounted to 547,000 m², thus around 2 million m² of potential development existed. The size of developments was increasing, the average floorspace rising from 2,440 m² to 3,859 m² in the period.[134]

A number of companies were emerging through innovation, takeovers of trusts as a vehicle for property investment and development, and through diversification. The asset base of Land Securities had grown from £0.001m to £11m by 1952.[135] Land Securities was primarily London based although an associate company, Ravenseft,[136] which was later to become a subsidiary, had started to develop bombed town centres designated as Red Areas.

MEPC had been diversifying away from housing investment into office investment and instigated its initial entry into the development market in 1955. The company also set up a Canadian subsidiary.[137]

Hammerson Property and Investment Trust was formed in 1953 by the takeover of the Associated City Investment Trust, which was a shareholding concern that became a vehicle to buy freehold office investments and pursue development.[138]

Slough Estates was already established and was consolidating earlier activities.[139] Other companies were important at the time too, but these companies were to become the largest companies by the 1970s, and illustrate the diverse origins of the emerging sector.[140]

Conclusions

The world economy was in the process of reconstruction, which was not straightforward. Insufficient was being produced for the potential markets, production having been dislocated by war. Physical destruction created further limitations. The world banking system was criticised for retarding reconstruction through conservative lending policies[141] and this was echoed in British banking. The Labour Government tried to facilitate the process of reconstruction initially. It used financial policies and indirect controls inherited from the war. The financial strategy led to economic problems, and the inadequacy of controls plus the partial dilution of cooperation between government and industry led to policy aims remaining unfulfilled. There were differences between the Labour and Conservative Governments, particularly at the level of political rhetoric, but the changing policies and strategies were carried out with considerable continuity between the governments. These general conclusions concord with the theoretical expectations during the aftermath of an economic crisis.

The construction sector benefited considerably from the surge of work during reconstruction and the major contractors largely consolidated their market position. The controls aimed at the sector had little effect on the industry, the indirect controls and the state of the economy having the most influence on their growth and output. The construction sector played an important part in providing the conditions for other sectors, particularly industrial sectors, to restructure their operations. This aided the completion of reconstructing the economy and the built environment as a prelude to renewed and sustained capital accumulation.

The property sector emerged after the war in a new form. The pre-war investors were largely superseded by a new investment and development sector, which had used the preconditions of wartime destruction to establish itself immediately after the war and had created the conditions between 1948 and 1955 for large scale development programmes. The emergence of this sector was necessary to facilitate the administration of national and international companies and to speed up and realise profits in the sphere of circulation by rebuilding the environment, especially in London, to meet these new demands and receive the surplus profits in the form of rents derived from these activities. The financial sector, through the insurance companies, had forged links with property companies which were to be crucial in the financing of future development on a large scale.

The circulation of capital and especially the realisation of surplus value is of central importance in an era of capitalism characterised by crises of overproduction. The built environment plays an important role in this respect. The use of offices facilitates the speed up in the sphere of circulation and greater demands were to be placed upon office use in four respects. First, the demand for floorspace was to increase quantitatively and qualitatively, thus reflecting the growing importance of the sphere. Second, the sphere was highly centralised, London being the focus, although some decentralisation occurred later. This occurred because, third, competition was to increase in the effort to gain advantage over competitors by speeding up the circulation and hence realisation process. Fourth, as the tendency for profit rates to fall ushered in crisis, competition intensified in this sphere to gain advantage to stave off the effects instead of facilitating expansion as had previously been the case.

The implication for the property market was that property was now considered as an asset that would appreciate; in other words, potential rental growth was being capitalised and yields were falling. This was a reversal from the pre-war and wartime experience in the property market.

The licensing system had not posed a severe restraint on development at this time. Although some pent up demand existed when the controls were lifted, demand prior to 1954 had largely been satisfied. Their removal was undoubtedly an important psychological turning point at a time when the future demands were being anticipated by property companies and in this respect their removal acted as a trigger to increased development activity.

The state played a significant role in the reconstruction period, but it had diminished in comparison to the wartime role. Private industry was making less demands on the state compared to the demands for support during crisis. The state no longer needed to intervene directly on such an extensive scale, indirect controls being pursued with varying success in the main, to facilitate the restructuring of the economy.

The reconstruction of the economic base of the nation state had largely been achieved in this period, and thus the conditions for sustained capital accumulation had been established, ushering in a period of prosperity.

6

Development and construction during prosperity

The period between 1955 and 1968 was one of relative prosperity, particularly in the 1960s, and the aim of this chapter is to demonstrate how development and construction responded and contributed to the British economy.

The chapter will consider development activity during the first post-war property boom between 1955 and 1964 and will then consider the aftermath of the boom between 1964 and 1968. Construction activity declined between 1955 and the turn of the decade, at least as far as the major contractors were concerned, and then expanded very rapidly until 1968 when there was a temporary decline in construction output (see figures 4.2 and 6.1).

The foundations already laid in the property sector enabled the sector to respond to the increased demand for new offices and retailing premises as the sphere of circulation restructured its operations to meet the needs of an expanding economy in terms of administration and profit realisation. A peak of development activity had been reached by the turn of the decade and takeover activity increased as capital concentration occurred and property investment and management were increasingly emphasised. The formal links with the financial institutions matured and government intervention tended to reflect market trends and reinforced the concentration in the sector.

The construction sector experienced a considerable boom in the 1960s. The expansion and restructuring of the sphere of circulation provided a very buoyant market, and many contractors began to undertake their own property development, having been financing the construction stage for developers. The industrial market began to improve in the 1960s and government capital expenditure increased substantially, producing a very large investment led construction market in health, housing, education and especially roads. Construction investment in the nationalised industries was low in this period and thus government expenditure was mainly concerned with providing the

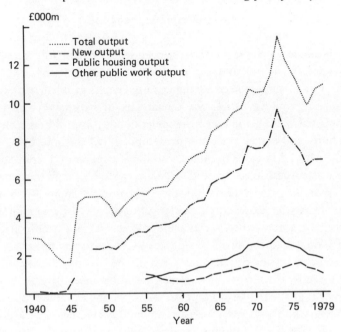

£000m

········ Total output
— · — New output
— — Public housing output
——— Other public work output

Figure 6.1. Total, new and public construction output at 1975 prices
Sources: Ministry of Works, Ministry of the Public Board of Works, Department of the
Environment.

infrastructure and utilities for production and infrastructure, services
and welfare facilities for a growing population.[1]

By 1968 rates of profit in industry were beginning to slow. Investment,
particularly state expenditure, had increased the proportion of fixed capital in the economy which was a tax on company profits over and above the
profitability realised from the benefits of the increased investment. The
proportion of constant capital to variable capital was therefore increasing, thus inducing a tendency for profit rates to fall. Statistically this can
be illustrated by the increase in the gross domestic fixed capital formation
in relation to the gross national product at factor cost which increased
from 17% in 1955 to a peak in 1968 of 21.4%.[2] The declining rates of
profit were leading to an overproduction in relation to the size of the
markets as the population increase had been catered for in market terms
and the establishment of new markets at home and overseas was
becoming increasingly constrained and competitive.

It will be shown, however, in this chapter and the following chapter
that the property and construction sectors once again do not exactly
coincide with the average in the economy as a whole. This is not because
these sectors act as a law unto themselves but is the result of their relationship to the rest of the economy.[3]

Economic context, 1955–68

At the moment when the economy seemed set to expand following the rise in consumer demand and the increase in investment in 1954–5, the economy again experienced a balance of payments problem in 1956–7 as imports grew and Keynesian-type demand led management pushed up the rate of inflation. This induced the government to put a brake on credit availability and deflate the economy temporarily,[4] the onus being on the management and unions in industry to boost exports and reduce wages.[5] There was success in restraining wage increases, although this seemed to have little long term effect on the reduction of imports;[6] however, employment was growing, particularly in office work where an annual increase of 3.2% per annum was achieved between 1951 and 1961.

No sooner had the problems of 1956–7 been overcome than a new balance of payments problem occurred in 1961. A pay pause was introduced in July 1961 to try to correct the imbalance.[7] It was, however, apparent that successive attempts to stimulate the economy followed by deflationary measures from the government had created over the decade a series of 'stop–go' economic cycles. The Conservative Government's strategy of short term interventionist policies had failed and so it initiated 'indicative planning', which was aimed to stimulate a more even pattern of growth over five year periods through voluntary cooperation between the government, industry and the unions.[8] The result was the setting up of the National Economic Development Council (NEDC) which became active in 1962.[9] By 1963 it was apparent that it had adopted a rival role to the Treasury, which was more concerned with economies rather than the economics of the nation state. Although the Chancellor sympathised with NEDC, it lost some of its impetus after 1963.[10] It had advocated a growth in the gross domestic product of 4% per annum, whereas the actual was 2.9%, a growth in total fixed capital investment of 5.3%, whereas the actual was 4.4%, and public investment of 7.0%, whereas the actual was 6.4%.[11] Public investment was one of the few areas to do well, but this added to the problems because private industrial investment fared badly, thus not producing or reaching the profits to pay for the increased public expenditure. So the government's deficit financing increased, which led to further stop–go measures and the outbreak of another balance of payments crisis in 1966 as exports failed to reach expectations.[12]

The introduction of NEDC had stolen the interventionist initiative away from the Labour opposition, but its failure led industry reluctantly to welcome the newly elected Labour Government in 1964 and links between government, industry and the unions flourished until the problems of 1966.[13] A Labour Government was returned to power espousing the scientific and technological revolution which could be achieved through indicative planning leading to 8% growth in the economy. Its other election pledges depended on achieving this growth rate and the Department of Economic Affairs (DEA), which was ranked in status although not in practice above the Treasury, was set up to coordinate this political and economic aim through industrial, regional and incomes policies.[14] The DEA shared a number of similarities with the Ministry of Production and, indeed, its structure was influenced by war experience.[15]

NEDC became a forum for discussion between employers and unions while the main economic policies became enshrined in the National Plan which was aimed to correct the balance of payments, repay government debt and generate internal trade. Although the government persuaded employers and unions to sign a statement of intent on productivity, prices and wages there was no strategy to increase exports.[16] This was the principal weakness in the Plan, but it was still believed that it could be successful until the renewed balance of payments crisis in 1966. The government increased its borrowing to over £400m and the bank rate went up to 7%. Austerity measures were introduced including a wage freeze, public expenditure cuts and a devaluation of sterling. Relations between government and industry became sour. Employers had lost faith in the policies, the unions felt downgraded within the state due to the wage restraints, and the days lost in strikes nearly doubled between 1967 and 1968, many of the strikes being unofficial, which concerned the Confederation of British Industry (CBI) and the Trades Union Congress (TUC). There was general concern about the possible consequences of government policies, the Ministry of Labour commenting to the Donovan Commission, 'if trade union leaders accept [the Prices and Incomes Bill] there is a risk that they will cease to be regarded by their membership as representative of their interests, and their influence and authority may be transferred to unofficial leaders'.[17]

The period had been one of relative prosperity, although all attempts to sustain an equal growth rate had failed. However, the period of prosperity was coming to an end in the second half of the 1960s, as rates of profit fell in industry, industrial militancy and unemployment grew, austerity measures and capital investment cutbacks were imposed, and the balance of payments problem was renewed. The nation state was beginning to witness the effects of falling rates of profit due to low productivity and an overproduction of commodities in relation to the markets available. Efforts made to increase productivity and increase exports to overseas markets could no longer keep at bay the tendency for the rate of profit to fall due to an increase in the national organic composition of capital, especially through state capital expenditure. This had been rapidly leading to overproduction which became the cause of crisis in its own right.

Property and development, 1955–64

Finance for the property markets

The deflationary measures of 1956 had a dampening effect on the growing development impetus, but the indirect consequences were favourable to development. The credit restrictions drove developers closer to the financial institutions while potential building users preferred to use their money capital to invest in their primary activity rather than use or raise capital for owner occupancy. Developers were using the financial institutions as a source of finance, not from mortgages but increasingly in sale and leaseback arrangements, which had already been used by many industrialists and had been pioneered by Charles Clore's City and Central in the property investment market. Its use for development was becoming more widespread, which is reflected in the increase in property and ground rentals compared to mortgage provision (see table 6.1). Contractors, such as Wimpey and Sir Robert McAlpine, were increasingly financing construction, often on a partnership basis with equity sharing for each development.

Table 6.1. *British Assurance Association members' investment in property, 1955–8*

	Total investments £m	Equities %	Mortgages %	Property and ground rentals £m	%
1955	4,430	15.4	12.0	360	8.1
1956	4,790	16.1	13.1	400	8.1
1957	5,149	17.2	13.4	446	8.5
1958	5,530	18.5	13.6	496	8.9

Source: Whitehouse, 1964.

It was nonetheless at this stage that the market was expanding, yielding high development profits. Having discounted site and construction costs, the capitalised rental amounted to 28% of the assets in 1956, 43% in 1958 and 38% in 1960 in the City of London.[18] Prime yields in 1956–7 were in the region of 7.5% for offices and 5.5% for retailing properties. The expansion finally established the new property sector which received a Stock Exchange listing in 1957.

Table 6.2. *Development in the City of London, 1952–8*

	Offices		Total	
	m²	(sq. ft)	m²	(sq. ft)
1952	109,624	1,180,000	143,069	1,540,000
1953	74,600	803,000	74,600	803,000
1954	101,449	1,092,000	101,449	1,092,000
1955	44,778	482,000	44,778	482,000
1956	101,820	1,096,000	101,820	1,096,000
1957	194,258	2,091,000	200,761	2,161,000
1958	139,167	1,498,000	150,966	1,625,000
Total	765,696		817,443	

Source: Investors Chronicle, 1959.

London was the centre of development activity and the majority of developments were offices, mainly for private companies, the breakdown for the City being given in table 6.2. Although the market was centralised in the City and Greater London, suburban centres were beginning to pave the way for more decentralised activity, in particular Croydon. Ravenseft, for example, was building shops and offices in Chester, Crewe and South Shields in 1956.[19] After the reconstruction of devastated town centres New Town development also provided a development market for companies like Ravenseft. Other centres were expanding: for example Leeds increased its stock of offices by 11.5% between 1955 and 1960,[20] although information on the proportion undertaken by development companies is unavailable.

In the period between 1957 and 1960 the balance of payments problem was being overcome and temporary deflationary measures gave way to inflationary tendencies again. The developers had been driven into the hands of the financial institutions by credit restrictions and the need to have substantial financial backing if development programmes were to be further expanded. The financial institutions also wished to benefit from investments which kept pace with or exceeded the overall inflationary trends. The *Investors Chronicle* commented:

The granting of straightforward mortgages are a thing of the past. Equity shares and fixed returns have been demanded by insurance companies as they have wanted to benefit from the 'anti-inflationary principle' too. Property companies have benefitted from these arrangements because they have received preferential treatment during the credit squeeze even though they give up some of their income. The long term expansion remains the priority.[21]

Property companies would expand in the longer term because of the

Table 6.3. *Properties and loan capital, 1951–60*

	Properties £	Total income £	Loan capital £
1951	339,878	15,950	157,057
1952	352,880	28,059	181,389
1953	416,265	91,958	199,790
1954	508,201	126,248	199,088
1955	1,479,651	194,542	436,316
1956	4,215,956	307,880	1,629,881
1957	3,175,051	407,616	1,464,969
1958	4,392,413	560,799	1,899,756
1959	5,328,252	609,552	2,644,882
1960	13,719,435	1,203,564	7,812,734

Source: Investors Chronicle, 1960a.

relation of office development and investment to the centralisation and expansion of capital circulation functions in the economy. The current trends of demand were indicative of the underlying process. Property companies were gearing themselves to meet these demands. Table 6.3 shows the rapid expansion of property investment and development companies as the income and the capitalised rental or capital asset values grew, but most significant is the dramatic increase in short and long term borrowing by property companies in the second half of the 1950s as links between property companies and financial institutions began to mature.

The financial institutions had taken an equity participation in specific developments, usually in the region of 5–15%.[22] This began to complicate the theoretical division between building and ground rent. Ground rents had been stagnant during the century, but sales and leasebacks potentially permitted the institutions to receive not only the ground rent and a rate of return on their loan capital but also a portion of the building rent.

Insurance companies were also beginning to take a shareholding or equity in entire property companies by obtaining the shares or the option to convert loans into shareholdings. Shareholdings are given for some of the major companies in table 6.4. By 1960 equity participation in individual schemes or company shares or both had become commonplace. The financial institutions were growing and the property markets constituted an important investment outlet in the spread and mix of their investments in this period of general prosperity.

The property markets, 1958–60

Although a peak of development activity occurred between 1958 and 1960, planning approvals continued to anticipate an expanding market.

Table 6.4. *Insurance company shareholdings in property companies in 1960*

Property company	Insurance company	Equity %	Conversion
Amalgamated Securities	Guardian	Small	—
Baranquilla Investments	Pearl	10.0	+ option
Berkeley Property and Investment Company	Prudential	23.5	—
Brixton Estate	Clerical, Medical	17.1	—
Capital and Counties	Norwich Union	8.4	—
Central and District	Prudential	4.4	—
City Centre Properties	Pearl	20.4	—
	Legal and General	JV	
Edger Investments	Prudential	6.6	Yes
Land and House	General Accident	25.0	+ option
Land Securities	Legal and General	6.0	Yes
London, City and Midland	Sentinel	48.0	—
London and Westcliffe	Sentinel	57.9	—
Oddenino's Property	Pearl	16.5	—
Sackville Estates	Provincial	6.6	—
Scottish Metropolitan	Guardian	Modest	—
Second Covent Garden	Eagle Star	8.2	—
Shop Investments	Clerical, Medical	26.2	—
Town and City Properties	Prudential	5.6	—
Western Ground Rents	Clerical, Medical	16.0	—

Source: Whitehouse, 1964.

The London County Council approved 418,060 m² (4.5m sq. ft) in 1961 and 278,706 m² (3m sq. ft) in 1962, a total of 4,645,113 m² (50m sq. ft) having been approved since the war.[23] The market was becoming more competitive as more property companies forged links with institutions and as more became listed on the Stock Exchange, off-loading their assets through the market to avoid tax in order that development activity could be expanded to the full. Capital assets were beginning to show signs of rapid growth (see figure 6.2 for a sample of companies). Rentals had already begun to take off as many of the investments made by property companies had been bought at prices which did not reflect the forth-coming lease reversions. Their full impact on capital assets had not been appreciated by investors at this time. Prime yields were in the region of 7.5% for offices and 5.5–6.0% for retail units, while industrial yields were higher at 10%. Office and retail development and investment were becoming increasingly concerned with the capital growth in assets as well as rental income derived from the property market, the capital assets

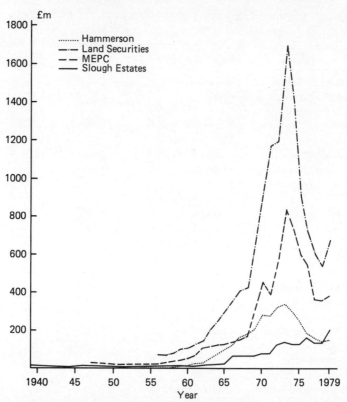

Figure 6.2. Property company capital assets at 1975 prices
Source: Company Annual Reports and Accounts.

being valued on the basis of future rental income in an inflationary economy rather than on current rental income.

Landowners were aware of these changes and so building leases to property companies, although remaining at 99 years or being increased to 125 years, were incorporating 30 year ground rent review periods.[24] However, ground rents have not kept pace with yields on whole properties,[25] but this should be expected because ground rents are derived theoretically from the surplus rent over and above the average rate of profit in the sector in the short term and in the economy as a whole in the very long term, although sales and lease periods complicate this notion in practice.[26]

During this expansionary phase new developments were no longer pre-let prior to construction. Development was taking place ahead of letting because of the high demand for space in the sphere of capital circulation due to its growing significance in the economy. The time lag between development, completion and letting and the eventual extent of demand for space to facilitate the acceleration of capital circulation and profit realisation did lead to a subsequent threat of an oversupply of offices.

In London a number of developments were under way, the City having some of the most notable developments. Property companies were not so active in the City as elsewhere in London, but the City of London Real Property Company, Felix Fenston's Metropolitan and Provincial, and Harry Hyam's Oldham Estates had a number of schemes. The peak of completions in London occurred in 1958 although the City experienced its peak in 1960.[27] This is due in part to five large City schemes along Route 11, which involved a number of agents (see table 6.5).

Table 6.5. *Five developments on Route 11*

Development	Developing agent	Area m²
Moor House	City and Central	14,500
St Alphage House	St Alphage Investment Co. (Wingate 25%; McAlpine 40%[a])	27,551
Lee House	Centrovincial, Metropolitan and Provincial Properties	15,375
Royex House	Oldham Estates[b]	15,508
40 Basinghall Street	Hammerson[c]	17,185

Notes: a. Sir Robert McAlpine provided building finance in addition.
  b. In association with Wimpey.
  c. In association with Wates and Phoenix Assurance.

Sources: Marriott, 1967; Barras, 1979a.

Out of central London Croydon was beginning to show signs of expansion. Croydon's Corporation Act of 1956 enabled the local authority to 'develop either themselves or by selling or leasing to others land bought under the bill and not required for street works requirements'.[28] The authority could therefore positively initiate development, and by 1959 the first three new office blocks had been completed.[29] These would have a demonstration effect that offices located on a mainline route out of London would be in demand for many companies as headquarters or as offices for the more routinised administrative and clerical functions.

Elsewhere in the country it was retail development which was the most significant. In the early 1950s Ravenseft had a virtual monopoly, but other companies were beginning a challenge: Arndale, Hammerson, Laing Properties, Murrayfield, and Town and City along with Ravenseft becoming the six major town centre retailing developers by 1964.[30]

By 1960 the market changed, mainly due to the relationship between the financial institutions and property developers and investors rather than the changing relationship between the property[31] and building owners and building users. Indeed, if there was any relationship it was an inverse one whereby the development market had reached its peak, although it was still very active, while the financial investment in property was still increasing in a self-reinforcing fashion.

In the period between 1960 and 1963 the established links between development companies and the financial institutions reached maturity. The sale and leaseback was not only established as a means of raising finance but was also in common use. Property companies with expanding development programmes could not justify repaying interest on loan capital out of rental income and so the leaseback was more suitable.[32] Institutions used their financial position to obtain equity in schemes or in property companies. These were now established demands, the institutions realising that once rental reviews became more frequent, dropping from 33 or 21 year intervals to 14 year intervals in the mid-1960s, the future rental growth potential expanded.[33] Property developers were further driven towards the financial institutions by the renewal of the balance of payments problems in 1961, while simultaneously institutions were obtaining representation on property company boards.[34] Some insurance companies such as the Prudential spread their investments using sale and leaseback and accepting shares in a company, while others concentrated their activities.[35] The advantage of these arrangements from the viewpoint of the property companies was that they were in a more favourable position compared to competitors. They had the finance to expand to meet the demands in the property market. Companies like Land Securities who had pioneered links[36] could now dominate a share market which had expanded dramatically since the sector was first listed in 1957. They were well placed in a development market, which was becoming increasingly competitive, and would also be well placed to benefit from the concentration of capital through mergers and takeovers, which was certain to gather momentum once demand for new development slowed.

Limits in the property market

Equity participation in property companies by the institutions has the same effects as a rights issue,[37] that is, it dilutes the equity which is only acceptable to the investor if it is believed that the finance will sustain further growth.[38] However, it was just this notion that investments in property were always sound which had become established. The notion became established because financial institutions consciously wished to make safe investments, and unconsciously convinced themselves that

Table 6.6. *Net acquisitions of investments by insurance companies*

	Total £m	Equitics %	Govt securities %	Other %	Property and ground rentals	
					£m	%
1962	559.5	15.4	26.6	48.9	50.9	9.1
1963	616.8	19.2	15.7	54.9	62.8	10.2
1964	686.7	22.7	12.8	55.9	58.7	8.6
1965	658.0	13.1	7.2	66.2	89.1	13.5
1966	650.3	15.9	3.3	62.8	117.0	18.0
1967	761.3	13.1	28.8	45.6	95.3	12.5
1968	894.8	25.0	13.4	48.2	119.4	13.4

Source: Financial statistics, Panmure Gordon, 1976.

these existed, which seemed justifiable as returns currently exceeded the rate of inflation. There was no obvious reason to suppose that the long term returns would not continue to do so and this would be reflected in the capital asset value of the investments.

A number of problems arise from this belief, and it is necessary to state how these circumstances arose. The financial institutions, initially the insurance companies and latterly the pension funds, had been expanding rapidly. The adoption of Keynesian-type policies of demand led management plus an emphasis on individual savings provided the material basis for the expansion of insurance and pension funds at a time when people and companies put behind them the adversities of war and reconstruction and were looking forward to a future which seemed more secure and prosperous despite the stop–go cycles in the economy. The notion that 'you've never had it so good' was in full flow. Keynesian-type policies which led to inflation in turn led to the financial institutions looking to increase their long term investments outside the equity and government security markets. Tables 6.6 and 6.7 show how the interests in property were increasing.[39]

Their beliefs, however, were grounded on the basis of continued growth in the whole economy, which in retrospect has not occurred, and specifically the continued demand for buildings, particularly offices. The specific demand was already being satisfied with the peak in completions occurring during 1958 in London and 1960 in the City with a threat of an oversupply of offices looming on the horizon. The financial institutions ignored this trend, their decisions being governed by the flow of money into the funds rather than the state of their investment markets.

While it is true that an increase of institutional investment in property

Table 6.7. *Net acquisitions of investments by pension funds*[a]

	Total £m	Equities %	Govt securities %	Other %	Property and ground rentals £m	Property and ground rentals %
1963	428	48.4	(3.3)	48.4	26	6.1
1964	450	46.2	1.1	46.0	30	6.7
1965	489	35.8	11.2	45.0	39	8.0
1966	533	36.0	7.0	48.0	48	9.0
1967	516	38.2	13.2	33.3	79	15.3
1968	588	49.1	2.4	32.7	93	15.8

Note: a. Pension funds assets are assessed by market value in this table compared to the book value method of assessment used by insurance companies.

Source: Financial statistics, Panmure Gordon, 1976.

development has the effect of increasing differential building rent II, there are limits to the extent to which this rent can be realised, which depends upon the performance of the building users in the national and international economy. Differential building rent II derived from investments on one site occurs if the building is let and thus the user believes their long term profitability will be enhanced in that building. Differential building rent II will also be derived if a number of successive development investments are made in an area thus making the area more 'prime', in other words enhancing profitability directly or indirectly through linkages, close contacts and area status. The functional advantage for the property companies was that the increased commitment by the financial institutions provided them with greater security and financial backing should an oversupply of property occur.

The implications for the property market were dramatic. Prime yields on offices fell from 7.5% in 1959 to 6% in 1963. Prime shop yields fell from 6% in 1959 to 5.5% in 1963, although industrials remained around 10%, indicating that the market for this boom was primarily located in the sphere of capital circulation rather than production, a higher yield indicating slower rental growth, and thus less surplus profits in the sphere of production from which rent is derived. The impetus behind property investment by the institutions was the future anticipated rentals rather than the current rental income, which could be realised as a result of rent reviews. Average yields had been about 1% above the yields of consols, gilt edged securities being the traditional long term investment which had lost ground to property investments. However, property yields were falling although this was due to the notion of its long term security as an investment rather than a perceived weakness. Hence property investments continued to receive institutional money despite the lower yields, this phenomenon being called the reverse yield gap. Boggis *et al.*[40] comment:

The advent of rent reviews converted property into a hybrid between gilts and equities, and the 'reverse yield gap' developed, when investors recognised that the potential rental growth, which could be tapped by using rent reviews, merited a rate of return below gilts where no income growth was possible, i.e. the potential future rental growth made an income stream from property more valuable in capital terms than the same quantity of initial income derived from gilts.

In other words anticipated future rental was capitalised into the capital asset value of the properties rather than being realised in money terms. This does, however, erode the link between capital asset values or capitalised rental and the rental of the properties. I have supported the generally accepted view that the price of a property is the capitalised rental of the building (and land) over its expected lifetime. While the capitalised rental is distorted by inflation it should still be reflected in the actual rental income at each stage during the lifetime of the building. The belief that money is safe in property investments begins to create the potential for an economic dilemma if the capital asset value always reflects future rental growth which is never actually paid but is always notionally deferred into a capitalised form. In other words rentals are continually capitalised in asset form and are not actually realised. The possibility of this occurring arises as yields drop, reflecting the disjuncture between long term investments in property and the current and future demand for property, which has parallels with the Keynesian notion of the state deficit financing the economy, although in this case the realisation of rentals is deferred rather than the repayment of debt.

The property markets, 1961–4

The credit squeeze in 1961 was aimed to restrict investment and the Chancellor, Selwyn Lloyd, particularly wished the financial institutions to curtail loans for 'speculative building, property development, and other purposes not vital to exports and production'.[41] In fact the squeeze, initiated through raising the bank rate from 4% in 1959 to 7% by 1961, merely reinforced links between developers and the insurance and pension funds, thus stimulating rather than curtailing property investment financing. Government policy therefore reinforced the economic trends in this respect.

During the early 1960s the development boom continued although it had passed its peak at this time. The majority of sites which were available due to wartime damage had either been developed or were 'spoken for'. Sites had to be assembled over long periods of time for developers to undertake redevelopment schemes. This was an important feature of the London development market with companies like Stock Conversion and Hammerson undertaking this lengthy procedure, but it was not an opportunity open to all developers. Others formed joint companies with industrialists who wished to redevelop their sites and relocate activities elsewhere. For example the Watney Mann Stag Brewery was leased to City and Victoria Property which was 51% owned by the City of London Real Property Company and 49% owned by Sir Robert McAlpine. However, supply was beginning to catch up with demand, particularly in London, and rental and capital asset growth slowed.

Development was becoming more competitive. The margin of profit on each development, although considerable, had been decreasing. Barras[42] estimates that developments completed in the City of London in 1962 fell from the pinnacle of 43% to 38% by 1964 and to 35% in 1966.

Expansion could not be achieved on a large scale through property investment because existing building owners had become aware of the potential growth rental reversions yielded,[43] and development for sale had become less profitable as development profits were subject to tax on sale since the advent of section 22 of the Finance Act, 1960.[44] Expansion could be sought through takeovers or through increased development activity outside the London market.

Looking more closely at the London market first and specifically the City of London, development activity was still at a high level in the early 1960s. Table 6.8 details the developments in the City. Table 6.9 gives a breakdown of the involvement of property companies in City development until 1964.

Table 6.8. *Development in the City of London, 1960–8*

Year of completion	Number of schemes	New floor-space m²	Previous floor-space m²	Av. size of scheme m²
1961	24	165,446	41,231	6,894
1962	23	126,189	40,980	5,486
1963	17	103,294	29,380	6,076
1964	12	162,180	53,620	13,515
1965	11	93,359	20,880	8,487
1966	15	125,806	58,882	8,387
1967	11	116,957	30,147	10,632
1968	7	67,288	59,346	9,613

Source: Corporation Architecture and Planning Department, adapted from Barras, 1979a.

Table 6.9. *Property company involvement in major City developments*

	Number of schemes
City of London Real Property Company	3
Metropolitan and Provincial	4
Oldham Estates	3
Hammerson	2
Town and City	1
Bridgeland	2
Wingate	1
City and Central	1
Centrovincial	1

Source: adapted from Barras, 1979a.

There were four very large development schemes in the City. The BP headquarters was developed by Baranquilla, the Metropolitan and Provincial subsidiary, in conjunction with the Church Commissioners. Involvement with the Church Commissioners and other large private landowners was one way round the problem of finding or assembling large sites for development. Draper Gardens was another example, developed by Oldham Estates. The two other large developments did not involve property companies. The Barbican was a very large scheme initiated by the City Corporation and the Paternoster development near St Paul's was undertaken by the Church Commissioners in conjunction with the contractors Wimpey, Laing, and Trollope and Colls, each of which had a 20% equity in the scheme.[45]

One aspect of development at this time was that bargains were being struck between the developers and the authorities whereby developers would yield up pieces or strips of land for road improvement schemes on the understanding that the development density for the original site area could be included on the smaller site. Stock Conversion's Euston Centre and Oldham Estates' Centre Point are the classic examples. Both Marriott and Jenkins[46] seem critical of this and it has been the subject of emotive political objection,[47] which appears to contradict the overt and covert wishes of leftist political opposition for increased state involvement in the sphere of planning and landownership.[48]

Planning permission in Greater London continued to exceed the development under construction and the demand in the market. In 1960 47,380 m^2 of space was under construction with a further 60,386 m^2 of outstanding planning permission and in 1964 130,993 m^2 of space was under construction with a further 166,296 m^2 of outstanding planning permission.[49] The abolition of the Third Schedule loophole on post-war property in 1963 was therefore merely of technical interest rather than consequence. Planning permission posed no general obstacle to development and the market was beginning to show the symptoms of a future oversupply of floorspace as institutional investment continued to be pumped into property. The restructuring and expansion of the sphere of capital circulation in the centre during the period of prosperity were completed and the property sector therefore was experiencing the first signs of crisis in the form of a potential oversupply.

The decentralisation of development reflected attempts to speed up capital circulation away from the centre and meet the demands for routinised functions in the sphere of circulation which could be separated from and did not need a central location. The trend towards decentralised development, and hence geographical diversification for developers, began in the early 1960s. It occurred mainly in the sphere of retailing. Ravenseft, the subsidiary of Land Securities, had had a virtual monopoly of this market, but other developers increasingly began to look outside London for new development markets as margins narrowed in the London market.

Local authorities had been trying to attract developers to town centres but with little success. Bradford, for example, had been replanning its town centre since 1946. In retrospect, the scepticism and doubt may seem strange considering this was an era of demand led management, with low levels of unemployment and hence high levels of consumer spending. Additionally, as Walter Flack of Murrayfield realised, town centres had not been redeveloped during the century and therefore were outmoded.[50] Hammerson paved the way by entering into negotiations with Bradford in 1956, announcing a deal in 1959. Being amongst the first into the partnership field they received a high yield on the development, although yields had fallen by 1961 as a large number of schemes were negotiated and under way.[51] Although competition for town centre redevelopment schemes increased, investors remained somewhat sceptical of their success, not only because of the competition, but also because they were still uncertain whether a demand existed.[52] However, it certainly did, a further indication being the growth of supermarkets in the early 1960s (see table 6.10). The Bull Ring in Birmingham, developed by the Laing subsidiary Laing Properties, and the Elephant and Castle, now owned by Ravenseft, were the first completely covered town centre developments in this country.[53] Some of the town centre developments were not very successful financially, the early ones due to ill considered designs and the later ones frequently due to poor or secondary locations as local authorities competed to initiate development in the civic prestige stakes, some authorities having more than one

Table 6.10. *Growth in supermarkets*

	Numbers	Increase %
1956	100	—
1958	175	75
1960	367	111
1962	996	171
1964	1,628	63
1966	2,500	53

Source: Supermarket Association of Great
Britain, quoted in Marriott, 1967,
p. 237.

development. This only contributed to the scepticism of investors, but the scepticism was not decisive in the long term as an increasing number of developments were initiated which induced higher levels of competition and lower yields.

The decentralisation of office development was also beginning to show. In Leeds, for example, the total office stock increased by over 20% between 1960 and 1965, of which around 30% of the applications came from property companies and 26% from institutions. In Bristol the office stock increased by over 80%, of which around 40% of the applications came from property companies and 27% from institutions.[54]

Additionally some tentative moves had been made into the overseas development market. Conditions were and are not the same in terms of operation of investment and development markets in economic and policy terms and few companies have been successful overseas, particularly at this time. Land Securities, through Ravenseft, decided to undertake development in Canada but withdrew in 1961, having made losses,[55] and has not expanded overseas since, deciding to remain in the markets they know. Hammerson on the other hand invested in Australia, using finance raised locally, and has since been one of the few companies to sustain overseas investments and development. Overseas markets are an essential means of expansion in an era dominated by overproduction as the motor of crisis. However, the majority of property companies believed that the same rate of surplus profits could not be yielded as (capitalised) rental because they did not have the knowledge to realise the rentals in overseas markets, Hammerson being one exception.

The other means of expansion, as development activity could not be sustained indefinitely, was through takeovers. A number of private property companies had been acquired in the late 1950s and early 1960s by public property companies, but with competition increasing a concentration of capital within the sector would become necessary from the viewpoint of property companies. It had already become an issue for investors. The *Investors Chronicle* stated: 'We have long taken the view that there are too many companies in the property share market. That there will be, and has to be, a rationalisation is undoubted, but that this rationalisation has been delayed by the 1960 Finance Act is also equally clear.'[56] While the Act may have been ambiguous whether the buying of a portfolio through takeover meant the vendor was subject to tax on the property asset value, I maintain the main reason development activity still dominated over investment activity was that sufficient expansion could be maintained for the time being. One large merger was, however, taking place in 1960–1 between Jack Cotton's City Centre Properties and Charles Clore's City and Central Investments. This was an exception rather than the rule, but the *Investors Chronicle* was correct in predicting that takeovers needed to and would occur to sustain expansion in the face of shrinking development markets.

In summary, the demand for development was in cessation by 1964, and, if the market in the sphere of circulation remained unconstrained, an oversupply would occur because the size of the institutional funds was governing the flow of finance into development rather than the size of the development market. The sphere of capital circulation had restructured and expanded. The increasing centralisation of this sphere was one result. Development markets to meet the demands of the sphere became more limited, especially in the centre in and around London. Decentralised markets were opening up as efforts were being made to reduce the cost of circulation functions, accelerate circulation away from the centre and realise surplus value. The limits to expansion in the economy were fast approaching and so the limits for development during expansion were also approaching. Development itself increases the organic composition of capital in the economy and is a cost against surplus value in the sphere of circulation which has to be weighed up against the benefits in facilitating the realisation of surplus value into profits in absolute terms and in relation to competitors. Overproduction was on the horizon and the property sector's experience of overproduction, oversupply, was potentially present.

The boom had largely bypassed the sphere of production, but in the sphere of circulation it was impressive with rentals increasing from the late 1950s by 140%[57] to around £20 m^2 in the City and £15 m^2 in the West End in 1960 for prime office rents.[58] The total value of property shares quoted on the stock market had risen from £103m in 1958 to

£800m by 1962.[59] Developers had largely avoided paying tax because their property assets were not liable to tax unless they were sold.

The government had been one of the main users in the reconstruction period but during this period of general prosperity it was particularly the large international companies, especially oil companies, who sought locations in London. In central London 5.3 million m² (58m sq. ft) had been built since 1948, of which 3.6 million m² (39m sq. ft) had been built between 1955 and 1963.[60] In the City 1.5 million m² (17m sq. ft) had been built between 1945 and 1964.[61] Of this development around 50% had been carried out by property development companies[62] and during this period the majority were being developed ahead of letting.[63] The number of quoted companies on the Stock Exchange had increased from 111 in 1958 to 183 by 1964, their total capital value rising from £103m to £730m in the same period.[64]

Pointers to the future were the growth in decentralised development nationally and to some extent internationally, the need for capital concentration among property companies and the potential oversupply in the existing London development market.

Property and development, 1964–8

In this short period the development market changed rapidly and dramatically. I shall argue that a series of government interventions curtailed the development boom in London, thus avoiding an oversupply of offices occurring. These interventions, which provided a stick to stimulate decentralisation, were backed up by the carrots of public capital expenditure on infrastructure and related services, enhancing a growing trend towards office decentralisation and town centre redevelopment for expanding retailing.

The changes permitted the continuation of a relatively high level of development activity, but at an absolutely lower level, and so the result of increased competition for development and reduced investment opportunities led to a redistribution of existing investment through a wave of takeovers producing the capital concentration in the sector desired by investors. The state therefore facilitated sustained development activity, but the increased competition and capital concentration in an effort to maintain capital accumulation are the theoretically anticipated effects in a period of prosperity which is giving way to a crisis of falling rates of profit and overproduction. The relationship between the financiers of development, who were now investors in property developments and development companies in their own right, also changed during this period because of the changing market conditions.

Finance for the property markets

With the exception of 1967 insurance company investment in the property sector increased (see table 6.6) and an even more dramatic increase in investment was seen by the pension funds (see table 6.7). The pension funds were becoming major property investors in their own right, although their total market value holdings still only amounted to £310m compared to the insurance companies' total book value of £1,211m in 1967. Insurance companies and pension funds were now becoming directly involved in property. They began to bypass property companies, not only for investments, but also for development, many now acquiring their own development expertise internally or through the takeover of property companies. This was in part due to the lower ebb of the market between 1964 and 1968 while the flow of funds into the institutions continued unabated (see tables 6.6 and 6.7), but it was also due to the changing taxation laws.

Insurance companies pay tax at reduced rates and pension funds are exempted from a considerable proportion of tax on investment income. The Finance Act, 1965, introduced corporation tax. The tax was aimed to induce internal growth and, therefore, the generation of profits for retention rather than distribution to shareholders became the object.[65] For property this could be reflected in capital assets or capitalised rentals rather than in profits for retention. This was an ideal situation for the financial institutions who were more interested in capital growth than current income, and was a situation in which they reduced their dependence on the property company while simultaneously benefiting from their preferential status. However, these circumstances widened the gap between the capital assets, being a reflection of rentals in their capitalised form, and income. In this case capital growth was induced by financial mechanisms rather than being a reflection of perceived future rental growth. Whereas the reverse yield gap constantly deferred by implication the future realisation of rents, this procedure led to a current rental growth being deferred until the future (which may again be potentially deferred). Problems stored up for the future were therefore increasing as the general period of prosperity drew to a close.

The property market

The situation was not severe for property companies – indeed government action unintentionally led to an increase in rentals and assets while preventing an oversupply of offices. An oversupply would have been serious because the institutions through sale and leaseback were taking few risks, the developer being responsible for letting and realising the rent, and offices cannot be exported should a national oversupply occur. Yields began to rise by 0.5–1.0%, except in the industrial market, and prime rentals rose around £50 m^2 in the City, £35 m^2 in the West End and about £12 m^2 on average outside London by 1968 (cf. figure 6.3).[66] Capital asset values also rose. The principal reasons for these outcomes were that government policy prevented an oversupply depressing the market, particularly at a time when the returns on development were in decline.

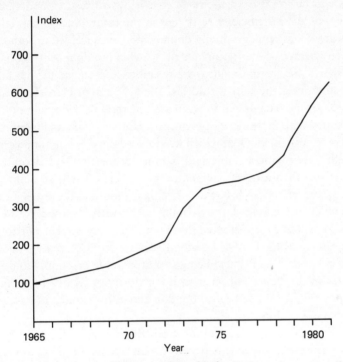

Figure 6.3. Rental index
Source: Investors Chronicle Hillier Parker, 1981.

The property sector had already begun to decentralise its development programme. The Conservative Government set up the Location of Offices Bureau in 1963 to try to decentralise employment. The effects of this will be considered later, but it was the incoming Labour Government which built on Conservative policy aims, and in a dramatic way. The National Plan had a strong regional content and the restriction of all new office development in Greater London imposed by the Department of Economic Affairs, in what is commonly known as the Brown Ban, was part of the strategy. The ban was imposed on November 4, 1964, literally overnight. Property companies were expecting something and there had been a general acceptance that a Labour Government would be elected. Property companies had not looked forward to the prospect, but as Nigel Broackes of Trafalgar House recognised, 'the Conservatives no longer had a coherent or relevant theme'.[67] In fact the ban favoured the property sector. Companies which had overcommitted themselves were unable to expand their development programme, while those schemes under way would gradually be left without an oversupply posing a threat. Patrick Galvin commented: 'The most obvious, and immediate effect of the ban on new offices will be to push up the rents of existing offices in London.'[68] The supply would be artificially restricted in the future and so capital asset values grew and rents gradually doubled and even trebled in some cases. The ban affected all developments on which a building contract had not been signed before midnight on November 4. Because people did not know how long the ban would last there was a rush to sign building contracts, some backdated, to ensure a long term development potential. Companies with large development programmes, such as Hammerson's £40m programme, much of which was located outside London, were little affected. Centrovincial, Star and Samuel Properties had decentralised their activities while other companies such as Max Rayne's London Merchant Securities, Nigel Broackes' Trafalgar House and the Levy's Stock Conversion had managed to sign building contracts.[69] However, the companies to benefit the most were those with large investment portfolios in London, such as the City of London Real Property Company, St Martins and Law Land,[70] MEPC also being in a favourable position. Land Securities was in the best position with the majority of its development programme located outside central London and its investment portfolio concentrated in London.

The growth in rentals resulting from the Brown Ban pulled back to some extent the divergence between current rental and future anticipated capitalised rentals in the institutions' portfolios as yields increased, thus reducing the reverse yield gap. Asset values also grew partly because the low yields had held back capital growth. While this seems to conflict with the above it was a short term effect although capital asset values continued to expand later, but this was due to takeovers and mergers. Not only was the Brown Ban concerned with regional unemployment, but concern had also been expressed about the very high rentals being paid by building users. The ban in this sense can be seen theoretically as preventing the growth of differential building rent II which developers and their financiers largely control themselves through successive investments of capital in the same area, so pushing up the rentals of existing property in the area more than the benefits realised in profit terms of current users. However, the result of the ban was to constrain London as a possible location for users. Users were now prepared to pay the additional rent in order not to lose advantage, or to gain advantage over competitors. Rentals therefore increased like an access charge, which theoretically can be seen as transference of differential building rent II to absolute building rent.

Following the Brown Ban the issuing of Office Development Permits (ODPs) was required for schemes of 278 m^2 (3,000 sq. ft), 13 schemes out of 21 being refused in 1965 and 4 schemes out of 13 in 1966, but after that time refusals eased with only 6 out of 28 schemes being refused in 1968. The Location of Offices Bureau, the Brown Ban and Office Development Permits can therefore be said to have had a smoothing effect on the development market. Developers were putting forward fewer proposals as they waited for the existing development supply to be completed and let. The restriction raised the profits on each development from 56% in 1964 to 79% by 1966.[71]

The introduction of the Land Commission in 1967 brought back a betterment levy. It could have acted as a material, if not a psychological, deterrent to further development as the taxing of differential building rent II once again would have had the same effect as increasing absolute ground rent from the developers' viewpoint. However, in practice the levy was not paid prior to its abolition.[72]

Croydon and other suburban and peripheral locations to London located on transport nodes became important development markets. Development in Croydon had been under way on a massive scale in the early 1960s, although few schemes were completed before the Brown Ban. In consequence Croydon was not adversely affected by the Brown Ban. Ravenseft had the largest single scheme, the Whitgift Centre, the site of which was leased to them by the Whitgift Foundation for 96 years. The scheme, financed by the Church Commissioners, was built by the locally based contractor, Wates,[73] and contained 32,515 m^2 (350,000 sq. ft) of offices.[74] Significantly, Rothschilds, the bankers, rented offices, thus de-centralising their headquarters out of London. This was the first major move from London of a main banker's office.

The extent to which the Location of Offices Bureau (LOB) actually contributed to office decentralisation is debatable, but decentralisation did occur, although 80% of moves were within 40 miles of central London. One main reason for decentralisation, the reduction of costs, could be achieved in two ways. The reduction of overheads could be achieved through lower rents and rates, even though postage, telephone and travel costs could be increased. Rhodes and Kan estimated that the total annual reduction of overheads per employee was in the region of £545. The second reduction could be achieved by restructuring the workforce. Reducing the number of people employed was not a prime means but undoubtedly salaries were lower outside the main urban centres, especially London. Rhodes and Kan estimate companies made an average annual saving of £105 per employee.[75] It was therefore found that the growing efficiency in terms of systems and office machinery used created a series of more routinised functions, which did not require constant contact with other concerns or constant supervision by head office staff, and hence decentralisation was favourable in these cases.

Office developments increased in other locations, sometimes for the above reasons, sometimes for coordinating greater regional penetration of national markets, and sometimes because regionally based companies had been expanding. State agencies decentralised a considerable proportion of their activities, particularly in 'development areas'. Leeds increased its stock of offices by 24.7% between 1965 and 1970, developers and institutions accounting for around 50% of the developments.[76] In Manchester property developers accounted for 50% and the financial institutions 18% of the planning applications between 1966 and 1969.[77] In Bristol 60,812 m² (654,580 sq. ft) of new office space were developed between 1964 and 1968 with property companies and financial institutions accounting for around 75% of the applications.[78]

The development market had therefore been curtailed in the centre with decentralised development the main thrust for expansion, but the total market was insufficient to sustain the expansion of the sector. Consolidation and rationalisation through capital concentration became necessary.

Capital concentration

By far the most important activity during the years 1964 to 1968 was the rapid surge of takeovers. Takeovers had taken place in the late 1950s and to some extent in the early 1960s, but as the *Investors Chronicle* had stated, a concentration of capital was necessary to rationalise the share market.[79] However, the conditions now prevailed whereby property companies sought to expand through takeovers. There were declining development opportunities and declining rental income as the institutions increasingly took an equity in schemes and the taxation changes promoted concentration.[80] The concentration was dramatic. In 1960 the ten largest property companies owned 20% of the assets in the sector. By 1970 this had been increased to nearly 50%.[81]

The advent of corporation tax brought in by the Finance Act of 1965 acted as an incentive for property companies to reinvest their profits rather than pay them out to shareholders as dividends and so the capital assets grew, a process which was accelerated by the Brown Ban. Investors had little reason to increase their shareholding as increased dividends were not forthcoming and hence for a potential takeover bid shares were a fraction of their value in relation to the assets, sometimes discounted as much as 40%. In a few cases companies relied upon new share issues to raise finance for possible expansion because the financial institutions were increasingly investing directly in property. The company wishing to instigate a takeover could buy the new shares, which might be facilitated by the fact that new issues dilute existing shareholdings and so existing shareholders may accept an offer for their shares or support a takeover bid in order to increase the share value once more.

A number of companies took advantage of these circumstances, the most notable being the property company Trafalgar House, which not only extended its property activities but diversified into construction, housebuilding and later into hotels and shipping.[82] Star (Great Britain) took over a number of companies including Felix Fenston's Metropolitan and Provincial Properties in 1968.[83] Land Securities was responsible for the most significant takeovers. The company acquired two of its largest competitors, City Centre Properties in 1968 and the City of London Real Property Company in 1969, for £65m and £143m. These takeovers involved the acquisition of prime London property investment portfolios which had been undervalued, Land Securities' capital assets increasing from £202m in 1968 to £498m by 1970 (£430m to £952m at 1975 prices; see figure 6.4). The City of London Real Property also had a considerable reversionary potential in its leases to generate further income. Land Securities would take over a company provided two criteria could be satisfied. First, the company required to increase its portfolio with investments compatible with its existing portfolio, particularly properties located in the City or West End of London. Any investments which were uncomplementary would be sold, especially overseas investments. Second, the portfolio must have land or property with long term development potential. Other benefits, although not the main criteria for a takeover bid, might include the acquisition of low rate debentures or the use of a tax loss and the raising of liquidity through the sale of under-valued, uncomplementary properties. The delays in obtaining ODPs for the Ravenseft development programme and the halt to new development in London made the company 'acute' to the potential for pursuing growth through takeovers.[84]

Land Securities' other takeovers included County and Urban Properties, Burlington Estates, Haymarket House and Nathan Brown Estates.[85] Nathan Brown Estates are industrial developers and this takeover marked Land Securities' only sustained diversification outside

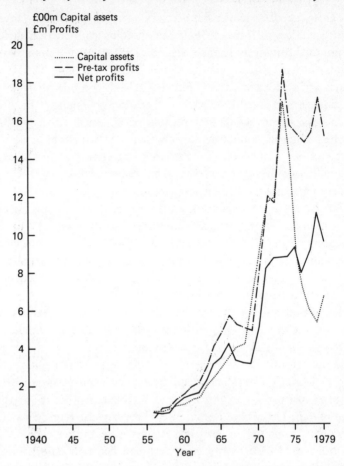

Figure 6.4. Land Securities' capital assets and profits at 1975 prices
Source: Company Annual Reports and Accounts.

the London market since the takeover of Ravenseft in the mid-1950s, although industrial development remains a small part of Land Securities' interests. A further £15m 6.25% fixed interest loan was arranged with the Liverpool Victoria Friendly Society and another £15m advanced by Legal and General in 1965 to finance the development and takeover activities. All of the developments in London were being completed prior to the Brown Ban.

Land Securities' portfolio in 1968 is broken down in table 6.11, which shows the considerable development potential should an upturn occur in the market. Land Securities' asset gearing had been higher at the turn of the decade compared to the sector as a whole because of its large development programme, but by 1965 this had been decreased from above 70%

Table 6.11 *Land Securities' portfolio, 1968*

	Central London £m	London suburbs, outside London £m
Properties completed	97.715	61.408
Properties uncompleted and undeveloped	14.331	28.676
Total	112.046	90.084

Source: Land Securities Annual Report and Accounts, 1968.

to nearly 60%, compared to 53% asset gearing for the entire sector. Following the Brown Ban and the takeovers, Land Securities' assets increased and loans were concurrently being repaid lowering the asset gearing to 54% in 1968 compared to 56% for the sector. The financial gearing had fallen during the early 1960s as fixed interest loans were repaid and the stock market overvalued the company, but it was increased again to 263% in 1965 and 315% in 1967 as the £30m loans were arranged for expansion.[86]

The company was therefore in a strong position both during the 1964–8 period and for future expansion. Unlike other companies, the sale and leaseback had not been favoured, so a higher degree of independence was maintained from the financial institutions, which was in their favour as the institutions were increasingly bypassing the property companies for their investments by investing directly into property. The company was not, however, lacking in money capital to finance expansion, seeking arrangements for long term fixed interest loans from the life departments of insurance companies which were more interested in long term capital growth than current income derived from equity shares.[87] Only Central Holdings Ltd and the Legal and General held more than 10% of Land Securities' share capital.

Land Securities had become the largest company in the sector, its total assets comprising 7% of the sector in 1968 and 11% in 1969. The location of its prime investments in London, the completion of existing developments in London being unaffected by the Brown Ban and its longer term development programme located outside London placed the company in a very advantageous position for further expansion. The company also had the finance to take the opportunities and benefited from the process of capital concentration in the sector. Land Securities was able to pursue a slightly different market strategy, in so doing gaining sector dominance. The case also clearly illustrates through comparison the main sector trends.

In summary, capital concentration and diversification, both geographically and in the type of development undertaken, were the main features of the period between 1964 and 1968, government intervention and policy preventing an oversupply of space and creating the conditions for capital concentration. The links with the financial institutions had matured and were now in relative if not absolute decline, the institutions bypassing the property companies to an increasing degree. The individual development market remained relatively passive compared to the growth in and restructuring of the sphere of capital accumulation. These features are those which theoretically are a prelude to a crisis in profit rates and market penetration.

Construction, 1955–68

The general period of prosperity in Britain was also a very prosperous period for contractors, particularly the large contractors who were being asked to construct more complex and diverse projects than ever before. The export of commodities is a major means of economic growth and although buildings cannot on the whole be exported the construction capability can, and construction firms were beginning to seek more work overseas, especially by the late 1960s. However, the main expanding construction markets were the internal British markets. The internal markets grew out of the capital accumulated because of and as a result of reconstruction activity in the economy, but also the population increase created new needs in terms of housing, services and infrastructure which were translated into demand. A considerable amount of this translation was undertaken by the state, public sector work accounting for around 50% of all construction work during the period (see figure 6.1).

The late 1950s was a relatively stagnant period in the sector with new work rising from £1,170m in 1955 to only £1,514m by 1959 (£3,277m to £3,912m at 1975 prices; see figure 4.2). The significance of construction in relation to the economy as a whole remained around 17% as measured by the gross domestic fixed capital formation as a percentage of the gross national product at factor cost (see table 5.4). Gross trading profits for the sector increased from £86m to £116m between 1955 and 1959 (£291m to £369m at 1975 construction prices), and profit margins remained around 13% (see table 5.5).[88]

The 1960s saw a substantial increase in construction work, particularly public sector work (see figure 6.1). All new work increased from £1,653m in 1960 to £3,090m by 1968 (£4,206m to £6,588m at 1975 prices; see figure 4.2). The significance of construction in the economy grew from 17% to a peak of 21.4% in 1968 (see table 5.4). Gross trading profits for the sector increased by £95m at 1975 prices between 1960 and 1968. Profit margins rose from 13.1% in 1960 to a peak of 15.1% in 1964, falling back to 9.6% in 1968 (see table 5.5).

Construction costs and productivity

The 1950s were a relatively fallow period, but as other industries began to sustain capital accumulation the investment in fixed capital was increased in the sphere of production and particularly in the sphere of circulation. Relaxation of the controls by 1959 increased work but competition remained intense.[89] The bank rate was reduced, government borrowing was increased and the market grew. Construction output in the industrial market tailed off somewhat between 1962 and 1964 but the commercial market expanded during the early 1960s as the property boom gathered momentum.

However, the growth in the market was not always reflected in higher rates of profit. Construction costs began to rise. Increased raw material costs were one reason and the other was increasing labour costs. The increase in costs on the one hand gives a false impression of the extent of increased activity (cf. figures 4.2 and 6.1) and on the other hand squeezed the margins of the contractors. Margins in the sector as a whole fell by over 1% in 1961 and 1962 and this is reflected in the margins of one major contractor, Taylor Woodrow, whose margins fell from 8–9% in the late 1950s to 5–6% between 1960 and 1965, although losses on some contracts and profits not matching turnover on nuclear power contracts were contributory factors.

Labour costs were a serious problem at a time when all public and many private contractors were on a fixed price basis, yet inflation was rising at a faster rate than at any previous time. Contractors needed to increase productivity in spite of and because of the increase in workloads. The government became concerned about this problem, the Minister of Building and Public Works, Geoffrey Rippon, commenting in 1962: 'I am bound to express some misgivings about the industry's readiness to face the challenge that I believe now faces it. Unless productivity rises dramatically, the industry will not be able to meet the country's building needs.'[90] In fact productivity increased by 28% between 1963 and the end of the decade, but wages increased by 50% (70% in manufacturing industry) over the same period.[91] The use of labour-only subcontracting increased from 1955 onwards, the Phelps Brown report[92] estimating that 20% of the workforce in the sector was employed in this way. The effect that this had on increasing or retarding productivity can only be surmised, but it had little long term effect on wage increases because the shortage of labour during the 1960s ensured that contractors had to compete between themselves and other sectors to secure labour.

In addition the labourforce became increasingly aware of its strengthening position, demanding improved wages and conditions. One of the notorious contracts was the large Barbican site in the City of London. A number of contractors experienced protracted labour disputes. The Taylor Woodrow subsidiary, Myton, was one contractor which had just regained profitability when labour militancy plunged it back into losses. The Taylor Woodrow chairman, Sir Frank Taylor, commented:

We – and we are not alone – have been subject to the activities of some disruptive elements which, although small in number, have a big effect and are no good to our industry. They are acting contrary to the real interests of trade unions, they are flouting the authority of the industry and, by provoking unofficial stoppages, time wasting and go-slow tactics, their work is disruptive and ruinous.[93]

Indeed the site was closed in 1966 under *force majeure* and was reopened a year later with union cooperation and a reorganised workforce after the Report of the Court of Inquiry upheld the decision of closure.[94] The contracts were renegotiated with the Corporation of London so as to give contractors a short term likelihood of breaking even and a long term possibility of realising profits, although losses continued in the short term.

Construction markets, productivity and state intervention

Indicative planning of the 1960s had little direct effect on construction. NEDC was mainly a talking shop and a separate division was not included for construction until 1965 when one for building and one for civil engineering were incorporated, but again with little effect. The National Plan of the subsequent Labour Government also had little effect on construction directly. Although the Plan stated that a 25% increase in national output between 1964 and 1970 would require the construction sector to expand by 31%,[95] the aims of the Plan were not achieved. However, the important point was that it was believed. Although its main aim was to prevent the stop–go economic cycles, the construction sector, despite Lewis and Singh's claims,[96] did not suffer from this phenomenon in the 1960s.[97] Output continued to increase and the fall in industrial construction and public housebuilding in the early 1960s was compensated by the increase in commercial construction and private housebuilding (see figures 4.2 and 6.1). Indeed, the renewed balance of payments problem, the credit squeeze and increase in the bank rate in 1965–6 did not have an immediate effect on the construction sector. The 'great deal of excess capacity, much of it concealed'[98] is not uncovered either in the figures for total output in the sector (see figures 4.2 and 6.1) or for individual companies.

Indicative planning did have an indirect effect on construction. The demands, public and private, on the construction sector were increasing as industry expanded and the banking, commercial and retailing sectors were restructuring their space requirements. The desire to curb increased construction costs, particularly due to wage increases and labour supply, and the need to increase productivity led to initiatives to bring the sector into the 'swinging sixties' on the back of the technological revolution.

I have argued that the construction sector cannot be considered backward. Indeed, it is highly advanced, being very flexible, able to respond to periods of high demand and cope with periods of low demand as an absence of contracts induces underproduction. The industry was experiencing demands exceeding any previous period with a wide variety of work. While the flexibility of the sector may have been under the greatest strain, especially in terms of labour supply, and indeed may have been unable to meet the full demands being made, it was not backward but only different from other sectors. The fears in the sector and the desire of government to bring the sector up to date through the development and introduction of industrialised building and flow line or mass production under factory conditions eroded the very flexibility of contractors which they required for long term survival. Indeed the large investment in fixed capital created extensive problems for contractors even during this very prosperous period as the factory capacities exceeded the size of the market.

The architectural profession, influenced by the Modern Movement, had long been pressing for industrialised building, but it was the contractors who took up the idea, mainly in the sphere of housing. Both political parties advocated large housebuilding programmes: 500,000 houses a year were the target and nearly 50% of these were supposed to be built by local authorities. This was potentially a large market and the major contractors wished to obtain a considerable share of this market but feared they did not have the capacity using traditional methods with the 'wet' trades.[99] The use of industrialised building appeared to offer one solution to increase productivity, reduce labour requirements and squeeze out smaller sized competitors using traditional methods, provided the new techniques became acceptable.

Laing was in the forefront of the introduction of industrialised building. It already had the Easiform system which it had adapted into other proprietary systems for high rise housing, schools, hospitals and industrial buildings called Laingwall, Laingspan and Storiform. Strictly speaking, these are systems rather than industrialised building. They are predominantly site methods of construction, whereas prefabricated units made under factory conditions and assembled on site constitute industrialised building. Laing acquired licences in 1962 for two industrialised building methods, 12M Jespersen from Denmark and Sectra from France.[100]

Meanwhile government enthusiasm for industrialised building had been increasing between 1960 and 1964. Financial assistance was not given at this stage, but the political competition to increase housebuilding continued unabated, even though the targets were not reached. Contractors had a rather naive view of the gap between policy aims and practical implementation at this stage,[101] and Laing in particular was very conscious of its status as the second largest contractor in Britain. Senior management was more concerned with prestige and liaison with government than managing the current affairs of the company and planning for the future.[102] It became a serious problem for Laing, as they severely overcommitted themselves in industrialised building.

Laing, encouraged by government statements, began the construction of three factories for 12M Jespersen production at a cost of over £2m. The construction of these factories was aimed at getting an early and hence large share of the market. Their success depended on a demand for 6,000 houses per year.

What had been forgotten was that industrialised building had succeeded in Scandinavia and Russia, and later in Germany and France, because little other choice was available, their building materials industry being less well developed than the British counterpart. In addition, they only succeeded with considerable state intervention in the sphere of finance and land use planning.[103] What was assumed by contractors in Britain was that the market would reach target figures and probably expand in the future.

A number of other contractors began to invest in systems, for example Taylor Woodrow and Mowlem. The Taylor Woodrow subsidiary, Myton, in a joint venture with Ready Mixed Concrete, formed Taylor Woodrow–Anglian in 1963. Using licences for the Danish units of Larsen and Nielsen they set up two factories with a capacity of 4,000 houses per year,[104] although the maximum number of starts achieved was 1,907 in 1967.[105] This initial success encouraged them to build two further factories, raising capacity to 6,500 houses each year with a turnover of £6m required. However, orders fell and turnover did not exceed £5m.[106] A host of contractors initiated or obtained licences for industrialised building methods as table 6.12 details. Contractors had been further encouraged by the election of the Labour Government in 1964 with commitment to council house construction and the setting up of the

Table 6.12. *Industrialised building and systems for local authorities and New Town housing*

Company	No. of houses built			
	1965	1966	1967	1968
Amey Group[a]	—	—	32	0
Bath and Portland	—	106	10	118
Bovis[b]	—	462	142	0
Concrete Ltd	1,595	2,733	2,573	3,624
Costain	10	519	338	0
R. M. Douglas[b]	94	128	128	128
W. & C. French	—	120	4	0
Higgs and Hill[a,c]	—	—	—	0
Kier	—	6	0	30
Laing[b]				
Easiform and Storiform	2,320	3,184	3,482	1,700
Sectra	505	333	730	10
12M Jespersen	—	133	765	1,588
Mitchell Construction[c]	—	—	—	0
Mowlem	519	460	657	1,472
Sir Lindsay Parkinson	88	722	599	621
Taylor Woodrow[a]	406	664	1,088	879
Trafalgar House	8	12	95	141
George Wimpey ('no fines')	12,241	12,085	14,690	11,836

Notes: a. System operated through associate company.
      b. Also had substantial non-housing industrialised building systems.
      c. Licences obtained to use Camus method which was not subsequently used.

Sources: Ministry of Housing and Local Government; Savory Milln, 1970; Scrimgeour, 1973.

National Building Agency to promote industrialised building in 1964. The technological fix of building high rise units spilled over from the notion of the technological revolution the government claimed it could induce.[107] Financial subsidies were introduced, a 24 storey tower block receiving a subsidy of £6,000 a year while equivalent low rise housing received £800 per year.[108]

The traditional and systems[109] housebuilding fared well but industrialised building did not. The increase in productivity and labour saving was not as extensive as had been hoped and the cost of construction was therefore high. Additionally, too many systems had been put on the market. These were not standardised and the local authorities did not favour any particular method as had happened in the reconstruction period. Competition was intense, but even if standardisation had taken place the market did not materialise to justify the fixed capital investments. A large proportion of the domestic fixed capital formation in the industry at this time can be attributed to investments in industrialised building factories.[110] This investment doubled between 1960 and 1965 to £145m per year. Contractors had therefore forsaken their flexibility and began to suffer from self-induced overproduction in relation to the size of the market. Colossal losses were incurred. Following the general economic problems of 1966–7 government expenditure on housing was reduced, and the collapse of Ronan Point in 1968[111] gave the government the symbolic means to initiate further cuts on grounds of safety and cost against a growing vocal background of the social problems of high rise living. A large number of factories were subsequently closed as the market almost completely collapsed. The attempt, like previous attempts, to model construction on other production methods failed and was destined to from the beginning because of the industry's relation to the market.

Some moderate success was achieved in school building. The Scola and Clasp systems were primarily used, having been selected by educational authorities[112] and erected by contractors such as Wates. School building peaked in the late 1950s and again between 1964 and 1968.[113]

Public construction markets

Other public building contracts included universities and hospitals. In fact there was an oligopoly in public works contracts as contractors had to qualify to get on to tender lists on the basis of their size, turnover and experience in work. This created ideal conditions for the very large contractors. Governments were committed to high levels of public investment and profit margins could be maintained between 5% and 7%. The length of contract for private work was usually 12–18 months, but public contracts tended to extend to 2.5 to 3 years. The length of contracts and volume of work therefore provided continuity of work and insulated the sector from short term fluctuations in interest rates.[114]

Contractors endeavoured to obtain 50% of their annual turnover from public contracts. Much of the work was heavy civil engineering. Power station contracts remained important, in particular nuclear power station construction. The Suez crisis of 1956 alerted western countries to their oil dependency in the Middle East.[115] A number of consortia emerged to undertake the new nuclear power programmes. Laing was in the AEI–Thompson consortium, which soon disbanded. Sir Robert McAlpine was in another, which is one of two surviving consortia. The other consortium involves Taylor Woodrow, who with their wartime partners Babcock and

Wilcox[116] and English Electric, formed British Nuclear Design and Construction[117] and successfully carved out this construction market along with McAlpine. Both Taylor Woodrow and McAlpine had a long standing experience and knowledge of concrete technology, vital in this type of work. The construction of nuclear power stations did not always yield average profits and the lack of continuity in government programmes[118] induced irregular annual turnover figures for the companies.

The most substantial public works programme was the construction of roads and motorways. McAlpine concentrated on power station contracts, as did Taylor Woodrow,[119] along with hospital and tunnelling contracts and did not enter the road building programme,[120] but most of the other major contractors entered the field. Central government capital expenditure on roads increased from £40m in 1960 to £108m by 1964, and reached a peak in 1968 of £275m.

Costain, Wimpey and Laing were prominent in the early stages of the programme, but other medium sized contractors began to specialise in road building or aspects of road building, increasingly gaining a share of the market and squeezing the more diverse contractors' profit margins. Costain's share of the market was declining in 1965, although it continued to remain an important road contractor. Medium sized companies such as Monk, who entered the market in 1960,[121] along with W. & C. French and Sir Alfred McAlpine, were responsible for fragmenting this market in the late 1960s. Wimpey and Laing found they were making losses in order to stay in the market and eventually withdrew.[122] W. & C. French had road contracts valued at £30m in 1969 and had become the third largest road contractor. Sir Alfred McAlpine (Marchwiel) built roads with Leonard Fairclough undertaking the bridge building. Fifty per cent of Sir Alfred McAlpine's turnover was motorway works, 90% of their turnover being public sector contracts. The consortium was second only to Monk, who had become the largest road builder at the end of the decade.[123] Fairclough later entered joint ventures with Amey Roadstone and Cementation.[124]

Private construction markets

Private contract work in civil engineering and industrial building did not reach the same levels as public sector work (cf. figures 4.2 and 6.1), but the entire construction market was buoyant and industrial companies were wishing to ensure an early completion of work. This led to the use of the negotiated, package deal and turnkey contracts in place of competitive tendering. The negotiated contract usually meant an earlier start and finish to the project, which gave client companies an edge over competitors and yielded above average rates of profit in the longer term. The package deals usually involved design and build, contractors entering into liaison with clients at an early stage, while turnkey contracts involved everything from the design and construction to the supply and installation of all equipment and plant.

These forms of contract became very important in industrial work such as mechanical and process engineering and the complex multimillion pound projects. As McGhie states: 'One year saved in overall time could mean the difference between acceptable capital turnover, minimum interest payments, increased market penetration in advance of competitors, and decline or even failure.'[125] Contractors further accelerated contracts for clients on site by the greater use of critical path analysis to 'crash' projects[126] and other management techniques coordinated from head offices with the increasing use of computer technology. Contractors and unions included protection against unanticipated wage increases on work during negotiated contracts, new collective bargaining agreements only taking effect at the start of new contracts.[127]

Commercial construction was growing slowly and steadily. This continued after the Brown Ban in 1964 as existing projects and projects under contract went ahead. Much of the work was for property companies, the Bovis subsidiary Gilbert–Ash undertaking a £94m construction programme for Town and City in 1968, for example.[128] The City of London was one of the largest construction markets. During the property boom Trollope and Colls[129] received the largest share of the market with four projects, Wimpey and Taylor Woodrow had three each, Costain two, Higgs and Hill one and Sir Robert McAlpine one.[130]

A large number of contractors began to enter into property development directly. Links had already been formed with other companies to undertake development such as Costain's joint ventures with the Rank Organisation through Rank Property Development.[131] Contractors had also seen the successes of property companies while contractors had been financing the building, even though this was undertaken through joint and associate companies such as Grosvenor–Laing, PIC–TW and Wimpey's various involvements. Additionally, the contractors were reaping the rewards of very high levels of construction activity, yet with general policies to keep overheads and hence fixed capital investment to a minimum, large liquid and general reserves were being accumulated.

Investment in property development was given an added stimulus by the advent of the slowing down of new construction work during the late 1960s in Britain, particularly in the public sector, as the first signs of recession began to show (see figure 6.1).[132] At least 8% of the major contractors' work is usually undertaken for property companies and this can rise to 15%. The direct investment in property brought two things. First, it maintained construction activity at a high level near to the 15%, while simultaneously increasing the asset backing of contractors and yielding a flow of rentals which provided liquid as well as asset insulation from recession, yet not threatening the flexibility contractors required in relation to the construction markets.

Wimpey, contrary to general belief, did not directly enter into property development until 1976 through its revival of Wingate.[133] This is probably because Wimpey had primarily expanded through internal financing and therefore employed reserves in other ways. Laing, although it had property interests dating back to the 1920s, built up a large scale development programme slowly. While Laing was one of the major town centre developers, it is probable that the problems of industrialised building eroded its reserves; it had also suffered losses on the Bull Ring Shopping Centre in Birmingham. Hence the main thrust of its development and investment came at the end of the 1960s and in the beginning of the 1970s.

Taylor Woodrow entered development later than some other contractors, the principal medium being Taylor Woodrow Property, but built up a portfolio from a low basis very rapidly. A comparison between the interests of some contractors is provided in table 6.13.

Private housebuilding was beginning to expand rapidly in the late 1960s. The major contractors, with the notable exception of Wimpey, undertook little private housebuilding, although most had a small housebuilding subsidiary. Contracting and private housebuilding had become two distinct types of operations,[134] the former working to contract and the latter producing for sale. Laing and Costain were to rely on housebuilding in the late 1960s and early 1970s due to the poor performance of their contracting divisions in Britain in the latter half of the 1960s.[135]

Overseas construction markets

The first signs of recession in industry, the relative reduction in public sector work and intensified competition in an increasingly segmented market, especially on the road programme, led some of the major contractors to seek diversification into overseas markets. Overseas construction had received a minor boost during the fallow period of the late 1950s. Overseas construction earnings contributed £70m in 1955, which rose to £125m by 1960, making it the fastest growing export industry,[136] and reached £182m by 1968.[137] Construction was being financed internationally. American companies had entered the market to the tune of £280m by 1960.[138] Costain was the largest British overseas contractor, making full

Table 6.13. *Main property interests of selected contractors in Britain*

	1964	1965	1966	1967	1968
Costain					
Property valuation	n.a.	5.9	7.5	10.8	11.4
Rental income	n.a.	n.a.	0.4	0.4	0.4
Laing					
Property valuation	3.1	3.1	3.2	3.5	4.2
Rental income	0.4	0.4	0.4	0.5	0.6
Mowlem					
Property valuation	n.a.	n.a.	3.5	2.7	1.2
Rental income	n.a.	n.a.	0.1	0.1	0.1
Taylor Woodrow					
Property valuation	0.1	1.6	2.6	3.3	6.1
Rental income	n.a.	n.a.	0.2	0.3	0.4
Wimpey[a]					
Property valuation	n.a.	n.a.	6.2	6.7	8.8
Rental income	n.a.	n.a.	0.1	0.2	0.3

Notes: n.a. Not available.
   a. No direct interests.
Sources: Savory Milln, 1970; Phillips and Drew, 1971; Scrimgeour, 1973.

use of the Export Credits Guarantee Department.[139] Costain was under-taking a number of mechanical and process engineering contracts in a joint company with William Press.

Other contractors were beginning to expand abroad, particularly in the Middle East by the late 1960s, sending people out to assess the markets.[140] Costain, who already had a substantial foothold in the overseas markets, was beginning to negotiate some of the large contracts which would sustain it in the 1970's.

Capital concentration and diversification

Capital concentration continued in the sector mainly because the type of demand was to a large extent only within the capability of the larger contractors, although the increased competition from medium sized companies reduced the market penetration of the majors at the end of the 1960s. The growth of the sector in relation to the economy as a whole has been indicated by the gross domestic fixed capital formation rising to 21% of the gross national product at factor cost by 1968 (see table 5.4). Additionally two construction companies were in the top 100 companies in Britain in 1968 whereas none had been in 1948.[141]

Contractors had tried to increase their market penetration by setting up new regional offices, particularly to obtain health and education contracts. Takeovers were also pursued.

The main wave of takeovers occurred between 1967 and 1969. The principal reason for a contractor to take over another company is diversification.[142] Examples of takeovers in 1968 were Bovis Holdings' takeover of A. E. Farr for £1.6m in order to diversify into road building and Taylor Woodrow's acquisition of Octavius Atkinson for £0.1m[143] in order to maintain the continuity of supply of structural steelwork for Arcon exports once Stewarts and Lloyds had withdrawn from the Arcon consortium.[144] Trafalgar House's acquisition of the London based builder Trollope and Colls was one of the unusual takeovers as it is a rare diversification of a property company into construction. While contractors were diversifying forwards into property to increase their asset backing, to absorb liquid reserves and to try to insulate themselves from recession, property companies have seldom diversified back into construction. The principal reason is that a flow of profits, albeit in the longer term, does not have the same complementary effect to the property company as asset backing does for the contractor. When property companies require greater liquidity it tends to be in a shorter term than the construction process and stage payments generate. Trafalgar House is probably the exception because it develops for sale and is therefore more concerned with income and realised profits, achieving its diversity through takeovers outside the property market. Trollope and Colls were primarily prestige office contractors, much of their work being for developers.

While this wave of takeovers did not induce large scale capital concentration, it was important for market diversification, while setting up regional offices and seeking work overseas were aimed at geographical diversification at a time when construction orders were beginning to slow in Britain, and prosperity in the economy as a whole began to falter. Table 6.14 gives a breakdown of some of the leading contractors' diversity at the end of this period against the background of their overall performance in the market outlined in table 6.15.

In summary, the period was generally prosperous, and also prosperous for contractors. After an initial stagnant period in the late 1950s, markets expanded and turnover was reflected in profit records in most cases, with the notable exception of the rise and demise of industrialised building. Output was high and the demand for building labour outstripped supply, giving rise to labour militancy. As markets began to decline, particularly in the public sector, contractors tried to diversify

Table 6.14. *Estimated breakdown of leading contractors' turnover* (%)

	Building	Construction	Civil engineering[a]	Materials	Plant	Property	Overseas	Others[b]
Bovis Holdings	82	—	6	—	1	10	—	1
Cementation	—	27	58 mining	—	—	—	(41)	—
Costain	27	—	18 + 4 mining	—	—	—	40	5
Laing	43	—	22	15	—	—	13	7
French	16	—	25 + 49 road surfacing	—	—	—	7	6
Kier	4	—	61	—	—	—	20	15
Marchwiel	27	—	55	—	—	—	10	10
Mowlem	43	—	42	—	3	—	9	7
Taylor Woodrow	26	—	47	2	—	3	—	7
Trafalgar House	10	60.5	—	—	—	—	—	39.5
Wimpey	50	—	32	—	—	—	14	4

Notes: a. Includes mechanical, chemical and process engineering.
  b. Companies' classifications differ, and some activities do not appear. For example, Laing's property activities may be included under 'building' and Wimpey's housing activities under 'building', while they are placed under 'others' for Trafalgar House.

Source: Savory Milln, 1970.

Table 6.15. *Record of leading contractors*

	Total turnover £m			UK turnover £m[a]			Pre-tax profits £m			Pre-tax profit margins %			Market share %			Financial gearing %		
	1966	1967	1968	1966	1967	1968	1966	1967	1968	1966	1967	1968	1966	1967	1968	1966	1967	1968
Bovis	n.a.	41.1	52.4	—	—	—	0.4	0.7	1.1	—	1.8	2.1	—	1.4	1.7	144	181	81
Costain	61.0	72.0	86.0	n.a.	48.0	51.0	0.7	1.1	1.9	1.1	1.6	2.2	1.3[b]	1.6	1.6	202	194	173
French	n.a.	26.8	29.0	n.a.	23.8	27.2	0.3	0.4	0.6	—	1.5	2.2	—	0.8	0.8	28	37	89
Kier	n.a.	18.0	18.6	n.a.	n.a.	n.a.	n.a.	0.6	0.2	—	3.5	1.1	—	—	—	n.a.	28	13
Laing	102.0	99.0	99.0	—	—	—	0.0	0.8	1.3	0.1	0.9	1.4	3.7	3.4	2.3	21	18	12
Marchwiel[c]	n.a.	36.9	41.0	n.a.	n.a.	n.a.	1.8	1.8	2.2	—	5.1	5.4	—	—	—	1	1	1
McAlpine[c]	n.a.	n.a.	41.0	—	—	—	2.0	2.9	1.7	—	—	7.1	—	—	1.3	27	16	13
Mowlem	26.4	31.3	35.7	n.a.	n.a.	n.a.	0.5	0.8	0.2	1.8	2.5	0.5	—	—	—	20	17	19
Taylor Woodrow	65.0	74.0	71.0	50.0	62.1	60.3	4.3	3.3	3.4	5.8	4.5	4.9	1.8	2.1	1.9	80	91	40
Wimpey	180.0	190.0	200.0	n.a.	165.3	171.7	6.1	6.5	7.5	3.4	3.4	3.7	—	5.6	5.5	35	40	24

Notes: n.a. Not available.

a. A dash indicates the majority of turnover in the total turnover column is UK based.

b. Estimate.

c. This is the Sir Robert McAlpine Company, Marchwiel being Sir Alfred McAlpine.

Sources: Compiled from Company Annual Reports and Accounts; Savory Milln, 1970; Central Statistical Office.

geographically, through takeovers and property development. Competition had intensified with the expansion of the medium sized contractors. The strategies were largely successful and thus had staved off the effects of the incipient crisis.

Conclusion

Both the construction and property sectors had benefited from and contributed towards the prosperity. Government intervention had on balance favourable effects on the property sector through controls while construction was directly affected due to the considerable increase in capital expenditure. This led commentators to place too much weight on the importance of public sector contracts for the continued expansion of the sector;[145] however, the contractors were already responding through geographical and market diversification.

General prosperity was showing the first signs of faltering by 1968. This increase in investment, particularly fixed capital investment by the state, much of which involved construction, was inducing a tendency for profit rates to fall in industry. Overproduction in the economy in relation to the size of the internal and external markets was occurring, which now threatened prosperity. The effect of this, which added to the situation, was an increasing amount of labour unrest inducing a proliferation of unofficial strikes.

As the following chapter will show, the property and construction sectors remain untypical of other sectors in the economy and were able to sustain their activities at a high level despite the deepening of the recession in Britain.

7

First phase of crisis

The end of the 1960s witnessed the first signs of falling rates of profit in industry heralding the end of the general period of prosperity and the beginning of a period of austerity as economic crisis escalated in the world economy. The experience was uneven, differing from nation to nation. In Britain this included reduced investment in industry, overspending and increased debts of the state plus increased labour unrest, much of which was initiated unofficially. The national organic composition of capital had been increased, financed through state debt and high taxation to a large extent, which had given rise to falling rates of profit. This was already apparent, but overproduction was taking on a causal role, the effects of which were not in full view at the opening of this first phase of economic crisis.

This chapter focuses upon the first phase of economic crisis from the late 1960s until the late 1970s. Although a precise date cannot be given to the end of this first phase, the election of the Conservative Government in May 1979 is a convenient marker because the change of government also brought a change in the dominant social, political and philosophical thinking. This broke with the previous Keynesian influenced thinking which had dominated since the second world war, even though the recessive economic trends have not been materially reversed. The definition of a first phase is derived from the theoretical unfolding and deepening of economic crises and the subsequent restructuring.

Each sector experiences economic crisis in different ways. Most industrial sectors experienced the tendency for rates of profit to fall as state expenditure drained profits, leading to an overproduction of commodities in relation to the size of markets. Overcapacity was closed down and an underlying growing unemployment gathered momentum throughout the decade to emerge again as a major political issue.

The experiences of the construction and property sectors were different. The construction sector experiences crisis as one of underproduction because its relationship to the market is based on working to contract rather than producing ahead of sale, while property companies experience crisis in terms of overvaluation for investment and oversupply for development. However, both sectors fared well compared to the economy as a whole. This is not because they are exceptions to the rules but because of their relationship to the national and international economy during the first phase of crisis. It is these relationships which this chapter will explore by analysing the sectors as a whole.

Economic context, 1968–79

The Labour Government lost credibility at the end of the 1960s as profit rates fell and labour unrest grew. Lereuz comments:

At all events, the deterioration in the climate of industrial relations, the most obvious sign of which was the proliferation of unofficial strikes, was having a depressing influence on British industry between 1969 and 1970, particularly since the government capitulated over its industrial relations reform in May 1969 and followed this by a strategic withdrawal over prices and incomes in October. These two episodes were widely seen as political defeats. Both must have had their impact on the outcome of the 1970 election, for they lost Mr Wilson the support of the marginal voters without regaining the approval of the left-wing militants.[1]

The removal of the Labour Party from government released the unions from the dilemma of siding with the government yet trying to incorporate the increasing demands of the workforce. The unions took a directly oppositional role to the incoming Conservative Government, which enabled them to channel industrial unrest into official disputes.

The period was characterised by industrial conflict between unions and employers and between unions. This included the ten week strike by the construction union UCATT and the miners' strike, which was the straw to break the Conservative Government's political back. Under the succeeding Labour Government unofficial strikes again broke out, this time in the public sector during 1978 as the unions were endeavouring to uphold the social contract whilst losing control of their membership. These unofficial strikes later became official and the so-called 'winter of discontent' became the downfall of the Labour Government in the election of May 1979 as once again the Conservatives rallied the marginal voters and Labour lost the support of militants.

The increase in labour unrest in the period is seen against a background of the inability of successive governments to arrest economic decline during the decade, the unrest further contributing to the decline. The austerity measures of the 'Selsdon Man' policies, the inflationary measures of the 'Barber boom' and the 1971 Industrial Relations Act of the Conservative Government failed. The changes in policy directions led to a fluctuation of interest rates which inhibited industrial investment and economic confidence, trends which were exacerbated by increases in the Public Sector Borrowing Requirement to finance state expenditure. Inflation continued to escalate.

The major international event of 1973 was the 'oil crisis' as OPEC states increased their rents on oil production in the face of growing Western bloc dependence on Middle Eastern oil. The miners' strike was the major national event to catch the public eye, but the crash of the booming property sector placed considerable strain on the financial system because of its strategic position in the circulation process during a period of overproduction. These events undermined the economy and further eroded political confidence in 1974.

The outgoing Conservative Government had announced reductions in public spending of £1,700m in total and the incoming Labour Government found it was forced to continue cutbacks. Prior to 1976 these were made in an *ad hoc*, and hence informal, way, but latterly reductions were formally announced as financial stringency was imposed by the International Monetary Fund as conditions for loans to Britain.

It is against this broad background that the property and construction sectors will be analysed.

Construction, 1968–79

The construction markets

Although the value of construction output increased throughout the period in current prices, once inflation is discounted it can be seen that construction output for total and new work declined in 1970 as the effects of devaluation in 1967 and cutbacks in public fixed capital expenditure worked their way through the industry (see figure 6.1). This was the construction sector's experience of the tendency for the rate of profit to fall in the economy. Output fell dramatically from 1974 to 1977 as the *ad hoc* and formal government cutbacks took hold. The tendency for the rate of profit to fall had given way to overproduction in the economy, the effects of which were working their way through to create further underproduction in the British construction market. Although output has risen subsequently it remains lower absolutely compared to the high levels in 1973 once inflation is discounted (see figures 4.2 and 6.1). As a result the importance of construction in relation to the British economy as a whole has declined since 1968. An indication of this is given by the reduction of gross domestic fixed capital formation to gross national product at factor cost from the high point of 21.4% in 1968 to 15.6% by 1979, the lowest point since 1952 (see table 5.4). Gross trading profits for the sector have also fallen once inflation is discounted and increased competition in the shrinking market has reduced profit margins for the sector[2] from 11.5% in 1969 and 12.2% in 1972 to 4.3% in 1978. These are the effects of the deepening economic crisis.

The major contractors had to a very large extent been insulated from the worst excesses of this decline. This was achieved through diversification into new markets, both geographically and through new contract work akin to construction or to the expertise contractors can offer. The result was that the major contractors to some extent maintained their turnover and did not experience a drastic decline in profit margins. Indeed the industry has been amongst the most successful on the stock market. As one stockbroker commented:

This has been achieved, paradoxically, in a period of steady and sometimes rapid decline in the UK construction industry (since the peak in 1973 the industry has experienced a fall in activity of 23%). Admittedly, overseas construction work has provided a major impetus but much of the growth has in fact been achieved at home as major companies have obtained an increasing share of the declining quantity of work available. The nature of contracting work itself – the lack of capital intensity, the protection afforded by price escalation clauses in an inflationary environment, the rapid generation of cash on construction work and the conservatism built into all those involved in the risky construction business – all contributed to getting the major contractors through the 1974 recession with little more than a temporary retardation in the rate of profits growth.[3]

The construction sector as a whole was beginning to feel the pinch by 1974, not just in Britain, but throughout Europe as a market worth £84 bn employing 7.8 m people, 8% of the total labourforce, declined.[4] The major contractors began to move down market, taking smaller contracts by the end of the decade, thus putting the pressure on the medium sized companies and so on. Although this strategy has been largely successful for the major contractors, the situation may in reality be worse as retention money held at the end of contracts, especially on overseas work, and claims on contracts were still coming through at the end of the 1970s. It is possible that stage payments and completions contributed 30% of pre-tax profits on contracting in 1975 whereas by 1980 claims and retention money could have amounted to as much as 70% of the pre-tax profits.[5]

At the beginning of the period labour was still in short supply and thus the use of subcontractors and labour-only subcontractors[6] was extensive. This subsequently allowed the industry to be more responsive to changing market conditions and also less responsive to the pay controls during the phases of the Industrial Relations Act, 1971. As workloads subsequently diminished, the sector was in a favourable position to slim down operations without the problems of redundancies and related labour disputes.

The increasing use of labour-only subcontractors was initially given a stimulus by the introduction of selective employment tax (SET) in 1966. This was replaced by the introduction of value added tax (VAT) in 1973 on which construction received zero rating, although the subsequent decline in the market led to increasing unemployment in the construction industry and so labour-only subcontracting was reduced, but not due to SET being superseded. Indeed labour-only subcontracting hid the extent of the unemployment in construction even though it was visibly higher than other sectors by the end of the decade. These are the results of the flexibility necessary for contractors to face the effects of crisis in the economy.

The sector has experienced a number of strikes during the period, the UCATT strike of 1972, the strikes on the construction of oil and gas platforms in the mid-1970s and the inter-union disputes at the Isle of Grain at the end of the period being notable examples. The twenty week UCATT strike in the summer of 1972 was over demands for £30 per week. Basic rates were raised from £20 to £26 for skilled operatives although a number of contractors, such as Bryant, settled independently, granting the full £30.[7] There was considerable intimidation during the strike leading to the flying pickets known as the 'Shrewsbury two' being convicted for criminal conspiracy. The dispute contributed to the undermining of the government's incomes policy.[8] Laing was singled out for special attention by the union resulting in costs exceeding £1m,[9] although Laing took the events in its stride, recognising the significance of the strike. Its chairman commented to shareholders:

Our management prefers to deal with well organised trades unions and thus hopes to shield our customers from the hazards of disorganised and unofficial action. In the very rare event of an official national strike such as occurred last year, this policy may operate against the Company but we are convinced that sound relations with properly elected union representatives are in the best interests of customers, employees and shareholders.[10]

The nationalisation of construction, or at least some of the major contractors such as Wimpey and Costain, became a political issue during the decade. There can be little reason for Sir Robert McAlpine becoming a publicly quoted company in 1972 under the name of a holding company, Newarthill, except to give the company an open market value for compensation purposes in the event of nationalisation, because the McAlpine family predominantly owns the company through trusts and retains management control. Similarly, the hiving of Laing Properties from the main contracting arm in 1978 can be seen as an attempt to protect family interests, especially as the move exposed the dependence of Laing on property interests to underpin profits. The nationalisation issue was heightened by a publication by the Labour Party in 1977[11] and was opposed by the industry through the formation of the Campaign Against Building Industry Nationalisation (CABIN) and the commissioning of evidence from the Economist Intelligence Unit.[12] Nationalisation transfers the ownership of capital from private concerns to the state and would therefore produce the largest concentration of capital seen in the construction industry, yet the relation of the sector to the market would of necessity remain fundamentally unchanged. Despite the intentions of nationalisation to induce continuity of work and employment this could not therefore be achieved and indeed is admitted by the Labour Party[13] in what is a key statement: 'The construction industry is characterised by flexibility and by diverse sources of initiative, and it is no part of our aim that these valuable qualities should be lost.' The social objectives are untenable through nationalisation and the sector neither has such a massive workload nor is in such a deep crisis that the conditions under which nationalisation has been justified in the past could be applied in this period. Nationalisation does not therefore permit the contradictions between capital and labour to be resolved and indeed would only be an opportunity for restructuring the sector under a process of forced capital concentration.

The housing markets

Public housing contracts have been dominated by Wimpey and Laing amongst the major contractors since the war with their 'no fines' and Easiform systems. The failure of industrialised building in the 1960s continued unabated in the early 1970s,[14] which gave Wimpey and Laing a short respite with their systems. However, the increased preference for low rise traditional building and more significantly the absolute decline in public housing programmes at the beginning of the 1970s and the 36% decline in the market between 1976 and 1979, coupled with the increasing use of timber frame housing, hit both of these major contractors severely.

Wimpey's performance in the sector has lagged behind that of its major competitors in Britain during the 1970s largely because of the decline in public housing. It was Wimpey's largest single national activity, but its share dropped from 12% of this market in 1970 to only 5% in 1977.[15] By 1974 timber costs were falling while wages were increasing and so contractors increasingly favoured timber frame construction to reduce costs and increase turnover. In 1973 only 3% of the local authority houses were timber frame but this increased to 8% by 1975,[16] and indeed Wimpey has recently introduced timber frame housebuilding.[17]

To some extent the decline in public housebuilding has been offset by the growth in repairs and maintenance, a large proportion of which has involved the refurbishment of public housing. Central government grants to local authorities boosted this work in 1974–5[18] and in 1978 the repairs and maintenance market generally grew by 16%, accounting for 38% of the total construction market by 1980.[19] Laing in particular has been well placed to penetrate the upper end of this market due to its strong regional orientation for building work[20] and there is evidence that it has been successful in this respect.[21]

Although public housebuilding is a production process, its use is concerned with working class consumption and reproduction. As the recession deepened during the decade, social policies were increasingly subsumed under economic policies and financial cutbacks aimed at the reproduction of capital first and foremost in terms of capital accumulation.

State building and civil engineering markets

While public housing work was tailing off the road, hospital and other state programmes remained comparatively buoyant at the beginning of the decade.[22] The major contractors, for example Taylor Woodrow and Laing, were heavily engaged in hospital construction, but contractors had been facing intense competition in the road programme from medium sized contractors such as Sir Alfred McAlpine (Marchwiel), Monk and French. The programme for new roads was a very large slice of the public sector market, consistently comprising 30% of total government expenditure on the gross domestic fixed capital formation. The medium-to-large sized contractors were now endeavouring to diversify their public sector work to gain an increasing share of government civil engineering contracts,[23] largely leaving government building contracts such as hospitals to the major contractors.

The major contractors had reduced their commitment to road contracts as many had made losses in the late 1960s due to specialist companies fragmenting the market and intensifying the competition. In 1976 Costain had reduced its involvement to one motorway contract, the £19.5m M4 contract in a joint venture with Cementation.[24] Wimpey similarly faced problems in the late 1960s and reduced its commitment to one or two road contracts, although the company had large indirect interests in the programmes through asphalting, which was estimated to produce a turnover exceeding £30m per annum in 1979.[25]

The profitability of all contractors in public sector work, but particularly the majors experiencing losses on motorway work, was threatened by rapid inflation on contracts exceeding two years which were on fixed prices. Eighty-one per cent of building contracts and 94% of civil engineering contracts were received through select or open competition,[26] and the rapid escalation of inflation in the early 1970s threatened their viability. This was added to by the construction strike in 1972, although according to one commentator[27] the wage increases had been foreseen at an early enough stage to be allowed for in tender prices. The situation was eased on the wages front by the prices freeze.[28] Contractors became largely insulated from inflation on public contracts after the introduction of the Baxter formula in November 1973, which linked contract prices to labour and material indices, whereby 80% of additional costs incurred due to inflation could be reclaimed.

The political demand for roads, hospitals and welfare construction was satiated by the mid-1970s even if the economic and social needs had not been satisfied.[29] These programmes therefore became the expedient target to reduce government expenditure. The effects of reducing fixed capital expenditure are more immediate, especially on new construction work, and so between 1974 and 1976 *ad hoc* or informal cuts, which were not explicitly announced, were implemented,[30] although these cuts were relative, the absolute cuts appearing in the formal explicit cuts of 1976–7. The first formal round of cuts particularly hit road programmes, nationalised industries, health and education. Further cuts between 1978 and 1979 were directed at these programmes again plus water and sewerage work. Central government expenditure on roads as a component of the gross domestic fixed capital formation fell from £492m in 1976 to £417m in 1978, although rising again to £570m by 1980. Total central government expenditure fell from £1,388m in 1976 to £1,229m in 1978, although rising again to £1,679m by 1980. These cuts mirror reductions in the Public Sector Borrowing Requirement, which peaked in 1975 at £10,480m and fell to £5,993m in 1977, although rising again to £12,244m by 1980.

Government found it more difficult to impose cuts on local and area agencies. One stockbroker commented in 1975: 'It is frightening to think as recently as October the Department of Environment for instance did not know how much was spent on capital account by the Water Authorities for the year to March 1975 let alone how expenditure was progressing in the current year.'[31] Water authority work, particularly concerning water and sewerage treatment, had been a growing market for contractors. Laing had entered this market in a joint venture with Degremont in the late 1960s in an aim to diversify public sector work, although in this case with little profitability even though work was buoyant until later in the 1970s. W. & C. French, and subsequently the amalgamated French Kier, had also entered this market. The drive to diversify into other markets was paramount to contractors endeavouring to maintain their overall market share at the expense of other companies. Market diversification was not always profitable, as in the case of Degremont Laing. Local authorities following their reorganisation in 1974 were larger and therefore potentially offered larger contracts that became increasingly attractive to major contractors. Recently economic stringency has resulted in these local agencies reducing capital expenditure. This expansion was therefore shortlived in the face of overproduction in the economy.

Energy related construction had been discontinuous during the decade. The demand for electricity was based on assumed high growth rates in the economy. The oil crisis gave a political stimulus to nuclear power station construction, but unrealised growth and cutbacks have led to demands being continually revised downwards and thermal and nuclear power station contracts were frequently postponed or cancelled. Taylor Woodrow and Sir Robert McAlpine continued to monopolise the nuclear power station construction projects. Following the restructuring of the industry by the Industrial Reorganisation Corporation[32] in 1966, Nuclear Design and Construction was controlled by the following agents:

Taylor Woodrow	4%
Atomic Energy Authority	20%
Industrial Reorganisation Corporation	26%
GEC–EE	25%
Babcock and Wilcox	25%[33]

McAlpine operated in the Nuclear Power Group,[34] which together were rolled into the British Nuclear Associates[35] under the National Nuclear Corporation in the mid-1970s, the ownership being:

GEC		30%
UK Atomic Energy Authority		35%
British Nuclear Associates		35%
comprising		
Taylor Woodrow	14.3%	
Clarke Chapman	28.6%	
Babcock and Wilcox	34.3%	
Robert McAlpine	7.1%	
Head Wrightson	8.6%	
Whessoe	5.7%	
Strachan and Henshaw	1.4%	

The lack of continuity in this market has pushed Taylor Woodrow to seek new energy related construction work such as the North Sea, wind energy, the Severn Barrage[36] and opencast coalmining in Britain and overseas. The Oldbury Magnox reactor offers some potential for export,[37] but the nuclear power programmes have not been developed with export markets in mind the way they have by Westinghouse in the United States.

Opencast coalmining has been expanding and so has the involvement of contractors both in Britain and overseas during the latter half of the 1970s and in the 1980s. Costain, Wimpey, Fairclough and Crouch were the most heavily involved in Britain in 1976 and the reserves are sufficient to maintain production rates until 1984.[38] This has been one of the few expanding state sectors for contractors in the late 1970s as the National Coal Board planned to increase opencast coalmining by 50% between 1976 and 1979. Contractors have endeavoured to capture a share of this market. Fairclough acquired Sir Lindsay Parkinson in order to diversify into opencast coalmining. Taylor Woodrow received the largest opencast coalmining contract in 1976 for the extraction of 12m tonnes of coal over ten years at Butterwell, Northumberland. The value of the tender was £130m.[39]

Other state programmes have been shrinking throughout the decade. New public housing work was worth £1,428m in 1969 at 1975 prices, a figure which has only been exceeded in two years during the 1970s. Other new public work peaked in 1973 at £2,942m and has continued to fall to £1,907m at 1975 prices by the end of the decade (see figure 6.1).

Contractors experienced increasing underproduction in these markets, the large contractors usually seeking 50% of their building turnover in the public sector and frequently over 50% of their turnover for civil engineering work. The situation was exacerbated by the already intense competition for public sector work between the large and medium contractors which emerged during the prosperous 1960s. During the early 1970s the road programmes were sometimes profitless for large and medium sized contractors alike. Monk began to diversify out of its reliance on road and other public sector work. W. & C. French, in contrast, after its merger with J. L. Kier, forming French Kier Holdings, over-extended its road operations requiring *ex gratia* grants totalling £9.5m and access to a £4.5m loan from the DoE to complete its commitments.[40] Competition for public contracts had switched from endeavours to obtain an increasing share of an increasing market during the 1960s to endeavours to maintain a share of a decreasing market. During the 1970s contractors were relatively successful in percentage terms but turnover fell absolutely. Underproduction became the dominant experience in these markets.

Private building and civil engineering markets

Private sector work was at a high level in the early 1970s, with the exception of industrial work, so commercial property development and the secondary private housing market were the principal stimuli.

Most contractors only have small private housebuilding subsidiaries with the notable exception of Wimpey and to a limited extent Laing. The private housing market suffered after the devaluation of sterling in 1967 and the large contractors subsequently reduced their interests in private housebuilding.[41] Although private housebuilding boomed between 1971 and 1973 this was largely only significant for Wimpey, and for Laing. Laing made large profits from land banking activities, having restructured its housebuilding operations to focus on the markets in the south east of Britain.[42] Private housebuilding made a large contribution to Costain's profit record at this time, but only served to highlight the poor building and less competitive civil engineering operations in Britain at the time.[43] Contractors have recently been increasing their private housebuilding operations, although to a very large extent this is overseas, particularly in the North American markets.

Laing has indirectly gained from the private housebuilding market in the last decade. In addition to its direct interests, it produces lightweight concrete blocks, especially Thermalite blocks. The company had been making them since the 1950s, and their easy handling and laying qualities made them increasingly popular, especially when materials were in short supply in 1973, but their high u-value or thermal insulation properties made them very successful after the 1973 'oil crisis'. Laing cornered a large proportion of this market due to the high initial investment costs inhibiting potential competitors entering the market.[44]

Commercial building had been steadily increasing throughout the 1960s (see figure 4.2) and received a boost from government grants for hotel building in 1971. During 1968–71 development margins were high as the limited development supply met a growing demand. Construction profit margins are generally higher for private sector building work compared to, say, public sector civil engineering work so as to offset a longer capital turnover period requiring more working capital.[45] However, the limited development activity which kept development margins high depressed construction profit margins as intensive competition on public sector work spilled over to affect private sector contracts.[46] This reflects on the one hand the demand to speed up circulation and hence high development margins and on the other hand the low level of demand for construction work and hence low construction margins, both of which are effects of overproduction in the economy.

The increased demand for commercial development, both office and retailing, induced a considerable rise in construction output in 1971–4 (see figure 4.2), but because of the long time lags between the decision to develop and completion the commercial construction boom occurred between 1974 and 1975 after the collapse of the property market (see figure 4.2). The rise in demand in this sphere was due to the strategic importance of the circulation process. Building users were endeavouring to speed up the circulation and realisation of profits in order to gain an advantage over competitors in a period of overproduction.

Attempts were made to speed up the development process through various package deal and negotiated contracts, one of the most notable being the management fee system operated by Bovis. This reinforced a trend towards the greater use of subcontractors by the contractors who placed more emphasis on management. Indeed the 1970s witnessed a dichotomisation. On the one hand complex building and civil engineering projects moved more towards management contracting, whereby the main contractor subcontracts all the work and the greatest flexibility of work is achieved for the contractor. On the other hand selective and open tendering was strengthened at the expense of negotiated contracts, especially in the sphere of production, as client companies became more cost conscious rather than aiming to be first into production, and therefore the market, through early completions. Costs were also being weighed up against the anticipated benefits from speeding up the realisation process in the sphere of capital circulation.

A further lag between the property boom and its related commercial construction boom was created by the 1972 building strike.[47] It may seem surprising that orders for new offices reached a peak in 1974. New offices formed 31% of new orders in 1970 and 49% in 1974, the reason probably being that developers and institutions were already committed at this stage, the costs of withdrawing being greater than the cost of continuing development programmes. In addition office and retail development remained at relatively high levels outside the London area for a while after the crash in the market in late 1973.

The boom did bring high profit margins for contractors. However, in the City of London two medium sized contractors obtained the largest share of the market: Trollope and Colls, the Trafalgar House subsidiary, with 7 contracts and Higgs and Hill with 3 out of a total of 21 schemes. Profits from commercial work take longer to be realised than other types of work and were therefore still underpinning contractor profits after 1975[48] and, indeed, commercial construction remained an important market in the late 1970s despite the end of the property boom (see figure 4.2).

Construction companies had been building up their own property portfolios in the previous decade but they expanded considerably during the 1970s. One of the principal reasons for contractors to enter property development was to provide work for the construction divisions and one of the principal reasons for entering property investment was to increase the asset backing of construction companies without threatening the flexibility of contracting in the face of underproduction. Indeed, rental income would help underpin profits in the event of declining turnovers.[49] An additional reason was that property companies were more highly rated than construction companies on the stock market. Property companies had assets valued in the region of 15 times their income flow whereas contractors had assets valued at about 7 times their income flow. An increase in development and investment activity would therefore enhance the contractors' stock market rating,[50] which would help raise equity capital for expansion at home and particularly overseas. Large scale expansion of development and investment activity was undertaken with low gearing. The conservative accounting and financing policies of contractors could not be threatened by the expansion of property activities. Their high liquidity as a result of their low money and working capital requirements, yet high profitability in the 1960s and early 1970s, kept asset gearing low, and the re-rating of the sector on the stock market kept the financial gearing low.

The low financial and asset gearing of contractors ensured that they did not suffer as a result of the crash in the property markets in 1973–4. Looking back in 1978 one stockbroker commented:

The position changed dramatically after 1974 when property values fell sharply but the contractors suffered relatively little because their conservatism had prevented them from exposing themselves unduly to the property market – for which they had been severely castigated by most outside observers only a few years earlier. Accordingly, in the recovery period in which we now find ourselves the contractors are extremely well placed given that so many of their competitors have disappeared as a financial force in the market place during the recession.[51]

Contractors were therefore in a strong position to select niches in the development market with high development margins after the property boom. Once the oversupply had been absorbed a wider range of developments could be undertaken, sometimes in association with financial institutions.

Wimpey was one of the last contractors to enter development directly.

The company entered direct development for the first time in 1976. Wimpey considered in 1974 that public sector work would tail off. The group was very liquid, in the region of £50m at the time, with overseas expansion being currently financed by creditors and pre-payments and so a development programme in the south and south east was initiated.[52] Wimpey bought the ailing Wingate Investments in 1976 and in 1977 formed Wimpey Property Holdings as the vehicle for its property interests. Development activity extended to Europe with the 50% interest in Ariel which became a subsidiary in 1979. The main feature was that this direct entry into development was undertaken at the bottom of the market and those companies active at this time obtained high development returns as the oversupply was eased.[53] Recent development included both commercial and extensive industrial development,[54] the development programme estimated to be in the region of £60m in 1979.[55]

As Taylor Woodrow had actually reduced its commitment to development since 1976 following its rapid expansion during the early 1970s, and Laing Properties was floated as a separately quoted company in 1978, the holding companies missed out on some of the improvements in the development market in the late 1970s.

Investment in new private industrial construction has fluctuated over the decade. Between 1969 and 1972 investment was in decline at 1975 prices (see figure 4.2). Investment in production improved in 1971–2, although this improvement was in relative decline compared to the economy as a whole as the gross domestic fixed capital formation to gross national product at factor cost declined from 17.1% to 16.8% in the period (see table 5.4). Certainly industrialised building did not keep pace with this limited improvement as only a 1.5% increase in activity occurred.[56] Laing, however, increased its industrial building orders by 6% in 1972 and by 44% in the following three months, although this can almost entirely be attributed to the contract for the British Steel Corporation's £10m steelworks at Redcar.[57] The decline in industrial investment is the anticipated response in theoretical terms, overproduction placing emphasis on the sphere of capital circulation, while increased productivity and the shake out of surplus labour occur in the existing buildings and through closures of production facilities.

Against the general background of declining investment in industrial buildings some areas of industrial and related activities did expand considerably during the 1970s. Warehousing is one example. Additionally, the specialised high technology work did not suffer the decline of mainstream construction work and profit margins on this type of work were good.[58] Mechanical, electrical and process engineering were the areas in which contractors were developing their expertise. This development is coupled with the decline in the pure or mainstream construction content in contracts in favour of a growing plant and associated mechanical and electrical content. This change of emphasis favours the large and specialist contractors who have a design and build capacity. The mechanical, electrical and chemical engineering division of Wimpey, for example, has expanded from a turnover of £20m in 1970 to £80m by 1978.[59] This market, however, is restricted:

There are, of course, limits to the extent to which civil engineering companies can invade the territories of the specialist process plant contractors since the oil and chemical companies are very reluctant to cut themselves off from the technological advances and the R & D effort of some of the major specialist companies. It does, nonetheless, present a natural diversification for civil engineering companies and this is already evident in the pattern of acquisitions and agreements which European contractors have increasingly entered into over the last two to three years in an attempt to move up the technology ladder and open up opportunities in markets not geared solely to levels of public capital expenditure.[60]

The diversification into other and new markets has been an essential strategy for contractors to offset the effects of underproduction as far as the total markets will permit.

The specialised work is frequently subcontracted by the main contractors. The flexibility in the construction labour market through the subcontracting system is once again seen as a vital component of the general flexibility contractors require to respond to crisis. While subcontracting can have a positive effect of diffusing or disciplining labour unrest, the mechanical, electrical and process engineering work can induce union action. The Costain chairman, Terrel Wyatt, commented: 'Wherever there is a very large contract and where both mechanical and building unions are involved there tend to be problems. Not only is there the problem of managing a large labour force but there are conflicting union interests.'[61] The divisions between unions help to manage the crisis by diffusing the possibility of united and concerted working class action and self-organisation.

Although a large proportion of mechanical, electrical and process engineering is overseas, a substantial proportion is located in Britain, of which the North Sea oil and gas industries constitute an important component of the work. From this basis the large contractors, who have been able to enter this growing market, have further diversified into on shore and off shore construction and general contracting work.

In addition to mechanical, electrical and process engineering for companies operating in the North Sea oil and gas markets some contractors entered into the construction of platforms. Expenditure on oil drilling rigs and related equipment had already reached a turnover of £100m per year for contractors by 1973.[62] The production of platforms for the North Sea reached £33m by 1973, which NEDO estimated would rise to £90m by 1976.[63]

Wimpey was the first to enter the platform market in a joint venture with the American general contractors Brown and Root in 1971. The company, called Highland Fabricators, was established to construct a £10m platform for BP in the Forties Field. A fabricating and pipe rolling mill was added later. Located at Nigg Bay the infrastructure cost was paid for by the state, the company only having to invest in specialist plant,[64] hence not infringing greatly on the flexible needs of contractors to keep fixed capital investment at a low level. The average turnover was £36.5m and average pre-tax profits were £2m between 1974 and 1977.

Laing and Sir Robert McAlpine also entered the platform construction market. Here too grants were given by the state to pay the infrastructure and capital costs. Laing in association with the French company Société Entrepose GTM pour le Travaux Pétroliers Maritime received one order from BP for the Forties Field and one from Signal Oil and the Gas Corporation for the Thistle Field. McAlpine Sea Tank used concrete construction as opposed to the traditional steel fabrication for their platform. Both companies experienced labour disputes, which retarded progress, and McAlpine had a number of design problems as the oil company's specifications changed, which led to short term losses in the region of £10m, although subsequent claims led to a return to profitability.[65] The main problem, however, was that the state had financed the yards, having misread the capacity of the market. The yards were set in competition with each other for new contracts at a time when oil company investment in the North Sea was being curtailed due to the Labour Party and Government policies for BNOC which were unpopular with the oil industry, while simultaneously competition from Norwegian and French yards was intensifying. The profitability of platform construction was therefore in question by the mid-1970s. Like the motorway programmes the first comers such as Wimpey received the highest profit margins. The state played an important albeit indirect role in the shortlived expansion of this market for contractors.

All North Sea contract work is a specialist and limited market which will become increasingly saturated.[66] Some later entrants to the market did, however, manage to carve out particular areas. Taylor Woodrow is the most notable example. Seeing the moderate and declining successes with platform construction its initial joint venture proposals with John Mowlem remained on the shelf. It identified that multinational oil companies were successful at exploration and extraction but had shortcomings in coordinating the diverse companies required to provide the means to extract the oil. Contractors had just this management expertise and so Taylor Woodrow decided not to undertake work directly but offer management contracts to oil companies.[67] This means that turnover is very high although profits are comparatively low, but so are the overheads and hence risks.

The management contract is the most mature form of contracting, offering the greatest flexibility to contractors and the greatest insulation from underproduction. It is the logical extension of the negotiated and design and build contracts, and is today being used in a wider variety of construction work such as office construction and airport terminal work. It is indeed a result of underproduction experienced by contractors in their continual efforts to stave off the worst effects of the crisis through product and geographical diversification.

Taylor Woodrow combined its successful identification of a market with the successful selection of companies to undertake work in joint ventures, so as to increase the expertise and therefore further decrease the risks. It has been argued that two very large companies such as Wimpey with Brown and Root are not always ideal, but Taylor Woodrow's joint venture with Santa Fe has been successful for both companies.[68]

Wimpey has also been involved through Wimpey Marine in providing off shore services through a fleet of forty barges, tugs, supply vessels and launches[69] which were largely loss making[70] until 1979, when profits were realised on a lower turnover. Taylor Woodrow has been successful in this market in association with James Finlay and Co. through Seaforth Maritime. Once again the successful selection of a partner paid off.

Although energy related work has been an important market during the 1970s it had probably reached a pinnacle by the end of the decade in terms of construction and related contract work although contractors such as Tarmac and Taylor Woodrow have entered into the seventh round of production licences in the North Sea in respective consortia, which may prove to be another successful diversification to alleviate some of the full effects of underproduction. However, these strategies are only alleviation, the experience of crisis being unavoidable and becoming more severe as each avenue of delay is exhausted.

Overseas markets

Another very important market during the 1970s has been the overseas construction business. Initially the main thrust came in the Middle East. British contractors anticipating the continued decline in construction work, particularly public sector work, in the 1970s decided to diversify, overseas work being a very important response. The restraint on dividend payments to shareholders benefited contractors in this respect because, while contract work in Britain requires little working capital and is largely creditor financed, the same is not so true for overseas work.[71] The liquidity through quick cash generation and the build up of reserves from the prosperous 1960s helped diversification into property and overseas markets. Dividend control reinforced this ability.

Table 7.1 details the division of the overseas markets during the 1970s. It can be seen that these markets have continued to expand. The North American market has continued to expand into the 1980s particularly in the spheres of housebuilding, development and opencast coalmining, but the major market has been the Middle East. It was the future decline of work in Britain that pushed contractors overseas, one of the most impor-tant contributory factors being the 'oil crisis' of 1973, which had the effect of increasing the liquidity of oil rich Middle Eastern states from the increased rents on oil. This filtered through to provide more work for British contractors overseas.

Although the market continued to expand in the Middle East until 1977–8, nearly constituting 50% of British contractors' overseas work during the 1970s, the profit margins have narrowed. The so-called 'jumbo' contracts for large scale infrastructure facilities had largely been ordered by the mid-1970s and smaller scale work became available, which induced some of the medium sized companies, such as Fairclough and Sunley, into the market. Despite the strategies to become more specialised, so fragmenting the market, competition has increased. This was further intensified with the entry of other international competitors. The decline of the European market by 1974[72] led to contractors from France, West Germany and the Netherlands entering these markets, although British contractors have largely competed successfully against them.[73] It was the contractors from the Far Eastern countries, such as Japan but notably South Korea, who successfully obtained an increasing share of the market using armies of disciplined low paid construction workers from their own countries.[74] The requirements that local contrac-tors should undertake more of the work arguably enhance the role of British overseas contractors, who form associate companies with local contractors to provide services and enhance capabilities and capacity.

British contractors had the largest share of the Middle Eastern market in 1969.[75] By 1978 it was being argued that they had not repeated the sustained successes of the British consulting engineers[76] due to intensified competition. This came at a time when oil revenues were declining and the construction market was showing signs of relative decline in the Middle East as the initial preconditions for industrialisation and

Table 7.1. Major overseas markets for British contractors

	Value of contracts obtained £m										
	1968/9	1969/70	1970/1	1971/2	1972/3	1973/4	1974/5	1975/6	1976/7	1977/8	1978/9
EEC	3	13	6	3	11	8	12	6	8	16	38
Rest of Europe	18	35	31	48	34	54	123	58	73	136	75
Middle East in Asia	37	47	53	42	64	210	519	494	851	793	619
Middle East in Africa	4	2	—	—	2	1	2	22	23	58	38
Rest of Asia	6	33	16	17	19	14	30	39	48	20	132
Rest of Africa	45	43	95	74	86	138	256	469	340	389	225
America	51	120	72	72	50	54	72	93	140	139	91
Oceania	68	40	37	41	58	75	70	99	105	94	81
All countries	232	333	310	297	324	554	1,084	1,280	1,588	1,645	1,299

Source: Department of the Environment.

development were being satisfied and the crisis took hold there in the form of declining oil revenues.

Costain has been the most successful overseas contractor with 40–60% of its turnover being overseas since the 1950s. They were working in the Gulf area before the second world war and therefore had long established contacts and experience. Wimpey entered the overseas market on a large scale later than some other contractors with its overseas turnover being 17% in 1975 rising to 40% by 1978,[77] yet its overseas turnover has remained at approximately the same as Costain throughout the 1970s.[78] Wimpey as the largest British contractor was insulated to some extent in the British market from underproduction due to its size and diversity despite declining workloads, for example housebuilding. This explains its delay in moving overseas to some degree, but its size and diversity permitted it to obtain a large workload in a short time. Costain had a low market penetration in the British market, but achieved above average profit margins and on a few contracts very high margins on overseas work as a result of its experience and early penetration of the Middle East market. Its other major contribution was in the field of finance. Contrary to popular belief Middle Eastern countries do not directly use oil revenues to finance projects and Costain was instrumental in arranging finance for projects on the international money markets through the World Bank and other agencies at very preferential interest rates and completing the package with its work being backed up by the Export Credit Guarantees Department in Britain. The ability to put together financial packages was frequently the key to the markets in the early days for contractors.[79]

Other contractors, such as Taylor Woodrow, which had spread its overseas activities widely across different countries in former commonwealth countries,[80] were now able to obtain continuity of work in overseas markets. Taylor Woodrow undertook two highly profitable 'jumbo' contracts in a joint venture with Costain in Dubai, although the joint ventures between Wimpey and Laing in Saudi Arabia with Haji Abdullah Alireza in Iran were not very profitable, the latter for political reasons.

Overseas work has generally added to the profitability of contractors, the flow of profits still entering the accounts some years after the completion of each contract, but not all contractors have realised profits. Tarmac, for example, after a number of problems concerning management and the acquisition of Holland, Hannen and Cubitts experienced problems overseas, especially in Nigeria. The managing director commented:

We jumped on an overseas bandwagon at a time when most of our competitors were winning foreign work to compensate for the scarcity of contracts at home and were, apparently, making good profits. The trouble was that we got our timing wrong and hit the tail end of the boom. Apart from that, it was a mistake to build up a heavily asset-based operation overseas, so that we found ourselves with severe problems when it came to pulling back.[81]

The limits of overseas expansion are being reached. Although new markets are being opened up existing ones are simultaneously being saturated and characterised by intensive competition. The flow of work is not therefore expected to grow. As retention money and claims for past overseas contracts work their way through the accounts the impact of current and hence future overseas work will be more easily assessed. This geographical diversification cannot therefore overcome underproduction, this being the contractors' experience of the world wide crisis of overproduction.

Capital concentration

During the 1960s there was little or no capital concentration in the industry. It was characterised by the growth of the medium sized contractors. The large contractors were not squeezed in total as other markets existed and were expanding when competition intensified. In addition smaller sized companies increased their market at the turn of the decade, almost entirely at the expense of national medium and large sized contractors.[82] Companies employing up to 1,200 operatives increased their market share from 76% in 1967 to 78% in 1973 and companies employing over 1,200 decreased their share from 23.3% to 21.9% over the same period.[83] In part this increased share is due to the growth of smaller companies through takeovers between 1971 and 1974, which gave them a base for expansion. This, however, has been subsequently counteracted by major contractors expanding their regional offices to increase regional market penetration during the late 1960s and 1970s with the setting up of small works operations in the late 1970s as the large companies move down market as workloads fall.

One of the features of contracting is the flexible organisation. As a result falling turnover does not induce a wave of takeovers and a shake out of larger companies. On the one hand the low level of fixed capital investment, the use of subcontractors and redundancy amongst management personnel give contractors the flexibility to maintain profit levels with reduced turnover.[84] On the other hand large contractors can encroach on the markets of smaller companies, thus inducing a knock-on effect, the small and smaller companies being the most vulnerable and characterised by high bankruptcy rates in the sector. The effect on overt unemployment in the sector has been an increase of 9% reaching a total of 17% or

164,100 operatives between 1969 and 1979, the labourforce accepting the brunt of the crisis.

Takeovers in the construction sector are to a very large extent motivated by the need to diversify. Diversification can occur at the beginning of a boom in one market, and a takeover will be aimed to reap the rewards of high profit margins. Diversification can also occur during a slump in order to insulate the contractor and hence decrease dependence on particular markets.[85] Ideally the two will be dovetailed whereby the decline in one market will lead to diversification through takeover in an expanding market. This contrasts with other production sectors which frequently pursue takeovers to achieve economies of scale in one main activity, rationalising excess capacity in other activities. This characterises the different relation the construction sector has to the market compared to other sectors.

Many of the takeovers in the early 1970s involved smaller and some medium sized companies, a large number concerning private housebuilders in order to expand land banks.[86] Takeovers were at a low ebb in the mid-1970s, but have increased in recent years as the large contractors pursued diversification policies where joint ventures and associate companies were inappropriate.

In comparison to other sectors capital concentration has not been important quantitatively.[87] While some active markets still exist and contractors are able to maintain acceptable rates of profits by slimming down their operations and by using claims for extra work, money retentions held by clients on work done being paid, and capital reserves to underpin profits there is unlikely to be a shake out or an increase of capital concentration at the upper end of the sector.

In response to the declining levels of work in Britain the medium sized contractors had slimmed down their operations in the late 1970s.[88] Higgs and Hill, for example, decided to withdraw from civil engineering work which subsequently appeared to improve profitability.[89] The large contractors have been encroaching on the markets of medium sized contractors in the latter half of the decade, but the rationalisation of medium sized companies led to some resistance, and so the large companies have been rationalising their structure and personnel too. Wimpey reorganised its structure,[90] although its management along with Laing was considered too top heavy at the turn of the decade.[91] However, it must also be said that Laing and to a degree Wimpey have been successful at maintaining turnover during the 1970s against increased competition. This is partly due to their decision to extend their operations down market for which a large administrative and management staff is required. Taylor Woodrow on the other hand have maintained their operations without noticeably moving down market,[92] and indeed do not have a diverse regional organ-isation. One of the most notable countertendencies is Marchwiel (see table 7.2), which it can be argued has been rapidly transformed into a major contractor. Its high levels of efficiency and above average rates of profit have brought this result.[93] Its experience of expansion has been to increase its operations in a market which is experiencing long term overall decline.

Development, 1968–79

The property sector exhibited net growth during this period and thus sustained activity against the general economic trends of falling rates of profit and the overproduction of commodities for the size of the market. The reason for this is not that the sector breaks the rules, but its relation to the market is different.

When industry first experiences overproduction, the competition to sell commodities intensifies and the need to improve the administration and management of company affairs intensifies. The improvement of admin-istration applies to all sectors of the economy. The relocation of offices and retailing outlets and improvement of working conditions in new buildings can lead to gains over competitors, thus accelerating the circu-lation of capital and its realisation into profits. This period is therefore in theoretical contrast to the restructuring and expansion of the sphere of circulation which ushered in the first property boom of the late 1950s and early 1960s.

The theoretical effect is to stimulate the development of offices and retailing units and it is these features which have predominantly charac-terised the 1970s. Developers, property investors, financial institutions and share investors to a very large extent mistook this stimulus in property development as a motor of growth in the economy leading to a belief that investments in property were safe despite other general trends. They did not see the stimulus as a response to the deepening recession in the economy. The result was that development activity in the sphere of capital circulation was concentrated in a growing property boom between 1969 and the end of 1973. Table 7.3 shows the extent of this concentration of activity in the first half of the decade. The increase in retailing units may appear to be low, but the development of shopping centres had been proceeding after the end of the previous property boom up to 1964, and new shopping areas were often created at the expense of other older areas. The net increase in office space is a reflection of in-creased competition between national and international companies, particularly international banks and financial institutions locating in

Table 7.2. Record of leading contractors

	Total turnover £m					UK turnover £m					Pre-tax profits £m					Pre-tax profit margins £m					UK market share £m				
	'70	'72	'74	'76	'78	'70	'72	'74	'76	'78	'70	'72	'74	'76	'78	'70	'72	'74	'76	'78	'70	'72	'74	'76	'78
Costain	108	124	193	358	509	61	67	99	121	152	3.8	8.0	10.6	23.3	46.9	3.5	6.4	5.5	6.5	9.2	1.4	1.3	1.4	1.3	1.2
Fairclough	23	53	98	163	232	23	53	96	n.a.	n.a.	1.2	2.4	4.1	5.9	9.5	5.1	4.4	4.2	3.6	4.1	0.5	1.0	1.3	—	—
French	43	55	135	156	163	40	n.a.	n.a.	n.a.	n.a.	1.1	2.4	2.9	3.0	n.a.	2.6	4.4	n.a.	2.0	4.6	1.0	—	—	—	—
Kier	21	32				17	27				1.0	2.0				4.8	6.2				0.4	0.5			
Laing	113	160	246	406	483	—	—	—	—	—	2.8	7.1	7.4	16.2	14.7	2.5	4.5	3.0	4.0	3.0	2.8	3.2	3.4	4.6	3.0
Marchwiel/ McAlpine	56	60	98	182	187	—	—	—	—	—	2.7	5.7	5.2	10.7	13.5	4.8	9.4	5.3	5.9	7.2	1.4	1.2	1.3	2.0	1.7
Newarthill	66	79	132	174	147	66	74	128	169	144	2.3	3.1	3.2	5.2	9.2	3.6	5.0	3.1	1.8	4.6	1.6	1.1	1.4	1.5	0.9
Mowlem	39	47	75	109	141	30	38	63	n.a.	n.a.	0.6	1.6	1.8	4.2	5.9	1.7	3.3	2.4	3.9	4.2	0.7	0.7	0.9	—	—
Tarmac	143	194	322	510	723	127	171	265	n.a.	n.a.	7.6	12.7	17.7	22.5	26.4	5.3	6.5	5.5	4.4	3.7	3.1	3.4	3.7	—	—
Taylor Woodrow	97	132	229	413	393	77	103	149	263	234	4.3	7.6	10.4	20.9	23.9	4.4	5.8	4.5	5.0	6.1	1.9	2.0	2.1	2.9	2.1
Wimpey	225	242	380	652	853	185	190	294	442	510	6.0	14.2	33.4	44.4	57.2	2.7	5.9	8.8	6.8	6.7	4.6	3.8	4.1	5.0	4.7

Note: n.a. Not available.

Sources: Compiled from Company Annual Reports and Accounts; Savory Milln, 1973; 1977; Capel and Co., 1979; Grieveson, Grant and Co., 1981.

Table 7.3. *Net increases in floorspace*

	Total floorspace in England and Wales in 1978, million m²	Net increase %	
		1967–75	1975–8
Industrial	242	9	2
Warehousing	109	77	10
Commercial offices	42	45	10
Central government offices	6	10–11	1–2
Shops	75	9	3

Source: Department of the Environment.

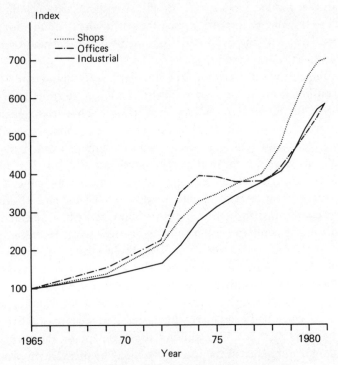

Figure 7.1. Shop, office and industrial rental indices

Source: Investors Chronicle Hillier Parker, 1981.

London. The large increase in warehousing also reflects the need to circulate physically commodities quickly in order to realise their value into profit. The relative increase in office and shop rentals compared to industrial rentals reflects their increased importance in the economy as well as reflecting the low level of industrial development (see figure 7.1). These are precisely the processes that the theoretical arguments anticipate.

The effects, if not the intentions, of government policies tended to reinforce the concentration of activity in the early 1970s. Government actually attempted to curtail activities through the introduction of the business rental freeze at the end of 1972 until spring 1975, and control activities through the introduction of Development Gains Tax and later the Community Land Scheme. It is superficially ironic that it was a Conservative Prime Minister, Edward Heath, who referred to the profits from property activity as the 'unacceptable face of capitalism', while it was the Labour Secretary of State for the DoE, Anthony Crosland, who recognised the integral part property played, stating 'a healthy market in commercial property is necessary for the achievement of the government's social and economic objectives'. In this Crosland was echoing the thoughts in the Pilcher Report[94] which the government commissioned to assess the effects of the proposed Community Land Scheme on commercial property development.

The competition to accelerate the circulation of capital and realise profits continued in the late 1970s, albeit at a lower absolute level. The main thrust in the late 1970s has been to rationalise overcapacity in industry, which reduces the level of activity in the economy as a whole, but commercial and retailing development continues. Even if rates of profit fall this does not mean that rents automatically fall. The advantages gained through certain locations and types of development can yield above average profit rates compared to operators located and working in the worst conditions, and these profits can potentially be translated into rents, which may compare with former and current rents. However, there are limits to the extent this can occur. The absolute fall in profit rates will eventually lead to pressure on rents. The Investors Chronicle–Hillier Parker Rent Index has shown recently that rentals are no longer keeping pace with the rate of inflation. Pressure was already on local authorities to reduce rates which had been increasing faster than the rate of inflation in most urban centres.[95] From the building user's viewpoint, rates represent a rent charge, and hence in the future there may be pressure on property owners to renegotiate contracts and leases to permit downward rental reviews in sectors and locations which are suffering badly in the recession.

Finance for the property markets

Finance for development activities continued to change during the 1970s. The sale and leaseback, although still common, was decreasing in significance. The claim that development companies and financial institutions were virtually indistinguishable by 1975[96] was an exaggeration. Although the property crash between November 1973 and March 1975

Table 7.4. *Investments by financial institutions in land, property and ground rentals*

Year	Insurance companies £m	Pension funds £m	Property unit trusts £m	Total £m
1968	119.4	93.0	40.2	252.6
1969	185.9	112.0	43.3	341.2
1970	197.5	97.0	24.8	319.3
1971	198.1	91.0	22.7	311.8
1972	131.1	121.0	38.9	291.0
1973	306.8	248.0	56.9	611.7
1974	405.1	305.0	14.5	724.6
1975	406.3	339.0	33.8	779.1
1976	449.7	520.0	71.2	1,040.9
1977	410.1	535.0	66.2	1,011.3
1978	549.1	590.0	109.4	1,248.5
1979	631.0	510.0	91.0	1,232.0

Source: Central Statistical Office.

involved close liaison and cooperation between agents, the division between development and finance remains as distinct as in most other activities concerning the financial institutions. Indeed at the end of the 1960s financial institutions were increasingly investing directly in property and property developers were increasingly seeking finance from the banks. Table 7.4 lends support to the argument. Although the investments concern all types of real estate, including agricultural land for example, the dramatic rise in investment in 1973–4 and again in 1976 is a reflection of the boom and crash in the property market, the financial institutions absorbing the crisis by buying the properties sold by property companies which were trying to reduce the deficit financing and very high gearing.

The Prudential, Legal and General, and Standard Life were all heavily committed to property investment. Other insurance companies such as the Commercial Union, Royal Insurance and Eagle Star were endeavouring to increase their commitment.[97] Some insurance companies and one pension fund, the Coal Industry Nominees (CIN), had directly undertaken development, but the institutional involvement remains largely investment rather than development. Property companies pay over 50% in tax on profits from rental income, whereas financial institutions are not liable to corporation tax and are exempt from capital gains tax on the sale of properties. On the other hand property companies can set interest on

borrowed money for development against tax.[98] This gives property companies with a large development programme an advantage over institutions and therefore served to reinforce the division between property
development by property companies and property investment by financial
institutions during the boom in the early 1970s.

The institutional investment in property has continued to increase in
total. However, by 1979 pension fund investment fell for the first time
since 1970 and the total investment by the institutions was static (see
table 7.4). This fall is more dramatic than the figures suggest. If the
fourfold rise in construction costs since the early 1970s as an increasing
percentage of the price of a property is discounted[99] along with the rise in
the capital asset value of properties, a net real or absolute reduction in
investment has occurred.[100] However, the trend appears to be upward
again[101] as the economic crisis deepens and property appears, if not an
absolutely safe investment, amongst the best long term investments from
the viewpoint of the financial institutions.

Property companies increasingly went to the merchant and clearing
banks for development and investment finance between 1971 and 1973.
Table 7.5 shows how this form of finance increased during the boom. The
investment of both the clearing banks and other banks increased dramatically between 1970 and 1973. In the subsequent period companies were
degearing operations by paying back loans. The table actually understates
the amount of bank lending to the large property companies, some of
whom sought finance on the international markets. For example, MEPC
used the Euromarkets in Deutschmarks and Eurodollars[102] to help provide money for development expansion in the 1970s and in so doing
bypassed the credit restrictions in Britain.[103] But the table overstates the
money lent to large property companies in respect of the 'other' column
involving merchant and Section 123 banks, more commonly referred to as
the secondary or fringe banks. These banks lent very large amounts to
smaller property investors, developers, dealers and asset strippers. They
were important, however, because they helped precipitate the collapse of
confidence in the sector. The growth in national and international credit
was itself a symptom of the deepening crisis of overproduction in the
world economy and property became a source of investment because of
the actual and anticipated growth in assets, whereas rates of profit were
falling in industry and the boom in credit devalued the value of money.

The large property companies were more dependent on the clearing
banks and international money markets. They also continued to pursue
sales and leasebacks, Hammerson being a notable example. This had the
effect of increasing the proportion of building rent through slicing
arrangements that went to the institutions. The reduced rental income

Table 7.5. *Bank lending to property companies*

	Net bank lending £m	Percentage of all lending to property companies	Clearing banks £m	Other £m
1970	30	1.9	−25	55
1971	262	11.2	157	105
1972	703	19.5	399	304
1973	1,265	28.9	223	1,022
1974	187	7.0	−6	193
1975	119	3.1	11	108
1976	−110	0.0	75	−35
1977	−322	0.0	−85	−237
1978	−245	0.0	15	−260
1979	−38	0.0	29	−67

Source: Compiled from Debenham, Tewson and Chinnocks, 1980b.

retained by the property company reduces its financial standing,[104] particularly as top slicing in developments is the least marketable in the event of selling remaining interests.

For the leading nine property companies, which accounted for about 50% of the asset values of the sector, over 50% of the finance was raised on long term loans, 17% from short term loans and 12% from issuing shares, from a total of £1,650m between 1968–9 and 1972–3.[105] Convertible debentures declined in popularity after 1970 and the issue of shares rose from £5.9m in 1971 to £29.4m in 1972, falling back to £1.4m in 1973 as the bank advances soared (see table 7.5).[106]

The raising of finance for large development programmes was made possible by the actual growing capital asset values of the sector in the late 1960s and early 1970s (cf. figure 6.2). These could be used as collateral for bank loans and could withstand some dilution through share issues. The capital assets were rising as demand increased, the supply still being in the pipeline; but the belief that the capital asset values would continue to increase was based on a mistaken view of the market. The money was available due to government policy and the operation of international banks. The Bank of England introduced a policy of competition and credit control in May 1971, although the emphasis was on competition rather than control. Having operated an informal cartel, the clearing banks competed to lend the available money. The money available rapidly expanded, first because the government printed money for investment into industry and, second, a large number of foreign banks located offices in London, thus increasing the money in the British banking system. The increase in money supply, known as the 'Barber boom', was not channelled into industry as industrialists hesitated about the prospects of expansion and investors were concerned about falling profit rates. A large proportion of the money was directed into property. A large proportion also entered the property markets indirectly through the secondary or fringe banks on back to back loans via the established banking sector. The secondary banking system was licensed by the Department of Trade, but was not under the control of the Bank of England, and therefore it was not known where the secondary banks were lending their money. The money supply increased by 50% between 1971 and 1973, but money invested in the property sector quadrupled (see table 7.5).[107]

The growth in money allocated for development increased activity on the stock market as investors believed finance would be translated into future capital growth, so property companies would easily raise finance through shares and share issues for further expansion. Future capital growth did not occur, as the property boom was a symptom of the crisis of overproduction rather than a motor to restore general economic growth. The result was the property crash as investors realised that their belief in capital growth was mistaken. The crash became self-reinforcing as confidence was lost.

After the crash in the property market degearing was the main aim of property companies, but finance again began to be sought after 1976 and new share issues were again pursued.[108] This continued in the late 1970s, £116m being raised by rights issues, including a £36.3m rights issue by Hammerson to acquire Reunion Properties.[109] This serves to reinforce the distinct and separate character of property companies from financial institutions at the end of the 1970s. The distinctions are the result of the relation different sectors have to the market and a reflection of the different strategies employed in their efforts to manage their experience of crisis in an era of overproduction.

The property markets

An initial development boom was instigated by the Development of Tourism Act, 1968, which gave grants of 20% for the construction of hotels up to a limit of £1,000 per bedroom between 1968 and March 1971. Planned investment in hotels exceeded £250m and a number of developers such as Edger Investments, Peachey Property, Town and Commercial, Capital and Counties, and Trafalgar House took advantage of these inducements.[110]

The property boom mainly concerned office development. It is commonly believed that ODP restrictions built up a latent demand for offices, which could only be satisfied once the right conditions prevailed, which was the task given to the incoming Conservative Government in 1970. In fact there is little evidence to support this view. Although ODP restrictions were relaxed in 1970, offices under 929 m^2 (10,000 sq. ft) not requiring permits, the number of applications for developments did not increase. In fact after the first few months of ODP control in 1965 refusals were lower at 12% between 1966 and 1969 compared to 1970–3 when they reached 21%.[111] The reason for the boom was the economic crisis of the tendency for the rate of profit to fall giving way to overproduction. This in its turn favoured development which would speed up the circulation of capital and its realisation into profit for prospective building users. The benefits derived from the use could potentially be translated into rents: in other words surplus profits over and above average profits could be resolved into rents. Average profits would fall as companies competed to realise their profits at the expense of others. New office developments facilitated this competition, but as average profits fell absolutely, surplus profits also fell absolutely, overproduction remaining the dominant characteristic despite the intensified competition. In the long term rents would fall, but in the short term the crisis induced a rise in rents.

Rentals were indeed rising in 1968–71, 'prime' rentals in the City increasing from £50 m^2 to £130 m^2, from £35 m^2 to £55 m^2 in the West End and from £12 m^2 to £17.5 m^2 in 'prime' urban centres outside London.[112] This induced an initial fall in prime office yields from 7% to 6.5% in 1969, but they rose again in 1970 as the overall finance from the institutions in property investment declined (see table 7.4). Yields are a reflection of future anticipated rental income and thus it was considered that future rentals would not substantially increase. However, current rentals were increasing notionally, although in actuality only some companies realised these rentals due to existing lease arrangements.[113] This only added to the stimulus to develop, the market being available due to the changing economic conditions yet further reinforced in the City of London by the major influx of international banks.[114] Between 1968 and 1979 over 200 foreign banks out of a total of 328 moved into the City in attempts to seek a share in the sterling, Eurocurrency and Eurodollar markets.[115]

The change in economic conditions was completed in 1971. The government, anxious about falling rates of profit in industry, decided to inflate the economy by increasing the money supply as measured by M3 in order to stimulate industrial investment. The result was an increase in financial investment in property instead. Bank borrowing became attractive to property companies as the bank rate fell from 7% to 6% interest on loans (see table 7.5). This induced a long downward trend in yields from 7.5% to

4.5% in 1973 as future anticipated rentals were considered to be favourable, rental review periods occurring at 5 year intervals compared to 14 years at the beginning and 7 years at the end of the 1960s.[116]

Rentals continued to rise notionally from £130 m² to £200 m² for 'prime' City offices between 1971 and 1973.[117] The rise in rentals induced property companies to revalue their portfolios. On the one hand undervalued portfolios could invite takeover bids, and on the other hand a revaluation of portfolios would increase the ability of companies to raise share capital to finance development or reduce the financial gearing. The revaluations also have the effect of reducing the asset gearing, all of which are stimuli for expanding development programmes.

Land Securities revalued its portfolio in 1971, the capital asset value of the company increasing from £498m to £681m (£952m to £1,183m at 1975 prices, see figure 6.4). Some companies' shares were priced in excess of capital assets[118] and, therefore, the pressure for the considerable upward valuations of assets was very strong, stimulated further by the demand for investment outlets by the institutions and banks. Land Securities raised £20.7m through a rights issue[119] and the subsequent revaluation of its portfolio was used as collateral to raise further finance, the chairman stating: 'market conditions were then favourable for raising finance on the United Kingdom capital market, at fixed rates of interest, without participation by the lender in equity or profits and that the opportunity should therefore be taken to launch a substantial funding operation. As a result arrangements have been completed for borrowing £53,500,000.'[120]

Land Securities was in a dominant market position to raise finance on preferential terms, but generally the increase in share issues in the sector rose from £0.1m in 1970 to £5.9m in 1971 and dramatically to £29.4m in 1972 as revalued portfolios improved the asset basis of companies.[121] Consequently the financial gearing of the sector fell from 121% in 1971–2 to 86% in 1972–3 and asset gearing fell from 59% to 49%.[122]

The increase in rentals brought resistance from some users in London during early 1971,[123] but as rentals continued to rise opposition grew and there was some scepticism as to the extent rises could continue.[124] Land Securities had taken a conservative view. Despite accusations that they were the 'sleeping giant' in the early 1970s they nevertheless had one of the largest development programmes[125] as the development finance raised indicated. However, they did not enter into deficit financing,[126] that is, borrowings which exceed the current ability of a company to meet its debts, which would rely on future rental and asset growth to pay or meet liabilities. The downward path of yields indicated the confidence in the market. Although it was perhaps a reflection of the growing euphoria in the market, stimulated by the massive increases in money availability from national and international sources, a large number of major companies were deficit financing development programmes even though the highly buoyant share market and the yearly revaluation of portfolios were tending to lower both financial and asset gearing respectively. This confidence continued to grow during the latter half of 1972 despite the increase in the bank rate from 5% to 9%. As the property sector and investors continued to look to the future anticipated rental and asset growth, the current interest rates appeared to be relatively unimportant.[127]

The developments being undertaken or planned at this time were largely by property companies; only 19 out of 154 various schemes were for owner occupation, banks and insurance companies being the main owner occupiers. In the City 49% of all schemes and 58% of the total floorspace developed were undertaken by property companies.[128] Land Securities undertook seven large schemes in the City through its subsidiary, City of London Real Property.[129]

Although insurance and pension fund investment for development was low at the time, developers were in many cases developing sites leasehold because vacant sites were not available and site assembly was a long process. Partnerships with other landowners were therefore instigated. Building users were now reluctant to tie up capital in property in order to minimise fixed capital investment in an era of overproduction and were therefore seeking rented accommodation, with the exception of some banks and financial institutions which needed long term investments.

The demand for space outstripped the supply in the late 1960s, so companies developing at this time reaped high rentals and development profits in the early 1970s. The increase in rentals continued unabated until December 1972 when the government introduced its emergency package to counteract inflation. One component of the package was a freeze on rentals for businesses. Businesses were feeling the pinch from increased rentals as they required to retain surplus profits to offset the fall in average profits, but the freeze was only effective on investment properties which had rental reviews and reversions in the near future. New offices were exempt from any controls. The rental freeze held back the capital asset growth of predominantly property investment companies, but rentals soared almost vertically (see figure 7.1) for new developments coming on to the market. Property companies with large development programmes stood to benefit considerably and companies which developed for sale rather than investment, such as Trafalgar House, were in the best position.

Companies without large development programmes jumped on the bandwagon and initiated schemes, which helps to explain why the commercial construction boom occurred after the crash in the property market at the end of 1973 (see figure 4.2) as these new development schemes reached the construction stage. At the end of 1972 278,706 m² (3m sq. ft) were on the market in the City and the immediate area, but this had been reduced to 9,290 m² (1m sq. ft) six months later, and so it seemed that the demand was considerable. Institutional money poured into the property sector in 1973 (see table 7.3), a major portion being for development, and the secondary banks were indiscriminately lending for property investment, development and asset stripping operations (see table 7.5) as the money supply increased the finance available for loans.

The dramatic increase in rentals led some developers to hold out for single tenants for large developments and hold out for even higher rentals. The most notorious example was Oldham Estates' Centre Point development in London. Other individuals and companies engaged in asset stripping and self-induced asset stripping as some industrial companies were worth more for their redevelopment potential than for their main activities. Jim Slater and John Bentley were the notorious names in this sphere.[130] These activities received considerable publicity and became political issues at the time. However, it must be said that leaving offices vacant and asset stripping were only made possible by the events of the early 1970s and they were neither causal processes at work nor the motor of the property boom at the time.

In October 1973 the government declared its intention to withdraw the freeze on rentals between 1974 and 1975, which gave a boost to the market.[131] This immediately reflected on the standing of property investment companies but also developers as current developments could be nearing completion at the time and be transferred to investment portfolios.

The financial institutions, the stock market and the property companies still had every confidence in the market despite interest rates rising 5.5%, until November 1973 when the Minimum Lending Rate (MLR)[132] was increased a further 1.75% to reach 13% and the government announced the introduction of development gains tax in December 1973,[133] which in effect was yet another tax on differential building rent II, mostly the portion that is derived from the advantages to the user from successive investments in the same area and is reflected in the 'prime' status of development locations.

The banking system came under threat at the same time as a result of the crisis in the economy and because of its very high level of commitment to property, especially amongst the merchant and secondary banks (see table 7.5). There was a dramatic spillover effect on to the property market to combine with the already declining confidence in the market.

Once again it was the increase in interest rates which was the trigger. The rise induced the main banks to ask for loan repayments from the secondary banks in order that they could maintain their liquidity.[134] This was necessary as the rise in interest rates was aimed to reduce the money supplied by government. However, a large number of secondary banks could not meet their liabilities. The first bank to collapse was London and County Securities in November 1973, and to a large extent its collapse was precipitated by large sums tied up in property investment and dealing.[135] Blocks of shares were distributed through 'warehousing' deals whereby it was guaranteed they would be bought back at a profit when the holding was taken over.[136] This was a form of 'creative accounting' and worked on similar principles to investing in property at yields lower than interest rates so that loans could only be repaid when the future and higher anticipated rentals were realised. This did not happen with property, nor did it occur for secondary banks' creative accounting.

The collapse of other secondary banks followed, such as the Cornhill Consolidated Group, Cedar Holdings and Twentieth Century Banking.[137] The extent of the involvement of secondary banks in property investment and dealing, usually through small scale operators, exacerbated their liquidity problems; however, the large clearing banks had also been active in property investment and development finance (see table 7.5).

The problem with the large scale financing of property activities is that property companies cannot realise their assets at short notice and were unable to repay loans at a time when repayments depended on future anticipated rental income. On the one hand the placement of a large number of sites, developments and properties on the market would have caused a collapse in that market. On the other hand secondary banks, being unable to meet their liabilities, would have squeezed the clearing banks, potentially leading to a run on deposits, thus threatening the entire banking and financial system.

These were the fears of the Bank of England and so it launched a 'lifeboat' of £2,000–3,000m. This was a fund available for the banking system to increase liquidity used to offset loans to property companies. All the funds made available were not used, its presence being as much a psychological one as a practical one. The 'lifeboat' fund was coordinated by Kenneth Cork of Cork Gulley and Co., an experienced liquidator, and it was agreed that the rescue operation would include underpinning property companies which would have gone into liquidation if they had to meet debts through immediate sales. This would prevent the market being flooded with investment properties at a time when an oversupply was building up in the pipeline due to the recent increase in development activity. The state, through the Bank of England, was therefore preparing to absorb this effect of the general economic crisis. In the event the crisis was absorbed by the financial institutions.

A number of property companies did collapse, for example the Lyon Group and Wilstar. The Lyon Group switched from property dealing to investment at the wrong time,[138] while William Stern of Wilstar had bought property when the current rental income was less than the interest on the loans.[139]

The capital assets of property companies were devalued in 1974, even the leading office development companies suffering a dramatic fall (see figure 6.2). The collapse of the market at the end of 1973 exposed the false confidence in it. The postponement of realising rental income to the future on the belief that rents would continue to rise in the medium term had been halted during the boom in the 1960s by the Brown Ban preventing an oversupply. In the 1970s this did not occur. The freeze on rentals only escalated development activity and reinforced the notion of continually capitalising future anticipated rental growth in a fashion where it would never be realised. Falling yields reflected this trend but the collapse started the upward rise in yields as it 'dawned with a vengeance that the continued sacrifice of current income for unrealised capital growth had been pointless'.[140]

The rise in yields was notional to some extent because there was little or no financial investment in the property sector in the first half of 1974 as investors took stock of the effect of the secondary banking crisis and the longer term implications of development gains tax. The fall in capital asset values was creating severe liquidity problems for a number of major property companies. The fall raised the asset gearing of companies. The overvaluation of portfolios had reduced the asset backing while borrowings reached a high. The revaluation of portfolios dramatically increased the asset gearing while interest rates were simultaneously high. Rentals fell for new property on the market, the supply of space on the market rising in the City of London from $65,030\,m^2$ (0.7m sq. ft) at the end of 1973 to $501,672\,m^2$ (5.4m sq. ft) by the end of 1975.[141] In practice rentals did not fall on investment properties due to the conditions of leases and tenancies, but the increased interest charges reflected on the pre-tax figures of companies.

Thus the liquidity of a number of developers was in jeopardy. Some companies were deficit financed. Town and Commercial went into liquidation while the English Property Corporation and Town and City, for example, faced severe problems.[142]

Virtually no property company escaped unscathed. Companies which had a large number of properties overseas were helped in their stringency, for example the English Property Corporation, MEPC and

Hammerson.[143] Companies which had low asset gearing such as Land Securities, which had not entered into deficit financing and had arranged some fixed interest loans, plus Stock Conversion and Great Portland Estates were better placed. Industrial developers remained relatively unscathed.[144] Companies with investment and development portfolios outside London were less badly hit and indeed the development market remained buoyant in other urban centres for some while after the crash. MEPC was again fortunate in this respect.[145] Despite these advantages MEPC was hit hard by the crash. It had been conscious of missing the first boom and was determined to capitalise on the second, therefore committing itself to a very large development programme. Having seen the changing circumstances in November the company borrowed more money to place on deposit. Even though it paid high interest rates it secured the liquidity of the company. MEPC also received £5.2m plus cancelled interest payments against £26m loaned to Wilstar and received a further £3,000 against deposits put through London and Counties Securities from the 'lifeboat'.[146]

A programme of sales was necessary for property developers to pay interest rates and repay loans. If this had occurred at once then the commercial property market would have collapsed completely because the assets would have been realised at low prices, which might have been insufficient to meet liabilities, hence increasing rather than reducing asset gearing. Loans were not recalled and a programme of sales was overseen by the Bank of England.

At first the institutions were reluctant to increase their property investments despite reversionary potential[147] even though they had traditionally taken the longer term view. Even Land Securities did not find immediate buyers for prime City properties.[148] The financial institutions did begin to buy property investments at prices which did not reflect reversions or the lifting of the freeze on business rentals. Initial purchases were therefore underpriced compared to the previous overvaluation a few months earlier. Property companies sold £2,000m of assets between 1974 and 1978 to the institutions under the 'lifeboat' scheme.[149] Town and City, Capital and Counties, and the English Property Corporation, for example, realised a substantial proportion of their portfolios. A total of £4,000m of assets were eventually sold to the institutions as the sector restructured.[150]

The institutions initially acquired property investments on preferential terms, but in the long term the problems of the banking and property markets were largely displaced on to the financial institutions. Although the property sector had been considerably diluted, the financial institutions were basing their investments on the criteria that property investments are secure long term investments which keep pace with or outpace the remainder of the economy, and that the capital asset value of their existing property investments must be protected in a weak market. Their level of commitment to property investment thus became self-fulfilling, whereby investment was governed by the inflow of funds rather than the market for users. This merely stores up problems for the financial institutions if a continued deepening recession induces an absolute fall in rentals. The financial institutions therefore largely absorbed the crisis experienced by the property sector, but this displacement does not solve this aspect of the crisis, although the institutions have not had to face severe consequences to date.

The events of the crash were to a large extent eclipsed in prominence by the 'oil crisis', the miners' strike and the loss of confidence in the Conservative Government. The events in combination mutually eroded general confidence. The 'oil crisis' had a more direct effect as the rents charged by oil rich states were in effect a tax on oil companies who were major users of property company offices. The increased oil prices gen-erally eroded profits across the economy and contributed to the fall in property rentals which became apparent in the economy in 1975. Prime office rentals in the City of London fell from £220 m^2 in 1973 to a low of £120 m^2 in 1976.[151] High interest rates contributed to the fall in rentals. High interest rates were followed by consols keeping in step and property yields rose to narrow the gap in investment terms, in other words to keep property competitive given the lower expectations of future rental growth.[152]

Falling rentals meant that the freeze was no longer necessary and was therefore lifted in March 1975. The tightening up on the number of ODPs issued after the crash[153] and the promise by the incoming Labour Govern-ment to take development land into public ownership[154] must be seen as 'stable door' policies in terms of actually achieving control over the boom conditions, although they performed a legitimation function in diffusing leftist political opposition by claiming something was being done. Development gains tax did have a restraining effect on developers, but this is being resisted: Land Securities, for example, has been continuing to negotiate payments.[155]

There was a higher level of development activity outside London after the crash, in part due to the dramatic increase in London rentals in the early 1970s promoting decisions to decentralise some activities, and in part due to a growing appreciation by developers of a rising demand for offices and shopping developments in an effort to accelerate the circula-tion of commodities in the economy. Indeed the percentage growth of office space in the south east was greater than the growth in London.[156] An oversupply of space in some urban centres, Birmingham for example, did occur later and development activity tailed off.

The sale of properties by property companies continued into the late 1970s, but the majority of the sales had been completed by the end of 1976. The asset gearing of companies became lower, aided by rights issues which boost liquidity and partially dilute assets. The lower gearing and hence the reduced borrowing achieved by 1978 minimised the dominance interest rates had on the performance of and investment into the property sector.[157] Office rentals were rising rapidly again (see figure 7.1), more so than the overall market indicated as far as property companies were concerned because a large number of rental reviews and reversions were bunched in the late 1970s.[158] The increase in rentals undoubtedly completed the degearing of property companies and led to a broadly upward trend in pre-tax profits even when inflation was discounted.

The capital assets did not fare so well. Although the trend appeared to be upward at the end of the decade (cf. figure 6.2), the portfolios of many companies were substantially reduced. While the financial institutions had investments in properties totalling £14,000m by 1980, 50% being in office investments,[159] the ten leading property companies had portfolios valued at £4,000m with a further £1,000m being accounted for by six other diverse groups such as Trafalgar House and London Merchant Securities.[160] A number of companies have been buying in freeholds to their leasehold property as the combined ground and building rent increases the control companies have over their investment, potentially projecting the rents beyond the life of the existing building and lease. This will be reflected in capital asset valuations.

The advent of rising rentals has placed a downward pressure on yields with the reverse yield gap between government stocks and property being wider than it has been. In 1979 prime office yields were 5% while consols were 12.4%.[161]

The property market has once again resurrected the criteria of investment being the future anticipated rental growth, which the market may not be able to sustain should the current recession deepen. The reverse yield gap is an indication of confidence in the future property market and the economy. It therefore differs from the early 1970s when the market was based not only on future anticipated rental growth, but also on a belief in the current market that had a self-generating and self-fulfilling drive, which sprang out of the poor performance of the rest of the economy rather than an actual sustained long term demand for commercial floorspace.

There is, however, some cause to believe a selective demand for new development will continue. There has been a demand for office space in the City of London and more recently on the City fringes from the insurance and banking sectors[162] and from multinational companies on the west side of London based on proximity to the capital and international air travel.[163]

Development activity has therefore resumed, albeit at a pedestrian rate and in selective locations and markets. Land Securities, although again being criticised for operating more like a trust than a property company, and MEPC had two of the largest development programmes in the country at the turn of the decade.[164] In contrast to development being undertaken prior to letting in the early 1970s, developments have to be largely pre-let.[165] In theoretical terms demands to accelerate the circulation of capital and realisation of profits through the use of new buildings could not be anticipated in advance. A number of companies embarked on development programmes, such as British Land, Chesterfield Properties, Greycoat Estates, and County and District (now part of Costain).[166] Developers raised £100m in 1979 through rights issues[167] which would mainly be used for buying in freeholds or development. Hammerson, although having considerable development potential in its portfolio, ceased new development in Britain after the introduction of development gains tax and has not subsequently resumed activities.[168]

The partial revival of development activity in Britain is likely to be sustained as the need to accelerate the circulation of capital in the economy will continue, although the circulation will relate to absolute lower levels of production.

The resumption of low key development may disguise to some extent the vulnerability of the property sector to falling rentals as rates of profit in the economy decline. Although it is true that 'Since rent is a first charge on profits under the terms of a normal commercial lease, a tenant is responsible for the full duration of the lease, profits from property companies are more secure than those of other companies which can fluctuate from year to year,'[169] the longer term rental growth may be restricted to more specific locations and building users where profit rates are maximised.

There has been increasing opposition to rate increases and in the longer term this may also filter into property rentals, particularly if companies experiencing declining profits do not manage to oppose rate increases successfully.

The financial institutions may not be too concerned about a short or medium term reduction in rentals, and they have continued to invest in property with a long term view. While this can induce an apparently short term buoyant investment market by simply investing in property in the absence of other investment outlets and by the need to protect existing property investments by underpinning the market, the long term security could prove to be an illusion if the past history of Europe is repeated. Invasion and wars devalue, destroy or redefine the ownership of property. This country only experienced devaluation and destruction in the last war. Even in the absence of war a long term deepening economic recession could induce a shortfall of rental income for financial institutions at a time when their financial commitments to investors are increasing as the population ages.

The position of the financial institutions is therefore different from the property investment and development companies. The distinction between property companies and the financial institutions, which some commentators claim to have been eroded,[170] remains. Property companies have investments, which would not meet with institutional criteria. Property companies are not dependent on institutional finance, the recent spate of rights issues being indicative of this, which is not to say the institutions are not an important source of finance. Property companies use different institutions for different projects, overseas development, for example, frequently being funded locally. Institutions do not coordinate their decisions and indeed there are different interests in and between institutions, especially in the insurance sphere. Institutional share-holdings in property companies do not imply integration. For example, institutions hold the majority of MEPC's shares but they are a disparate group, who meet under the umbrella of the Protection Committee. They have the power to intervene,[171] but the directors and managers of the company can equally use this forum to gauge the differences and agreements concerning issues on which institutional shareholders will vote.[172]

It is anticipated that takeovers will become a future source of expansion again for property and construction companies, but it is unlikely that the financial institutions will engage in takeovers[173] unless a property company has a portfolio solely of 'prime' property by institutional criteria. Very few companies would satisfy these requirements, Land Securities being one possible exception.

The industrial property market did not exhibit the same trends as the commercial markets. The decline in the rates of profit in industry resulted in little development taking place, although the commercial property market did have some effects on the industrial market. Current rentals were influenced to a small degree by the rest of the market (see figure 7.1). Future rentals reflected in yields were more affected as they rose and fell in sympathy with the rest of the market.[174] There was, however, a re-rating of the industrial market in the 1970s. There had been a 3% gap between commercial and industrial yields, but this had narrowed by 1% since the late 1960s.[175]

The falling yields in industrial property may in part be a reflection of growing institutional interest in industrial investment. It may also be due to the preferential tax allowances given against investment in buildings. While it has been thought that these allowances have not made a great deal of difference to the rate of industrial development, they undoubtedly benefit the industrial property developer. For example, Percy Bilton reduced its taxation by £0.7m and Slough Estates by nearly £0.55m in 1975.[176] In the case of Slough Estates this represented 16% of their net profit for 1975.

Industrial development has proceeded at a relatively even pace during the decade (see table 7.3). However, if industrial property is assumed to have a life of 25 years, 4% of the stock needs to be replaced each year, a position which is exacerbated by the fact that a very large proportion of existing industrial properties are over 50 years old.[177] Should the current recession end, a precondition for sustained recovery would be the large scale reconstruction of industrial property, even assuming that a further devaluation and destruction of buildings do not occur.

There has been a more rapid replacement and expansion of warehousing, sufficient to replace the entire stock every 25 years. This expansion of warehousing is a reflection of the increased competition to sell commodities ahead of competitors. An efficient storage and distribution network is essential in this respect. The growth of warehouse facilities around the international airports and on the main arterial routes is an indication of this. In the case of Britain the growth is associated with the increase in imported commodities.

Locations in the Reading and Slough areas are favoured.[178] Slough Estates, for example, has a growing warehouse component on its Slough estate occupied by companies such as National Panasonic and British Tissues.[179] In the mid-1970s it was usually American multinational manufacturers who were seeking premises, but by 1979 a large proportion of European and Japanese companies had sought industrial premises.[180]

It is possible that industrial development may continue at the current or even a higher level as rentals form a small component of the costs for companies, labour costs being the most critical factor. Indeed, the need to restructure production and distribution to reduce labour costs can involve relocation in new developments.[181]

The distribution between factories and warehouses is not always clear, particularly with regard to allowances. Any unit in which a process is undertaken, even if this is repackaging or the storage of commodities used in another production process, is an industrial unit and not a warehouse for allowance purposes.[182] The official figures for factory development may in fact have a high warehousing content.

The main demand for factories had been for units between 90 m² and 465 m². Although industrial developers have been developing some smaller units, the nursery units have been provided by other agents aiming to reduce tax liabilities.[183] While the needs of multinational companies and new industries may be new premises, the provision of industrial development would need to be on a larger scale in floorspace and quantitative terms as a precondition for the resumption of capital accumulation and the increase in rates of profit in the future. However, the deepening of this phase of economic crisis has prevented this occurring.

The overseas property markets have been more active than the British markets since the early 1970s. A number of property companies have endeavoured to expand overseas and have withdrawn. Some have been successful, usually pursuing a path of investment before undertaking development activity. The United States market is the most buoyant and has the largest potential.[184] Commonwealth countries, notably Australia and Canada, have been markets British companies have entered. Grosvenor–Laing was one example and the Taylor Woodrow subsidiary, Monarch, which was an indigenous company acquired by Taylor Woodrow, has been active in Canada. Slough Estates and Hammerson have been two of the most successful pure property companies in both Canada and Australia. Hammerson has a significantly higher proportion of properties overseas than any other company.

MEPC had a considerable portfolio in Canada which was sold as part of the degearing of the company in the mid-1970s. It has recently been expanding in the southern cities of the United States, but only 30% of its activity can be undertaken abroad at any one time because it must pay a dividend to shareholders in Britain.[185] The recent attempts to extend overseas expansion are a symptom of crisis, property companies trying to take advantage of markets in countries which have not reached the same depths in the recession.

Conclusion

The generally prosperous 1960s were very prosperous for contractors, although high turnovers were not always realised as profits. The large and the medium sized companies which shared out these markets became increasingly competitive during the 1970s as they carved out a total market which has declined since 1973 (see figure 4.2).

The construction sector has therefore been experiencing underproduction which at the end of the period was largely being displaced on to smaller operators. This has continued subsequently, but the extent to which this can continue must be limited, especially as the Conservative Government elected in 1979 replaced capital expenditure allocations with cash limits and block grants. These have had a devastating effect on capital expenditure, particularly construction work, as local agencies try to protect their own employment and thus impose cuts on capital rather than current expenditure. These dilemmas are, however, an effect and not a cause *per se* of the deepening recession, thus marking a change which may be seen as the beginning of the second phase of economic crisis.

Overseas work has provided a large degree of insulation from the British market for the large contractors, but work overseas will probably not see a net growth and indeed may fall for British contractors as international competition intensifies.

Contractors had successfully managed to stave off the worst of the crisis, unlike many other industries such as the steel or car industries. This they achieved through market diversification and unemployment in the sector. Their flexibility has permitted this, but the limits to this are drawing to a close as opportunities become less as the crisis deepens. The full face of underproduction is now being experienced by the sector.

The property sector could have experienced more consistent growth for commercial development, but events in the national economy and misinterpretation by investing, financing, development and other agents led to an oversupply and overvaluation followed by a crash. The property boom was mistaken as a motor of growth in the economy rather than an effect of the crisis, in other words from a need to speed up the process of capital circulation, profit realisation and capital concentration.

The effect of this misinterpretation will probably be a continuation of ripples of under- and oversupply, an oversupply occurring in London markets at the end of the decade,[186] but a selective demand will probably be maintained for office and retailing developments as the need to accelerate capital circulation will persist in order to remain competitive. The resulting capital concentration may result in increased space demands by successful operators who will want buildings to meet current requirements rather than accept existing vacant space. The same will probably be the case for industrial development.

All development markets are likely to be at an absolute lower level and rents on many properties may fall in the long term because the property sector cannot avoid the crisis. There will be pressure to renegotiate leases to allow downward reviews in the future.

The financial institutions and property companies mutually influence the activities of each other, but they have not become integrated and this is not likely in the future. The role of the financial institutions has been to absorb the crisis as far as its effects have materialised in the property market. This is quite distinct from an integration of activities. There is likely to be far greater integration between contractors and property companies, contractors taking over developers. Costain, for example, has recently acquired County and District and it is thought likely that Wimpey will take over Stock Conversion when the current management retires.

The property sector will therefore be subject to change in forthcoming years through a process of capital concentration and falling rates of rent; however, property companies will remain a distinct sector in the economy.

Conclusion

The aim of this work has been to produce a history of the property and construction sectors in the British economy during the period beginning with the second world war and finishing at the end of the 1970s. The history is a synthesis of the theoretical and empirical material.

The second phase of crisis is well under way. The Keynesian notions of creating new internal markets within capitalism have failed and deflationary trends are being established. Austerity measures are being peddled by the right and left as a necessity for long term recovery, but no long term solutions have been posed, although the rhetoric of 'recovery' being around the corner or that 'alternatives' can be found abounds.

As overproduction deepens, the economic problems continue to raise international political tensions on the one hand and widespread social unrest on the other hand. Against this background the production and management of the built environment have occurred and will continue to occur. Growth has been and will become even more selective. Sectors of economic growth require new accommodation, while static and declining sectors restructure their operations. Restructuring can require new accommodation at the expense of old capacity or relocation where labour costs and other overheads are lower.

Overall, the trend of decline will increase competition in shrinking construction markets and rents will fall in total as profits fall. The surge of office development at the end of the 1970s and at the beginning of the 1980s did not amount to the major boom some had hoped for. It indicated the selective growth in this sphere, but more importantly indicated increased competition in the international financial markets and rationalisation through relocation of many national office based activities. Retail development and investment have remained sound because of deflationary price trends, increased personal indebtedness and the rationalisation of the high street through capital concentration, which has kept the retail property sector relatively prosperous.

The selective growth in developing and investing in the built environment has therefore been a product of the crisis. As the second phase deepens there will be less activity to finance, manage and translate into profit. Public and private administration and the profit realisation functions will need to be further rationalised in the economy. New technologies offer another avenue for rationalisation, which will have the long term effect on the efficiency and the type of work carried out in the built environment, and are likely to reduce the demand for new space concerned with administrative and circulation activities in the economy. Regardless of whether new technologies induce or reduce employment opportunities, the shrinking of the world market will reduce employment requirements in this sphere. This aspect of the economy is politically charged, but will have to be tackled eventually, resulting in the reduction of the level of development and the value of investments in the built environment.

It cannot be predicted whether this decline in development and devaluation of the building stock will happen gradually or be prompted by international events, such as the collapse of the international financial system due to national indebtedness or the escalation of national wars and political tensions, for example. In the meantime the property sector will continue to be more selective about development activity and definitions of 'prime' investments, and will concentrate through shake outs, mergers and takeovers.

The construction sector has been gradually reaching its limits of flexibility as underproducers in a period of overproduction. The lobby for increased capital expenditure will increase and future governments of either the right or left will have to initiate large scale capital projects, such as the telecommunications investments, defence and infrastructure investments. Economically, governments will not be able to afford this, but will not be able to neglect this arena politically, in order to create employment and prepare for growing international political tensions. These measures will not solve the crisis, but merely serve to phase it in, and hence attempt to manage the most profound social depths of the crisis.

The crisis of overproduction will therefore continue to deepen. Only the working class can halt the process through conscious action in response to the depths of crisis, knowing that reform in any form cannot arrest the process of impoverishment.[1] Such action is not inevitable,[2] and therefore in its absence capital would continue to prepare itself for the only solution it can offer. This solution would not be consciously sought but would be the result of endeavouring to manage, without avoiding, the crisis. The second phase of crisis has therefore begun, and the comment of C. Wright Mills[3] is even more appropriate today than at the time of writing: 'Humanity itself now lies before us, the super-nation at either pole concentrating its most coordinated and massive efforts upon the preparation of the Third World War.'

Notes

Introduction

1 Park *et al.* (1967) were the main exponents of this school.
2 Pahl, 1975; Rex and Moore, 1967.
3 Harvey, 1973.
4 Castells, 1977; 1978.
5 See Saunders (1979) for some pointers as to the different directions.
6 The work of Ball (1978), the Bartlett Summer School on the *Production of the Built Environment* and recent work of the Political Economy of Housing Workshop have been influential in this respect. In the sphere of property development Marriott's book (1967) and later Ambrose and Colenutt (1975) have paved the way for further consideration.
7 Mills, 1970.

1. Theories of crisis

1 Schmidt, 1971.
2 Timpanaro, 1975.
3 The outline will draw on the three volumes of *Capital* (Marx, 1954; 1956; and 1959) unless referenced otherwise.
4 Protectionism between nations, through import controls and taxes for example, is not a phenomenon which disproves the tendency towards the formation of an average and general rate of profit, but is symptomatic of nations' inability to maintain their industries' profitability in the formation of the general rate of profit; a position which is exacerbated in crises.
5 Credit relies on the future payment of wages and realisation of surplus value, and, therefore, is dependent on a belief that the system will be maintained. Credit has grown in importance in this century, particularly in the sale of the means of consumption, but in the nineteenth century money was in circulation from value appropriated from previous modes of production and this formed another stimulus to demand, which is absent today.
6 Cf. Braverman, 1974, and Aglietta, 1976.
7 The producers of the means of production, department I, can sell their commodities within the department or to department II producers.
8 The rate of surplus value is calculated by dividing the variable capital into the surplus value expressed as a percentage.
9 Marx, 1959.
10 Glyn and Sutcliffe, 1972.
11 Ibid., p. 65.

12 It is possible that the increase in the organic composition of capital will induce a further crisis. This anticipates the theory of the tendency of the rate of profit to fall, but in this instance the exacerbation of the crisis arises from a secondary cause.

13 Yaffe, 1973a.

14 Kalecki, 1971.

15 See chapter 2.

16 A number of writers have considered the ideas of Tugan-Baranovski from different stances: cf. Kalecki, 1967; Luxemburg, 1951; and Rosdolsky, 1977.

17 Hilferding, 1981.

18 Some may disagree in part with this comment if state planned societies are considered to be (potentially) socialist rather than state capitalist in organisation.

19 There has been a certain amount of 'points scoring' by claiming Kalecki made the developments prior to Keynes, but the most interesting and important point is that both worked on the same problems at the same time with similar ideas emerging rather than who came first. See Kalecki's work, *Selected Essays on the Dynamics of the Capitalist Economy 1933–1970* (1971), and Keynes' *General Theory* (1961).

20 See for example Kidron, 1970.

21 Baran and Sweezy, 1968.

22 Harvey, 1975.

23 Baran and Sweezy, 1968, p. 89.

24 Yaffe, 1973b.

25 Marx, 1959.

26 See note 8 of this chapter.

27 The rate of surplus value, s', is expressed in value terms as,

$$s' = \frac{s}{v}$$

but Marx usually expressed the rate of profit, p', in value terms too,

$$p' = \frac{s}{c+v}$$

whereas it is more accurately expressed in prices unless conditions ensure that values and prices are equal. This equation can be rewritten as

$$p' = \frac{p}{k}$$

where p represents the profit and k is the cost price of the commodity.

28 Marx, 1959, pp. 256–7. The passage continues by elaborating the argument, and in so doing, also gives a criticism of underconsumption theories: 'If it is finally said that the capitalists have only to exchange and consume their commodities among themselves, then the entire nature of the capitalist mode of production is lost sight of; and also forgotten is the fact that it is a matter of expanding the value of the capital, not consuming it.' There is, therefore, a difference between overproduction and underconsumption. Under-consumption states that there are no limits to the production of value and surplus value under capitalism but only to its realisation. Overproduction states that because of the limits to the production of surplus value under capitalism there is a related realisation problem.

29 The crisis can restrict this option which Marx recognised when he follows the

discussion with the famous quote: 'The *real barrier* of capitalist production is *capital itself*' (1959, p. 250).
30 Mattick, 1971; 1981.
31 Yaffe, 1973b.
32 Mattick, 1981.
33 Mattick, 1974, p. 19.
34 Kalecki, 1934.
35 Frank, 1980, p. 312.
36 Ibid.; Mattick, 1976.
37 Mattick, 1974.
38 Mattick, 1976.
39 Harre, 1970.
40 Cutler *et al.*, 1977.
41 See all references to Mattick.
42 Luxemburg, 1951.
43 Ibid., p. 335. See also note 28 of this chapter.
44 Ibid., p. 352.
45 Robinson, 1951.
46 Kalecki, 1967.
47 Ibid.
48 Mattick, 1981, p. 112.
49 Rosdolsky, 1977; Mandel, 1975.
50 Opponents to this notion have dismissed it by way of assertion rather than argument.
51 I appreciate those who believe the eastern nations to be (potentially) socialist will reject these statements and I shall offer no further arguments other than those already stated to persuade them otherwise, the aim being to clarify the theoretical position used in the historical analysis rather than engage in a political discussion of this kind.

2. Rents and property development

1 Massey and Catalano, 1978.
2 Marx, 1959, p. 619. Rent can be compared to interest to see which investments yield the highest rate of return. The stream of income is capitalised and the return calculated. Years' purchase does this, but it assumes the existence of rent (Marx, 1959, p. 623). The calculation aids the decision to be made between investments, a process which will contribute to the formation of average profits. This is complementary to the effects that ground rent has on the profits of capitalist land users. As Marx (1959, p. 624) points out, if the rate of return is low on land purchased, this is not because rents are too low but the capitalised rent or land price was too high; a point that could be missed if rent is treated as synonymous with interest.
3 The following analysis is based on Marx, 1959.
4 The rate of rent is the ratio of capital inputs, including the labour power, to the rent per hectare.
5 In the foregoing argument I have referred to differential rent II as opposed to differential ground rent II, which indicates the analysis is equally applicable to the formation of rent in relation to buildings. Absolute rent will be treated similarly.

6 The fact that differential rent II can only increase the price of production in periods of high demand for the commodities in question or in aggregate (Marx, 1959, p. 733, cf. p. 743) is frequently overlooked. This can act back on the production process to affect the relations between capital and labour, and between capitalist and landowner (cf. Ball, 1977).

7 Ball, 1977.

8 It is this point which lies behind the much quoted phrase '*landed property itself has created rent*' (Marx, 1959, p. 755).

9 There is controversy if this constitutes a separate category called monopoly rent, although in my opinion this is only a semantic point.

10 Marx, 1959, p. 771.

11 Bruegel, 1975; Murray, 1977; 1978.

12 Emmanuel, 1972; Harvey, 1974; Walker, 1974; Clark and Ginsburg, 1975; Edel, 1976; Lamarche, 1976; cf. Scott, 1976.

13 Howard and King, 1975; Ball, 1977.

14 Ball, 1977; Massey and Catalano, 1978, pp. 128–38, cf. Alonso, 1964.

15 Harvey, 1973; Byrne and Beirne, 1975; Lamarche, 1976.

16 Bruegel, 1975; Duncan, 1978a; 1978b; see Scott, 1976, cf. Murray, 1977.

17 Bruegel, 1975; Lamarche, 1976; Ball, 1977; Murray, 1977; 1978; Massey and Catalano, 1978, pp. 128–38, cf. Scott, 1976.

18 The difference between building rent for capital and labour will be discussed below.

19 Marx, 1959; Ambrose and Colenutt, 1975; Massey and Catalano, 1978.

20 Boddy, 1979; 1981.

21 Lamarche, 1976.

22 Massey and Catalano (1978) are absolutely right in this respect despite their ambiguity concerning property companies and their tendency to neglect the state as a landowner (cf. Ambrose, 1976; 1977).

23 Cf. Massey, 1973; 1977.

24 Cf. Lojkine, 1976; Preteceille, 1976.

25 The recent demands by users to reduce rates may be due as much to their inability to reduce rentals, hence differential building rent II, paid to building owners as high rates *per se* because tenancies cannot be renegotiated or contracts have upward rent review clauses only (cf. Debenham, Tewson and Chinnocks, 1980a).

26 I am not arguing this in architectural terms. It is not therefore a deterministic argument that form follows function and thus form determines function in design. I am outlining the limits and potential of use in terms of the appropriation and realisation of average and surplus profit.

27 The term building owner is used even though landlord or landlady are more common ones. This is because rented housing has the same divisions as other buildings and the landowner and building owner can be two different agents.

28 The sale of council houses can be seen as a means whereby the state has achieved the removal of absolute rent as a barrier and can therefore abdicate from its continued interest in housing rent on the same scale or cannot afford to remove the barrier.

29 These examples are based on Panmure Gordon and Co., 1976. See also Ratcliffe, 1978.

30 See chapter 1.

31 Harvey, 1978.

3. Construction and contracting

1 The two terms are usually used synonymously; however, while almost all construction companies are contractors, not all contractors are construction companies.
2 See, for example, the Department of Industry's *Report of the Census of Production: Construction*, the Department of the Environment's *Private Contractors Census*.
3 Ball and Cullen, 1980.
4 Ball, 1978; Smyth, 1982a.
5 Marx, 1954.
6 Ive, 1980.
7 Dobb, 1963; Landes, 1969; Foster, 1974.
8 Braverman, 1974.
9 Aglietta, 1976.
10 Taylor, 1947.
11 Aglietta, 1976.
12 Braverman, 1974.
13 These arguments have been expressed in terms of absolute rent and differential rent, but I have located them more precisely using the theoretical analysis provided in chapter 2.
14 Bruegel, 1975; Murray, 1977; and a number of French writers (see Scott, 1976).
15 Ball, 1978.
16 Colclough, 1965.
17 Duncan, 1978a; 1978b.
18 Duncan, 1978a, p. 30.
19 Ibid., pp. 29–30.
20 Ball, 1978.
21 Ibid., p. 86.
22 Boddy, 1978.
23 See chapter 6.
24 Direct Labour Collective, 1978; Ive, 1980.
25 Clarke, 1980.
26 Ball, 1978; Smyth, 1982a.
27 Friedmann, 1977; Schwarz, 1977; Elger, 1979.
28 Schwarz, 1977; Elger, 1979.
29 Braverman, 1974; Brighton Labour Process Group, 1977.
30 Elger, 1979.
31 Paulding, 1980; Tuckman, 1980.
32 Boddy, 1978.
33 Tuckman, 1980; Ball, 1980.
34 Ball, 1980.
35 Tuckman, 1980
36 Ive, 1980, p. 5.
37 Sugden, 1975.
38 Ibid.
39 See chapter 1.
40 Cf. Long, 1940; Lewis, 1960; 1965; Gottlieb, 1976; Walker, 1978; Blackaby (ed.), 1979.

41 HMSO, 1965; Lewis and Singh, 1966.
42 Tuckman, 1980.
43 Clarke, 1980.
44 Postgate, 1923; Cooney, 1954; Hobhouse, 1971; Cripps, 1978.
45 McGhie, 1981.
46 Ibid.
47 Cripps, 1980.
48 Ball, 1983.
49 Ball and Cullen, 1980.
50 McGhie, 1981.

4. Construction and the state during the second world war

1 Bowen, 1940; Bowen and Ellis, 1945.
2 HMSO, 1936.
3 Coad, 1979; Laing and Son Ltd, 1950.
4 Middlemas, 1979.
5 Kohan, 1952. Kohan's book *Works and Buildings* will be referred to repeatedly. It is a descriptive account of construction programmes and government machinery implementing these programmes, forming part of the official history of the second world war.
6 Ibid.
7 Ibid., cf. table 4.2.
8 Coad, 1979; interview with Sir Frank Taylor, founder and Life President of Taylor Woodrow, on Wednesday, January 28, 1981.
9 WORK 26/7/1 (1–41), Royal Ordnance Factory, Bridgend, PRO, London.
10 Wimpey, who presumably also asked to submit a price, had the lowest initial tender at £500,156, but supplementary drawings resulted in Wimpey revising its tender figure upwards while Sir Robert McAlpine revised its figure from £539,872 down to £525,141, thus winning the contract (WORK 26/7/1, Royal Ordnance Factory, Bridgend, PRO, London).
11 Ibid.
12 Ibid.
13 WORK 26/2/2, Royal Ordnance Factory, Bridgend – no. 11, PRO, London.
14 Coad, 1979.
15 Interview with Sir Frank Taylor, loc. cit.; Jenkins, 1971.
16 Company Annual Reports and Accounts.
17 Bowen and Ellis, 1945, p. 111.
18 See table 4.3, cf. table 4.2.
19 Sayers, 1956. The excess profits tax was aimed primarily at other manufacturing sectors, such as aircraft production (cf. Middlemas, 1979).
20 Sayers, 1956.
21 Kohan, 1952.
22 Ibid.
23 Hudson, 1948, p. 26.
24 Coad, 1979.
25 Laing and Son Ltd, 1950.
26 McAlpine and Sons, c. 1955.
27 For details of contracts and contractors for the Air Ministry in 1943 see WORK 46.7, Works and Building, PRO, London.

28 Kohan, 1952.

29 Barlow Report, 1940; Andrews, 1941.

30 For details of estimated expenditure on construction by county in England, Scotland and Wales in 1940 see Kohan, 1952, Appendix v, pp. 493–4.

31 Reith, 1949.

32 Kohan, 1952.

33 WORK 45/16, Central Council for Works and Buildings: Signed Minutes and Papers, 1941–2, PRO, London.

34 Jenkins, 1971.

35 This is the only period when agreement was reached between 'building' and 'engineering' sections of the industry.

36 *Manchester Guardian,* 1940.

37 *The Times,* 1939.

38 *Builder,* 1939a.

39 Bowen, 1951.

40 It later dropped the prefix 'Sub' from its title.

41 610.1.1, The Production Council and the Production Executive, Current Guide, Part One, Division 6 (ss. 601–99), Trade, Industrial Affairs, Communications and Power, PRO, London. The Production Executive was to have its functions assumed by the Minister of Production in February 1942.

42 Kohan, 1952, p. 59.

43 *Builder,* 1939b.

44 Bowen, 1951.

45 Reith, 1949, pp. 405–6.

46 Stuart, 1975.

47 House of Commons, 1940.

48 Bowen, 1951.

49 Ibid.

50 House of Commons, 1941; also quoted in Bowen, ibid., p. 126, and Kohan, 1952, p. 90.

51 116.1.5. Ministry of Works and Buildings 1940 to 1942 and Ministry of Works and Planning 1942 to 1943, Part One, Division 1 (ss. 101–99), Central Government and Common Services, PRO, London.

52 The first Director of the Building Programme was George Burt, Chairman of John Mowlem. It would be possible to construe a conspiratorial analysis concerning the interests of the industry being served by leading members serving in an official capacity. In my opinion this would be completely unjustified. There is no reason to suppose that two different functions cannot be performed by the same person even if the interests underlying each function are different (cf. Giddens, 1974, p. xii). Indeed, if there is any correspondence it will be that the interests of the nation state must take priority over the interests of an individual contracting company in order that conditions in which that company may continue to operate also continue.

53 Bowen, 1951; *Architects Journal,* 1939.

54 Bowen, 1951.

55 Kohan, 1952.

56 Walker-Smith, *c.* 1948.

57 Kohan, 1952.

58 *Builder,* 1941, various editions.

59 Hall, 1948.
60 The same point concerning interest and influence can be made about union representatives as was made concerning industry leaders (see note 52).
61 Quoted in Walker-Smith, *c.* 1948.
62 Marx House, *c.* 1941, p. 3.
63 Hall, 1948.
64 WORK 45/16, Central Council for Works and Buildings: Signed Minutes and Papers, 1941–2, PRO, London.
65 Middlemas, 1979.
66 This figure included work abroad.
67 Women were employed on site during the war. Women, it was agreed in October 1941, should not be less than 17 years old and receive 80% of the equivalent male wage. In 1939 15,700 or 1.3% of the total construction workforce were women. In 1945 24,200 or 4% of the total construction workforce were women (Hall, 1948). Boy labourers received full labourers' wages until 1941 when it was agreed that 15–16 year old boys would receive 40%, 16–17 year old boys would receive 50%, 17–18 year old boys would receive 75% and 18 year olds would receive 100% of the equivalent male wage (WORK 45/16, Central Committee for Works and Buildings: Signed Minutes and Papers, 1941–2, PRO, London).
68 Ministry of Works, cited in Kohan, 1952.
69 HMSO, 1942.
70 Ibid.
71 Ibid.
72 WORK 45/14, Central Council for Works and Buildings: Regionalisation Committee Signed Minutes and Report on the War Time Builders Emergency Organisations, 1941, PRO, London.
73 Quoted in Kohan, 1952, p. 200.
74 Ministry of Works, cited in Kohan, 1952.
75 Kohan, 1952.
76 Sayers, 1956.
77 Kohan, 1952.
78 Hudson, 1948.
79 Coad, 1979. It is interesting to speculate whether this liaison was instrumental in persuading or influencing Laing and Wimpey to re-enter the house-building market after the war. They were the only two major contractors to do so, although it was the public housing rather than private housing market they entered.
80 116.1.5. Ministry of Works and Buildings 1940 to 1943 and Ministry of Works and Planning 1942 to 1943, Current Guide Part One, Division 1 (ss. 101–99), Central Government and Common Services, PRO, London.
81 Ibid.
82 McAlpine and Sons, *c.* 1955.
83 Jenkins, 1971.
84 Rolt, 1958.
85 Laing and Son Ltd, 1950.
86 Interview with Terrel Wyatt, Chairman of Costain, on Friday, October 9, 1981.
87 Hawkey, 1948.
88 Wood, 1948a.

89 Kohan, 1952, although Bowen (1951) states that about 30,000 were employed.
90 Letter from Lord Portal to Ernest Bevin, October 26, 1943.
91 Kohan, 1952.
92 Jenkins, 1971.
93 Hawkey, 1948.
94 See Wood (1948a) for a list of the contractors.
95 Laing and Son Ltd, 1950; McAlpine and Sons, *c.* 1955.
96 Paury, 1948.
97 Wood, 1948b; Coad, 1979. Wood states that Wates built 12 Whale units, Monk 4 and Trussed Concrete Steel 2 units. He makes no mention of the 40 Whale units Coad states Laing built.
98 Hartley, 1948.
99 Ibid.; Jenkins, 1971.
100 Ministry of Works, cited in Kohan, 1952.
101 WORK 46.7, Works and Buildings, PRO, London.
102 WORK 45/21, Building Programme Joint Committee, Contracts Allocation Sub-Committee: Minutes and Papers 1942–5, PRO, London.
103 Ibid.
104 Ministry of Works, 1945.
105 Kohan, 1952.
106 Company Annual Reports and Accounts, 1944.
107 McAlpine and Sons, *c.* 1955.
108 WORK 45/21, Building Programme Joint Committee, Contracts Allocation Sub-Committee: Minutes and Papers 1942–5, PRO, London.
109 Powell, 1980.
110 Laing and Son Ltd, 1950.
111 Bowley, 1966.
112 Working Party on Building Operations, 1950.
113 Ministry of Works, cited in Kohan, 1952.
114 *Builder*, 1944.

5. The reconstruction period

1 Rogow, 1955.
2 Ibid.
3 Addison, 1975.
4 Coad, 1979.
5 See note 79, chapter 4.
6 Bowley, 1966.
7 'No fines' means that fine aggregate is excluded from the mix of concrete.
8 Bowley, 1966.
9 Ministry of Health, 1948.
10 Merrett, 1979.
11 Rosenberg, 1960.
12 Ibid.
13 Ibid.
14 WORK 45/56, Control of National Building Programme: Programme and Licensing Circulars 1–25, PRO, London.
15 Rosenberg, 1960.

16 WORK 45/57, Building Control Circulars 1–119, PRO, London.
17 HMSO, 1947; Merrett, 1979.
18 Mallalieu, 1956.
19 Merrett, 1979.
20 Interview with Terrel Wyatt, Chairman of Costain, on Friday, October 9, 1981.
21 Costain Annual Reports and Accounts, 1956.
22 HMSO, 1945a.
23 Lereuz, 1975.
24 Ward-Perkins, 1952.
25 Lereuz, 1975.
26 Ibid.
27 HMSO, 1945b; Morgan, 1979.
28 Dow, 1964.
29 Ibid.
30 Ward-Perkins, 1952.
31 Wigham, 1976.
32 HMSO, 1945c; Brady, 1950.
33 Interview with John Derrington, Director of Sir Robert McAlpine and Sons, on Monday, July 27, 1981.
34 WORK 45/56, Control of National Building Programme, PRO, London.
35 Interview with Sir Frank Taylor, loc. cit.
36 Rogow, 1955.
37 WORK 45/116, Interpretation of Statistics. Regional Programming Circulars 1945–1952 (RPO) 21–40, PRO, London.
38 Dow, 1964.
39 WORK 45/111, Building and Civil Engineering Joint Committee Circulated Papers JBC/P151, PRO, London.
40 Central Statistical Office.
41 Cole, 1947.
42 WORK 45/56, Control of the National Building Programme: Programme and Licensing Circulars 1–25, PRO, London.
43 Ibid.
44 Working Party on Building Operations, 1950.
45 Interview with John Derrington, loc. cit.
46 Interview with Nat Fletcher, Personnel Director, and Michael Buckland of Taylor Woodrow on Friday, May 15, 1981.
47 McAlpine and Sons, c. 1955.
48 Interview with John Derrington, loc. cit.
49 Laing and Son Ltd, 1950; Annual Reports and Accounts, 1948.
50 Coad, 1979.
51 Laing Annual Reports and Accounts, 1948; Laing and Son Ltd, 1950.
52 McAlpine and Sons, c. 1955.
53 WORK 45/56, Control of National Building Programme, PRO, London.
54 Taylor Woodrow Annual Reports and Accounts, 1948.
55 Merrett, 1979.
56 Taylor Woodrow Annual Reports and Accounts, 1952.
57 Merrett, 1979.
58 Cf. Merrett, 1979, p. 247.
59 HMSO, 1948.

60 Mallalieu, 1956.
61 *Economist,* 1949, p. 130.
62 Rogow, 1955.
63 Dow, 1964.
64 WORK 45/57, Building Control Circulars 1946–1950 LC1/46–119/50, PRO, London.
65 HMSO, 1950.
66 Quoted in Rogow, 1955.
67 *Financial Times,* 1951.
68 Mitchell, 1963; Dow, 1964.
69 Dow, 1964.
70 Mitchell, 1963.
71 Ibid.
72 Blank, 1973.
73 Dow, 1964
74 Rosenberg, 1960.
75 Working Party on Building Operations, 1950.
76 Rosenberg, 1960.
77 Ibid.
78 Morgan, 1979; see table 5.3.
79 Interview with Terrel Wyatt, loc. cit.
80 Wright, 1962.
81 Carter, 1961.
82 Cripps, 1980.
83 Ibid.
84 Coad, 1979.
85 Laing Annual Reports and Accounts.
86 Ibid.
87 Ibid.
88 Ibid.
89 Rosenberg, 1960.
90 Marriott, 1967.
91 Pollard, 1962.
92 Marriott, 1967.
93 Rosenberg, 1960.
94 Jenkins, 1975.
95 Jones Lang Wootton, 1980.
96 Jenkins, 1975; Marriott, 1967.
97 Marriott, 1967.
98 Reith, 1949.
99 Backwell and Dickens, 1978.
100 Ibid.
101 Reith, 1949; Uthwatt, 1941.
102 Addison, 1975.
103 Newman, 1980.
104 Jenkins, 1975; Massey and Catalano, 1978.
105 Jenkins, 1975.
106 About 50% of industrial development in DAs was being financed by the government (HMSO, 1947).
107 Marriott, 1967.

108 Ibid.
109 Whitehouse, 1964.
110 Marriott, 1967.
111 Interview with J. C. Harding JP, Company Secretary, and D. M. Millis, Finance Director, of Slough Estates on Wednesday, April 1, 1981.
112 Slough Estates Ltd, *c.* 1970.
113 Slough Estates Annual Report and Accounts.
114 Marriott, 1967.
115 Whitehouse, 1964.
116 Ibid.
117 Interview with Roger Baden-Powell, City Panel of Takeovers and Mergers, on Tuesday, December 16, 1980.
118 Boggis *et al.*, 1980.
119 Whitehouse, 1964.
120 Boggis *et al.*, 1980.
121 Whitehouse, 1964.
122 Ratcliffe, 1978.
123 A rights issue is an offer of new shares to existing shareholders on a *pro rata* basis to their existing shareholdings. They are often offered at preferential prices, but are usually used by companies as one of the last means to raise money capital and issues can have a diluting effect on the share value of a company (see Samuels and Wilkes, 1980; Firth, 1975). A scrip issue or bonus issue of new shares is distributed *pro rata* and free of charge to existing shareholders (Firth, 1975). They are issued by the company to shareholders instead of the annual cash dividend on each share. On the one hand this means that the shareholder does not have to advance any cash but receives a larger investment although the shareholding in the company remains the same in percentage terms. On the other hand the shareholder does not receive any cash but the liquidity of the company remains sound, and if the yield holds up so will the share price and dividend over the forthcoming year (Samuel and Wilkes, 1980).
124 Firth, 1975.
125 Interview with John Derrington, loc. cit.
126 Marriott, 1967; Jenkins, 1975; Broackes, 1979.
127 Ibid.
128 Holden–Holford plan, 1947, quoted in Barras, 1979a.
129 Dunning and Morgan, 1971.
130 Barras, 1979a.
131 Ravetz, 1980.
132 Marriott, 1967, p. 55.
133 Jones Lang Wootton, 1980.
134 Barras, 1979a.
135 Marriott, 1967.
136 Named Ravensfield prior to 1949.
137 Smyth, 1982a.
138 Ibid.
139 Ibid.
140 Ibid. for further details of these companies.
141 Mallalieu, 1956.

6. Development and construction during prosperity

1 Interview with Fred Wellings of Laing and Cruickshank on Tuesday, January 27, 1981.
2 Central Statistical Office; see table 5.4.
3 This has of course already been witnessed in the case of the construction industry which was one of the sectors to restructure its operations during the course of war, not only to meet the needs of the war economy but as a precondition for other sectors to restructure their operations during reconstruction.
4 Dow, 1964; Middlemas, 1979.
5 Blank, 1973.
6 Dow, 1964.
7 Lereuz, 1975.
8 Blank, 1973; Lereuz, 1975.
9 Simultaneously other consultative bodies such as the Economic Planning Board and National Production Advisory Council became moribund.
10 Lereuz, 1975.
11 Polanyi, 1967.
12 Lereuz, 1975.
13 Blank, 1973.
14 Lereuz, 1975.
15 The country was even divided into the same regions which were used during the war.
16 HMSO, 1965; Lereuz, 1975.
17 Quoted in Middlemas, 1979, footnote p. 439.
18 Barras, 1979a.
19 Land Securities Annual Report and Accounts, 1956.
20 Catalano, 1979a.
21 *Investors Chronicle*, 1960a.
22 Whitehouse, 1964.
23 Jenkins, 1975.
24 This later fell to 10 year review (Cadman and Austin-Crowe, 1978).
25 Barras, 1979a.
26 See chapter 2.
27 Cowan *et al.*, 1969.
28 Quoted in Saunders, 1979, p. 300.
29 Saunders, 1979.
30 Marriott, 1967.
31 The use of 'property owners' is to distinguish the empirical grey area developing whereby institutions were not only landowners but also had equity in the buildings, thus breaking down pure theoretical conceptions of landowners and building owners corresponding to ground and building rent and their being brought together through the act of property development.
32 *Investors Chronicle*, 1961a.
33 *Investors Chronicle*, 1961b.
34 *Investors Chronicle*, 1961a.
35 Barras, 1979a.
36 *Investors Chronicle*, 1960b; although Land Securities mainly forged links

through long term fixed interest loans with conversion rights rather than through sales and leasebacks, thus maintaining greater control over its portfolio, being owners of the ground rents, building rents and the value of the building.

37 See note 123, chapter 5.
38 *Investors Chronicle*, 1962a.
39 The compilation of figures for this era is on a different basis to Whitehouse's (1964) basis used in table 6.6 and therefore comparisons cannot be made absolutely, but the growth in property investment is clear.
40 Boggis *et al.*, 1980.
41 The Chancellor quoted in Whitehouse, 1964, p. 105.
42 Barras, 1979a.
43 *Investors Chronicle*, 1962b.
44 Broackes, 1979.
45 Barras, 1979a. Wimpey is frequently cited as a contractor who entered property development at an early stage, but as Savory Milln (1973, p. 355) points out, 'Wimpey's direct property development and investment activities are relatively small, its major interests being the 50% stake in Euston Centre Properties (jointly owned with Stock Conversion and Investment Trust) and the remaining $10\frac{1}{4}$% interest in Mr Harry Hyams' Oldham Estate Company,' 75% of which was sold in 1972. Wimpey had therefore been at the forefront of providing building finance in exchange for equity shares, and largely rode on the coat tails of the developers rather than being developers or investors in its own right.
46 Marriott, 1967; Jenkins, 1975.
47 See, for example, Counter Information Services, 1973.
48 To prelude this with the argument that the right kind of state is required to carry out the wishes of leftist opposition seems to me to ignore or misunderstand the functional effects of state intervention in any capitalist economy. The causal processes cannot be seen purely in terms of the role of the state in isolation from the conditions in the economy as a whole.
49 Annual Reports by the Board of Trade on the Control of Office and Industrial Development Act, 1965, quoted in Rhodes and Kan, 1971.
50 *Investors Chronicle*, 1962c.
51 Marriott, 1967.
52 *Investors Chronicle*, 1962d.
53 See Marriott (1967) for details.
54 Catalano, 1979a; 1979b.
55 Land Securities Annual Report and Accounts, 1961.
56 *Investors Chronicle*, 1961c, p. 396.
57 Interview with Patrick Galvin, de Zoete and Bevan, on Monday, November 10, 1980.
58 Ratcliffe, 1978.
59 Marriott, 1967.
60 Ibid.
61 Whitehouse, 1964.
62 Marriott, 1967. In the City only 12 out of 34 developments were undertaken by developers (Barras, 1979a).
63 Interview with Roger Baden-Powell, City Panel of Takeovers and Mergers, on Tuesday, December 16, 1980.

64 Marriott, 1967.
65 Broackes, 1979.
66 Ratcliffe, 1978.
67 Broackes, 1979, p. 96.
68 *Investors Chronicle,* 1964a.
69 Ibid.
70 Ibid.
71 Barras, 1979a.
72 It is interesting to note that Nigel Broackes had argued within the British Property Federation in favour of the Land Commission, on the grounds that something else would eventually be implemented in due course, and that it would have been better to lobby to make the Commission useful to developers (Broackes, 1979). In fact this strategy was later adopted when something else did arise – the Community Land Act – although this too was scrapped in 1979.
73 Saunders, 1975.
74 Land Securities Annual Report and Accounts, 1963.
75 Rhodes and Kan, 1971.
76 Catalano, 1979a.
77 Catalano and Barras, 1978.
78 Catalano, 1979b.
79 *Investors Chronicle,* 1961c.
80 Massey and Catalano, 1978.
81 Barras, 1979b.
82 See Broackes, 1979.
83 It changed its name to the English Property Corporation (EPC) in 1973.
84 Interview with Peter Hunt, Chairman of Land Securities, and D. H. MacKeith, Finance Director, Land Securities (Management) on Thursday, June 18, 1981.
85 Details are drawn from Land Securities Annual Reports and Accounts.
86 The financial gearing, the ratio of fixed interest loans to equity capital, excludes reserves attributable to ordinary shareholders in the calculation.
87 Interview with Peter Hunt and D. H. MacKeith, loc. cit.
88 This is calculated on the ratio between total output and gross trading profits, and will include small, specialised and miscellaneous works which have higher margins than contract work.
89 Costain Annual Report and Accounts, 1959.
90 Quoted in Hartshorn, 1963.
91 Savory Milln, 1970.
92 Phelps Brown, 1968; Clarke, 1980.
93 Taylor Woodrow Annual Report and Accounts, 1965.
94 Taylor Woodrow Annual Report and Accounts, 1967.
95 HMSO, 1965.
96 Lewis and Singh, 1966.
97 Ball and Cullen, 1980.
98 Lewis and Singh, 1966, p. 19.
99 Interview with Malcolm Brown, James Capel and Co., on Thursday, May 7, 1981.
100 Laing Annual Report and Accounts, 1962.
101 Interview with Malcolm Brown, loc. cit.

102 Interview with Bob Erith, Savory Milln and Co., on Friday, July 10, 1981.
103 Duncan, 1978a; 1978b; see also chapter 3.
104 Jenkins, 1971.
105 Phillips and Drew, 1971.
106 Ibid.
107 Interview with Martin Murch, Simon and Coates, on Tuesday, June 2, 1981.
108 Mellor, 1977. These subsidies for each storey above 6 storeys were abolished under the Housing Subsidies Act, 1967 (Cooney, 1974).
109 For example Wimpey's 'no fines' and Laing's Easiform; see table 6.12.
110 Interview with Malcolm Brown, loc. cit.
111 Ronan Point, in the London Borough of Newham, was constructed by Taylor Woodrow-Anglian. A gas explosion initiated 'progressive collapse', the entire side of one block collapsing. The courts and House of Lords have been deliberating throughout the 1970s who is responsible for costs. Taylor Woodrow-Anglian eventually lost, but in the meantime Taylor Woodrow sold their share to Ready Mixed Concrete.
112 Interview with Fred Wellings, loc. cit.
113 Seaborne and Lowe, 1977.
114 Interview with Malcolm Brown, loc. cit.
115 Hartshorn, 1957.
116 See chapter 4 for details on FIDO.
117 Jenkins, 1971.
118 Interview with Nat Fletcher, Personnel Director, and Michael Buckland of Taylor Woodrow on Friday, May 15, 1981.
119 Ibid.
120 They did undertake intersection construction (interview with Sir Frank Taylor, Founder and Life President of Taylor Woodrow on Wednesday, January 28, 1981).
121 *Investors Chronicle*, 1960c.
122 Interview with Malcolm Brown, loc. cit.
123 Savory Milln, 1970.
124 Ball and Cullen, 1980.
125 McGhie, 1981, p. 21.
126 See chapter 3.
127 McGhie, 1981.
128 Savory Milln, 1970.
129 Trollope and Colls was taken over by Trafalgar House in 1968.
130 Barras, 1979a.
131 Costain Annual Report and Accounts, 1959.
132 Michael Buckland, interviewed with Sir Frank Taylor and Nat Fletcher of Taylor Woodrow on Wednesday, January 28, 1981.
133 Laing and Cruickshank, 1980.
134 Ball and Cullen, 1980.
135 Smyth, 1982b.
136 *Investors Chronicle*, 1960d.
137 Savory Milln, 1970.
138 *Investors Chronicle*, 1960d.
139 Costain Annual Report and Accounts, 1965.
140 Interview with Fred Wellings, loc. cit.
141 Whittington, 1972.

142 Ball and Cullen, 1980.

143 Savory Milln, 1970.

144 Phillips and Drew, 1971. In fact the takeover was an error in retrospect as an overcapacity in structural steelwork and a fall in Arcon exports led Octavius Atkinson into pre-tax losses.

145 Lewis and Singh, 1966; Sugden, 1975.

7. First phase of crisis

1 Lereuz, 1975, p. 223.

2 This has been calculated on the basis of output to gross trading profits (see table 5.5).

3 Simon and Coates, 1978, p. 3.

4 Euro-Construct, 1977.

5 Interview with Malcolm Brown, James Capel and Co., on Thursday, May 7, 1981.

6 Labour-only subcontractors, colloquially known as 'lump' labour, are unregistered operatives who do not pay tax and national insurance contributions are not paid by contractors.

7 Savory Milln, 1973.

8 Wigham, 1976.

9 Savory Milln, 1973; Scrimgeour, 1973.

10 Laing Annual Report and Accounts, 1972.

11 Labour Party, 1977.

12 Economist Intelligence Unit, 1978a.

13 Labour Party, 1977, p. 45.

14 See chapter 6; Savory Milln, 1973.

15 Capel and Co., 1979.

16 Savory Milln, 1977.

17 *Building,* 1980; although it is unclear if this includes public housing.

18 Capel and Co., 1979.

19 Grieveson, Grant and Co., 1981.

20 Civil engineering work by contrast is centrally controlled.

21 See the 'Building and Civil Engineering' section of the *Financial Times* for new contracts in recent years.

22 Savory Milln, 1970.

23 Capel and Co., 1976.

24 Savory Milln, 1977.

25 Capel and Co., 1979.

26 Building and Civil Engineering EDC, 1975.

27 Scrimgeour, 1973.

28 Ibid.

29 Interview with Malcolm Brown, loc. cit.

30 Scrimgeour, 1975.

31 Ibid., p. 3.

32 This was a government initiation to rationalise and concentrate Britain's industry, particularly engineering sectors.

33 Phillips and Drew, 1971.

34 Newarthill Annual Report and Accounts, 1975; Jenkins, 1980.

35 *Sunday Times,* 1981.

36 Taylor Woodrow, 1981; *Financial Times,* 1981a.
37 Interview with John Derrington, Director of Sir Robert McAlpine and Sons, on Monday, July 27, 1981.
38 Savory Milln, 1977.
39 Ibid.
40 The merger had been undertaken to diversify company operations permitting larger contracts to be tendered for, but French lost its dominance in the group due to the problems over motorway and housing contracts plus land purchases at overvalued prices. Former Kier management took control and integrated the two companies (Savory Milln, 1977).
41 Phillips and Drew, 1971.
42 Smyth, 1982b.
43 Costain Annual Reports and Accounts.
44 Scrimgeour, 1978.
45 Capel and Co., 1976.
46 Savory Milln, 1970.
47 Scrimgeour, 1975.
48 Interview with Malcolm Brown, loc. cit.
49 See chapter 6.
50 Interview with Malcolm Brown, loc. cit.
51 Simon and Coates, 1978, p. 57.
52 Capel and Co., 1979.
53 Laing and Cruickshank, 1980.
54 Simon and Coates, 1978; Savory Milln, 1980.
55 Capel and Co., 1979.
56 Scrimgeour, 1975.
57 Scrimgeour, 1973.
58 Grieveson, Grant and Co., 1981.
59 Capel and Co., 1979.
60 Ibid., p. 13.
61 *Estates Times Review,* 1981a.
62 Savory Milln, 1973.
63 Building and Civil Engineering EDC, Construction Forecasts.
64 Capel and Co., 1979.
65 Interview with John Derrington, loc. cit.
66 Interview with Bob Erith, Partner in Savory Milln, on Friday, July 10, 1981.
67 Interview with Malcolm Brown, loc. cit.
68 Interview with Martin Murch, Simon and Coates, on Tuesday, June 2, 1981.
69 Simon and Coates, 1978.
70 Capel and Co., 1979.
71 Savory Milln, 1980.
72 Euro-Construct, 1977.
73 Capel and Co., 1978.
74 Interview with Nat Fletcher, Director of Taylor Woodrow, Friday, May 15, 1981. British contractors have largely used site labour from the poorer Arab countries and from Pakistan for Middle East contracts (Savory Milln, 1977).
75 Savory Milln, 1970.
76 Simon and Coates, 1978.
77 Capel and Co., 1979.
78 Capel and Co., 1978.

79 Interview with Malcolm Brown, loc. cit.; Jenkins, 1980.
80 Jenkins, 1971; 1980; Phillips and Drew, 1971.
81 *Financial Times,* 1979.
82 Capel and Co., 1976.
83 DoE, quoted in Capel and Co., 1976.
84 See, for example, Lea, Lansley and Spencer, 1974.
85 Ball and Cullen, 1980.
86 Smyth, 1982b.
87 Ball and Cullen, 1980.
88 Interview with Martin Murch, loc. cit.
89 Grieveson, Grant and Co., 1981.
90 Capel and Co., 1979; *Financial Times,* 1981b.
91 Interview with Bob Erith, loc. cit.
92 Interview with Martin Murch, loc. cit.
93 Simon and Coates, 1978.
94 Pilcher Report, 1975.
95 Debenham, Tewson and Chinnocks, 1980a.
96 Ambrose and Colenutt, 1975.
97 *The Economist,* 1978.
98 Boddy, 1981.
99 DoE, quoted in Debenham, Tewson and Chinnocks, 1980b.
100 *Financial Times,* 1980.
101 *Financial Times,* 1981c.
102 The Euromarkets are international money markets which grew up in the 1960s as multinational companies wished to raise finance on a scale to match their international operations. This the Euromarkets catered for, requiring little information, and were not tied to national taxation or capital control laws, such as those introduced in the United States in 1963. The Euromarkets doubled in size between 1973 and 1977 after international rise in oil prices and increased investment activity by OPEC countries (Samuels and Wilkes, 1980).
103 Interview with Alan Crowe, Company Secretary of MEPC, Wednesday, May 13, 1981.
104 *Investors Chronicle,* 1980a.
105 Hoare and Co., 1972.
106 Panmure Gordon and Co., 1976.
107 Broackes, 1979.
108 Panmure Gordon and Co., 1976.
109 Vickers da Costa, 1980.
110 *Investors Chronicle,* 1971a.
111 Barras, 1979a.
112 Ratcliffe, 1978.
113 Riddell, 1973.
114 Ibid.
115 *Investors Chronicle,* 1980b.
116 Sebag and Co., 1978; Boggis *et al.,* 1980.
117 Ratcliffe, 1978.
118 *Investors Chronicle,* 1971b.
119 *Investors Chronicle,* 1971c.
120 Land Securities Annual Report and Accounts, 1972.

121 Midland Bank Ltd, quoted in Panmure Gordon and Co., 1976.
122 Panmure Gordon and Co., 1976.
123 *Investors Chronicle*, 1971c.
124 *Investors Chronicle*, 1971d.
125 Interview with Peter Hunt, Chairman of Land Securities (Management), on Thursday, June 18, 1981.
126 Ibid.
127 Sebag and Co., 1978.
128 Ellis, 1978a.
129 Barras, 1979a.
130 Ambrose and Colenutt, 1975.
131 Sebag and Co., 1978.
132 The bank rate had been replaced by MLR as the principal determinant of interest rates.
133 Sebag and Co., 1978.
134 Riddell, 1975.
135 *The Banker*, 1974a.
136 Broackes, 1979.
137 Twentieth Century Banking was a subsidiary of Bovis, operating primarily in property. National Westminster sent a 'lifeboat' of £14m to the subsidiary with the condition that Bovis found a stronger financial partner (*Banker*, 1974b), so paving the way for the merger with P and O.
138 Ratcliffe, 1978.
139 *Observer*, 1979.
140 Sebag and Co., 1978, p. 28.
141 Sebag and Co., 1978.
142 Barras, 1979a.
143 Sebag and Co., 1979.
144 Ibid.
145 Interview with Alan Crowe, loc. cit.
146 Ibid.
147 Ibid.
148 *The Times*, 1974.
149 *The Economist*, 1978.
150 Barras, 1979b.
151 Ratcliffe, 1978.
152 Sebag and Co., 1978.
153 Barras, 1979a.
154 Labour Party, 1974.
155 Interview with Peter Hunt, loc. cit.
156 Barras, 1979a.
157 Economist Intelligence Unit, 1978b; Sebag and Co., 1979.
158 Sebag and Co., 1979.
159 Boggis *et al.*, 1980.
160 *Estates Times Review*, 1981b.
161 Boggis *et al.*, 1980.
162 Erdman, 1979.
163 Ibid.
164 Interview with Alan Crowe, loc. cit.
165 *Investors Chronicle*, 1980c.

166 *Investors Chronicle,* 1980d.
167 Erdman, 1979; Vickers da Costa, 1980.
168 Sebag and Co., 1979.
169 Quilter Hilton Goodison and Co., 1980, p. 3.
170 See, for example, Ambrose and Colenutt, 1975, and Boddy, 1981.
171 The power of intervention was used when Charles Hardie was replaced as chairman.
172 Interview with Alan Crowe, loc. cit.
173 Quilter Hilton Goodison and Co., 1980.
174 Boggis *et al.,* 1980.
175 Interview with J. C. Harding, Company Secretary, and D. M. Millis, Finance Director, of Slough Estates on Wednesday, April 1, 1981; Economist Intelligence Unit, 1978b; Ellis, 1978b.
176 Panmure Gordon and Co., 1976.
177 Boggis *et al.,* 1980.
178 Grant and Partners, 1980.
179 Interview with J. C. Harding and D. M. Millis, loc. cit.
180 Grant and Partners, 1980.
181 Ibid.
182 Sebag and Co., 1978.
183 Interview with Narish Gudka and Will Martin, Quilter Hilton Goodison and Co., on Tuesday, December 9, 1980.
184 Ibid.
185 Interview with Alan Crowe, loc. cit.
186 Ellis, 1980a; 1980b.

Conclusion

1 Luxemburg, 1970.
2 Ibid.
3 Mills, 1970, p. 10.

References

Addison, P., 1975. *The Road to 1945*. Cape, London

Aglietta, M., 1976. *A Theory of Capitalist Regulation*. New Left Books, London

Alonso, W., 1964. *Location and Land Use*. Harvard University Press, Cambridge, Massachusetts

Ambrose, P., 1976. *The Land Market and the Housing System*. Urban and Regional Studies Working Paper 3. University of Sussex

  1977. 'The Determinants of Urban Land Use Change'. In *Values, Relevance and Policy*, Fundamentals of Human Geography, Section III, Unit 26, Social Science Second Level Course, Open University. Milton Keynes, Bucks.

Ambrose, P. and Colenutt, B., 1975. *The Property Machine*. Penguin, Harmondsworth

Andrews, P. W. S., 1941. 'A Survey in Industrial Development in Great Britain since the Commencement of War', *Oxford Economic Papers*, no. 5

Architects Journal, 1939. Letter from Mr. George Hicks MP, General Secretary, Amalgamated Union of Building Trade Workers, December 14

Backwell, J. and Dickens, P., 1978. *Town Planning, Mass Loyalty and the Restructuring of Capital*. Urban and Regional Studies Working Paper 11. University of Sussex

Ball, M., 1977. 'Differential Rent and the Role of Landed Property', *International Journal of Urban and Regional Research*, vol. 1, no. 3

  1978. 'British Housing Policy and the House-Building Industry', *Capital and Class*, no. 4

  1980. 'The Contracting System in the Construction Industry'. Mimeo.

  1983. *Housing Policy and Economic Power*. Methuen, London

Ball, M. and Cullen, A., 1980. *Mergers and Accumulation in the British Construction Industry, 1960–1979*. Discussion Papers in Economics no. 73, Birkbeck College, University of London

Banker, The, 1974a. 'Danger Signals for Banking', vol. 124, no. 575

  1974b. vol. 124, no. 577

Baran, P. A. and Sweezy, P. M., 1968. *Monopoly Capital*. Penguin, Harmondsworth

Barlow Report, 1940. *Report of the Royal Commission on the Distribution of the Industrial Population*. Cmd. 6153, HMSO, London

Barras, R., 1979a. *The Development Cycle in the City of London*. Research Series 36, Centre for Environmental Studies, London

  1979b. *The Returns from Office Development and Investment*. Research Series 35, Centre for Environmental Studies, London

Blackaby, F. (ed.), 1979. *De-industrialisation*. Heinemann and National Institute for Educational and Social Research, London

Blank, S., 1973. *Industry and Government in Britain*. Saxon House, Farnborough

Boddy, M., 1978. 'Finance Capital, Commodity Production, and the Production of Urban Built Form'. Paper presented to the Socialist Economists Money Group
  1979. 'Investment by Financial Institutions in Commercial Property'. In *Land, Property and Finance*, ed. M. Boddy. School for Advanced Urban Studies Working Paper 2, University of Bristol
  1981. 'The Property Sector in Late Capitalism'. In *Urbanisation and Urban Planning in Capitalist Society*, ed. M. Dear and A. J. Scott. Methuen, London
Boggis, M. J., Baden-Powell, R. S., Evans, P. and Wyatt, A., 1980. 'Property as an Investment for Long Term Funds'. Paper presented at the Royal Institution of Chartered Surveyors Conference, July
Bowen, I., 1940. 'Building Output and the Trade Cycle (UK, 1924–38)', *Oxford Economic Papers*, no. 3
  1951. 'The Control of Building'. In *Lessons of the British War Economy*, ed. D. N. Chester. Cambridge University Press
Bowen, I. and Ellis, A. W. T., 1945. 'The Building and Contracting Industry', *Oxford Economic Papers*, no. 7
Bowley, M., 1966. *The British Building Industry*. Cambridge University Press
Brady, R. A., 1950. *Crisis in Britain*. Cambridge University Press
Braverman, H., 1974. *Labour and Monopoly Capital*. Monthly Review Press, New York
Brighton Labour Process Group, 1977. 'The Capitalist Labour Process', *Capital and Class*, no. 1
Broackes, N., 1979. *A Growing Concern*. Weidenfeld and Nicolson, London
Bruegel, I., 1975. 'The Marxist Theory of Rent and the Contemporary City', *Political Economy and the Housing Question*. Political Economy of Housing Workshop, London
Builder, 1939a. 'Bankruptcy of Builders', July 14
  1939b. 'Private Building and the War', September 29
  1944. 'Statement by Mr. R. Coppock, General Secretary of the NFBTO', December 8
Building, 1980. April 11
Building and Civil Engineering EDC, 1975. *The Public Client and the Construction Industries*. NEDO, London
Byrne, D. and Beirne, P., 1975. 'Towards a Political Economy of Housing Rent'. In *Political Economy and the Housing Question*. Political Economy of Housing Workshop, London
Cadman, D. and Austin-Crowe, L., 1978. *Property Development*. Spon, London
Capel and Co., James, 1976. *The United Kingdom Construction Industry 1976–1979*. London
  1978. *International Civil Engineering Contractors*. London
  1979. *Wimpey*. London
Carter, C. F., 1961. 'The Building Industry'. In *The Structure of British Industry*, vol. 1, ed. D. Burn. Cambridge University Press
Castells, M., 1977. *The Urban Question*. Arnold, London
  1978. *City, Class and Power*. Macmillan, London
Catalano, A., 1979a. *Office Development in Central Leeds 1960–1975*. Centre for Environmental Studies Working Note 533. London
  1979b. *Office Development in Central Bristol 1959–1975*. Centre for Environmental Studies Working Note 569. London

Catalano, A. and Barras, R., 1978. *Office Development in Central Manchester 1960–1975.* Centre for Environmental Studies Working Note 515. London

Central Statistical Office. *Annual Abstracts of Statistics.* HMSO, London

Clark, S. and Ginsburg, N., 1975. 'The Political Economy of Housing', *Political Economy and the Housing Question.* Political Economy of Housing Workshop, London

Clarke, L., 1980. 'Subcontracting in the Building Industry'. In *The Production of the Built Environment* 2. Proceedings of the Second Bartlett Summer School, University College, University of London

Coad, R., 1979. *Laing: the Biography of Sir John W. Laing, CBE (1879–1978).* Hodder and Stoughton, London

Colclough, J., 1965. *The Construction Industry of Great Britain.* Butterworths, London

Cole, G. D. H., 1947. *Local and Regional Government.* Cassell, London

Cooney, E. W., 1954. 'The Origins of the Victorian Master Builders', *Economic History Review*, vol. 8

1974. 'High Rise Flats in Local Authority Housing in England and Wales since 1945'. In *Multi-Storey Living*, ed. A. Sutcliffe. Croom Helm, London

Counter Information Services, 1973. *The Recurrent Crisis of London.* London

Cowan, P. *et al.*, 1969. *The Office.* Heinemann, London

Cripps, C., 1978. 'Construction and the Development of Building Capital'. In *Building Capital and Labour, Political Economy of Cities and Regions*, no. 2. Architectural Association, London

1980. 'Research of the Production of Housing: Some Methods and Questions Arising'. In *Housing, Construction and the State.* Political Economy of Housing Workshop, London

Cutler, A., Hindess, B., Hirst, P. and Hussain, A., 1977. *Marx's 'Capital' and Capitalism Today.* Routledge, London

Debenham, Tewson and Chinnocks, 1980a. *Office Rent and Rates, 1973–1980.* London

1980b. *Money into Property 1970–1979.* London

Direct Labour Collective, 1978. *Building with Direct Labour.* Conference of Socialist Economists, London

Dobb, M., 1963. *Studies in the Development of Capitalism.* Routledge, London

Dow, J. C. R., 1964. *The Management of the British Economy 1945–1960.* Cambridge University Press

Duncan, S. S., 1978a. *Housing Reform, the Capitalist State, and Social Democracy.* Urban and Regional Studies Working Paper 9. University of Sussex

1978b. *Housing Provision in Advanced Capitalism: Sweden in the 1970s.* Urban and Regional Studies Working Paper 10. University of Sussex

Dunning, J. H. and Morgan, E. V., 1971. *An Economic Study of the City of London.* Allen and Unwin, London

Economist, The, 1949. Speech at Workington by Sir Stafford Cripps, 22 January

1978. 'The New Leviathans: Property and Financial Institutions', Survey, June 10

Economist Intelligence Unit, 1978a. *Public Ownership in the Construction Industries.* London

1978b. *An Analysis of Commercial Property Values.* London

Edel, M., 1976. 'Marx's Theory of Rent: Urban Applications'. In *Housing and Class in Britain.* Political Economy of Housing Workshop, London

Elger, T., 1979. 'Valorisation and "Deskilling": a Critique of Braverman', *Capital and Class*, no. 7

Ellis, Richard, 1978a. *City of London Accommodation Survey*. London
   1978b. *Property Investment Report*. London
   1980a. *SW1 Office Accommodation Market*. London
   1980b. *West Central Office Accommodation Market*. London

Emmanuel, A., 1972. *Unequal Exchange*. Monthly Review Press, New York

Erdman, Edward, 1979. *Property Market Review 1979*. London

Estates Times Review, 1981a. 'Interview', August
   1981b. 'Sprightly "Dinosaurs" are Alive and Kicking', May

Euro-Construct, 1977. *The Medium Term Outlook for the European Construction Industry 1975–1980*. James Capel and Co., London

Financial Times, 1951. October 13
   1979. 'Tarmac Starts to Fill in the Cracks', November 9
   1980. 'Investment "Go-slow"', April 25
   1981a. 'Private Group Probes Severn Barrage Plan', July 24
   1981b. 'George Wimpey Dives £3m to £6m at Midterm', September 25
   1981c. 'Investment hits Peak', April 24

Firth, M., 1975. *Investment Analysis*. Harper and Row, London

Foster, J., 1974. *Class Struggle and the Industrial Revolution*. Methuen, London

Frank, A. G., 1980. *Crisis: in the World Economy*. Heinemann, London

Friedmann, A. L., 1977. *Industry and Labour*. Macmillan, London

Giddens, A., 1974. Preface. In *Elites and Power in British Society*, ed. P. Stanworth and A. Giddens. Cambridge University Press

Glyn, A. and Sutcliffe, B., 1972. *British Capitalism, Workers and the Profits Squeeze*. Penguin, Harmondsworth

Gottlieb, M., 1976. *Long Swings in Urban Development*. National Bureau of Economic Research, New York

Grant and Partners, 1980. *Report on the Industrial Property Market*. London

Grieveson, Grant and Co., 1981. *The U.K. Construction Industry*. London

Hall, D., 1948. *Cornerstone*. Lawrence and Wishart, London

Harre, R., 1970. *The Principles of Scientific Thinking*. Macmillan, London

Hartley, A. C., 1948. 'Fog Dispersal from Airfield Runways'. In *The Civil Engineer in War*. The Institution of Civil Engineers, London

Hartshorn, J. E., 1957. 'New Power for Britain – at what Cost?', *The Banker*, vol. 107, no. 373
   1963. 'Has Construction the Capacity Ned Needs?', *The Banker*, vol. 113, no. 451

Harvey, D., 1973. *Social Justice and the City*. Arnold, London
   1974. 'Class Monopoly Rent, Finance Capitals and the Urban Revolution', *Regional Studies*, vol. 8, no. 3–4
   1975. 'The Political Economy of Urbanization in Advanced Capitalist Societies: the Case Study of the United States'. In *The Social Economy of Cities, Urban Affairs Annual Reviews*, vol. 9, ed. G. Gappert and H. M. Rose. Sage, Beverly Hills
   1978. 'The Urban Process under Capitalism: a Framework for Analysis', *International Journal of Urban and Regional Research*, vol. 2, no. 1

Hawkey, R. W., 1948. 'Temporary Works at East India Dock, and South Dock, Surrey Commercial Docks, Port of London, in Connexion with the Construction of Concrete Caissons for the Mulberry Harbours'. In *The Civil Engineer in War*. The Institution of Civil Engineers, London

HMSO, 1936. *Statement Relating to Defence*. Cmd. 5107, London

1942. *The Allocation to Messrs. George Wimpey and Co. Ltd., during the War of Government Contracts in Scotland*. Cmd. 6393, London

1945a. *Statistical Material Presented during the Washington Negotiations, Accounts and Papers*, vol. XXI, 1945–46. Cmd. 6707, London

1945b. *Coal Mining, Report of the Technical Advisory Committee*. Cmd. 6610, London

1945c. *Capital Issues Control: Memorandum of Guidance to the Capital Issues Committee*. Cmd. 6645, London

1947. *Capital Investment in 1948*. Cmd. 7268, London

1948. *European Cooperation: Memoranda Submitted to OEEC*. Cmd. 7572, London

1949. *Economic Survey for 1949*. Cmd. 7647, London

1950. *Economic Survey for 1950*. Cmd. 7915, London

1965. *The National Plan*. Cmd. 2764, London

Hilferding, R., 1981. *Finance Capital*. Routledge, London

Hoare and Co., Govett, 1972. *Property*. London

Hobhouse, H., 1971. *Thomas Cubitt*. Macmillan, London

House of Commons, 1940. *Parliamentary Debates*, vol. 365, col. 1150, October 24. HMSO, London

1941. *Parliamentary Debates*, vol. 370, col. 177, March 19. HMSO, London

Howard, M. C. and King, J. E., 1975. *The Political Economy of Marx*. Longman, London

Hudson, P. G., 1948. 'The Development and Construction of Airfields and Runways for the Royal Air Force, 1939–1945'. In *The Civil Engineer in War*. The Institution of Civil Engineers, London

Investors Chronicle, 1957. September 12

1959. 'The World's Greatest Office Centre', March 27

1960a. 'Associations with Insurance Companies', April 29

1960b. 'Prophets in Property', September 2

1960c. March 25

1960d. 'Costain', November 18

1961a. 'Funds for Property', March 31

1961b. 'Finance for Property Companies', September 15

1961c. 'The Largest Property Group', January 27

1962a. 'City Centre Breaks Through', March 30

1962b. 'Some Observations on Property Finance', Property Survey, February 23

1962c. 'The Economics of Town Centre Development', Property Survey, February 23

1962d. 'Market Forces as much as Politics', Property Survey, February 23

1971a. 'Upsurge in Hotel Growth', March 26

1971b. May 14

1971c. 'Index Outpaces Earnings', March 26

1971d. 'What Land Securities' Figures Mean', August 27

1980a. 'Property is Going to be a Very Different Game in the 1980s', March 21

1980b. 'City Space Still Much in Demand', March 21

1980c. 'New Period of Growth for MEPC', November 7

1980d. 'Takeover Prospects an Important Factor', March 21

Investors Chronicle Hillier Parker, 1981. *Rent Index*. London

Ive, G., 1980. 'Capital Accumulation, the Built Stock and the Construction Sector: an Economic Overview'. In *The Production of the Built Environment* 2. Proceedings of the Second Bartlett Summer School, University College, University of London

Jenkins, A., 1971. *On Site*. Heinemann, London
1980. *Built on Teamwork*. Heinemann, London

Jenkins, S., 1975. *Landlords to London: the Story of Capital and its Growth*. Constable, London

Jones Lang Wootton, 1980. *Offices in the City of London*. London

Kalecki, M., 1934. 'On Foreign Trade and Domestic Exports'. In *Selected Essays on the Dynamics of the Capitalist Economy 1930–1970*. Cambridge University Press, 1971
1967. 'The Problem of Effective Demand with Tugan-Baranovski and Rosa Luxemburg'. In *Selected Essays on the Dynamics of the Capitalist Economy 1930–1970*. Cambridge University Press, 1971
1971. 'Class Struggle and Distribution of National Income'. In *Selected Essays on the Dynamics of the Capitalist Economy 1930–1970*. Cambridge University Press

Keynes, J. M., 1961. *The General Theory of Employment, Interest and Money*. Macmillan, London

Kidron, M., 1970. *Western Capitalism since the War*. Penguin, Harmondsworth

Kohan, C. M., 1952. *Works and Buildings*. Longman and HMSO, London

Labour Party, 1974. *Labour Party Manifesto*. London
1977. *Building Britain's Future*. London

Laing and Cruickshank, 1977. *Slough Estates Limited*. London
1980. *Wimpey and its Property Portfolio*. London
1981. *Hammerson*. London

Laing and Son Ltd, John, 1950. *Team Work: the Story of John Laing and Son Limited*. London

Lamarche, F., 1976. 'Property Development and the Economic Foundations of the Urban Question'. In *Urban Sociology: Critical Essays*, ed. C. G. Pickvance. Tavistock, London

Landes, D. S., 1969. *The Unbound Prometheus*. Cambridge University Press

Lea, E., Lansley, P. and Spencer, P., 1974. *Efficiency and Growth in the Building Industry*. Ashridge Management Research Unit, Ashridge Management College

Lereuz, J., 1975. *Economic Planning and Politics in Britain*. Robertson, London

Lewis, J. P., 1960. 'Building Cycles: a Regional Model and its National Setting', *The Economic Journal*, vol. 70
1965. *Building Cycles and Britain's Growth*. Macmillan, London

Lewis, J. P. and Singh, D. D., 1966. 'Government Policy and the Building Industry', *District Bank Review*, no. 158

Lojkine, J., 1976. 'Contribution to a Marxist Theory of Capitalist Urbanisation'. In *Urban Sociology: Critical Essays*, ed. C. G. Pickvance. Tavistock, London

Lomax, K., 1959. 'Production and Productivity Movements in the U.K. since 1900', *Journal of Royal Statistical Society*, Series A

Long, C. D., 1940. *Business Cycles and the Theory of Investment*. Princeton University Press

Luxemburg, R., 1951. *The Accumulation of Capital*. Routledge, London

1970. 'Reform or Revolution'. In *Rosa Luxemburg Speaks*, ed. M.-A. Waters. Pathfinder, New York

Mallalieu, W. C., 1956. *British Reconstruction and American Policy 1945–1955*. Scarecrow, New York

Manchester Guardian, 1940. May 18

Mandel, E., 1975. *Late Capitalism*. New Left Books, London

Marriott, O., 1967. *The Property Boom*. Hamish Hamilton, London

Marx, K., 1954. *Capital*, vol. 1. Lawrence and Wishart, London
    1956. *Capital*, vol. 2. Lawrence and Wishart, London
    1959. *Capital*, vol. 3. Lawrence and Wishart, London

Marx House, c. 1941. *Problems of the Building Industry*. Lawrence and Wishart, London

Massey, D. B., 1973. 'Towards a Critique of Industrial Location Theory', *Antipode*, vol. 5, no. 3. Reprinted in *Radical Geography*, ed. R. Peet. Methuen, London, 1978
    1977. 'Industrial Location Theory Reconsidered'. In *Values, Relevance and Policy*, Fundamentals of Human Geography, Section III, Unit 25, Social Science Second Level Course, Open University. Milton Keynes, Bucks.

Massey, D. B. and Catalano, A., 1978. *Capital and Land*. Arnold, London

Mattick, P., 1971. *Marx and Keynes*. Merlin, London
    1974. 'The Crisis of the Mixed Economy'. In *Economics, Politics and the Age of Inflation*. Merlin, London, 1978
    1976. 'Deflationary Inflation'. In *Economics, Politics and the Age of Inflation*. Merlin, London, 1978
    1981. *Economic Crisis and Crisis Theory*. Sharpe, New York

McAlpine and Sons, Sir Robert, c. 1955. *Sir Robert McAlpine and Sons*. Civil Engineering Publications, London

McGhie, B., 1981. 'The Implications of Project Management', to be published in *The Production of the Built Environment 3*. Proceedings of the Third Bartlett Summer School, University College, University of London

Mellor, J. R., 1977. *Urban Sociology in an Urbanized Society*. Routledge, London

Merrett, S., 1979. *State Housing in Britain*. Routledge, London

Middlemas, K., 1979. *Politics in Industrial Society*. André Deutsch, London

Mills, C. Wright, 1970. *The Sociological Imagination*. Penguin, Harmondsworth

Ministry of Health, 1948. *Housing Returns for England and Wales*. Cmd. 7442, HMSO, London

Ministry of Works, 1945. *Statistical Tables Relating to the Building and Civil Engineering Industries in War-time*. HMSO, London

Mitchell, J., 1963. *Crisis in Britain 1951*. Secker and Warburg, London

Morgan, K., 1979. *State Regional Interventions and Industrial Reconstruction in Post-war Britain*. Urban and Regional Studies Working Paper 16. University of Sussex

Murray, R., 1977. 'Value and Theory of Rent: Part I', *Capital and Class*, no. 3
    1978. 'Value and Theory of Rent: Part II', *Capital and Class*, no. 4

Newman, P., 1980. *The Formation of the 1947 Town Planning System*'. Papers in Urban and Regional Studies 4. Centre of Urban and Regional Studies, Birmingham

Observer, 1979. 'The World's Biggest Bankrupt', February 18

Pahl, R. E., 1975. *Whose City?* Penguin, Harmondsworth

Panmure Gordon and Co., 1976. *The Property Sector, 1976–1977*. London

Park, R. E. *et al.* (eds.), 1967. *The City*. University of Chicago Press

Paulding, J., 1980. '"Labour and Monopoly Capital", the Concept of Mode of Production', *The Production of the Built Environment 2*. Proceedings of the Second Bartlett Summer School, University College, University of London

Paury, R., 1948. 'Mulberry Pierheads'. In *The Civil Engineer in War*. The Institution of Civil Engineers, London

Phelps Brown, E. H., 1968. *Report of the Committee of Enquiry under Professor E. H. Phelps Brown into Certain Matters Concerning Labour in Building*. HMSO, London

Phillips and Drew, 1971. *Taylor Woodrow*. London

Pilcher Report, 1975. *Commercial Property Development*. HMSO, London

Polanyi, G., 1967. *Planning in Britain: the Experience of the 1960s*. Institute of Economic Affairs, London

Pollard, S., 1962. *The Development of the British Economy 1914–50*. Arnold, London

Postgate, R. W. P., 1923. *The Builder's History*. National Federation of Building Trades Organisations, London

Powell, C. G., 1980. *An Economic History of the British Building Industry 1815–1979*. Architectural Press, London

Preteceille, E., 1976. 'Urban Planning: the Contradictions of Capitalist Urbanisation', *Antipode*, vol. 8, no. 1

Quilter Hilton Goodison and Co., 1980. *Property Shares*. London

Ratcliffe, J., 1978. *An Introduction to Urban Land Administration*. Estates Gazette, London

Ravetz, A., 1980. *Remaking Cities*. Croom Helm, London

Reith, J. C. W., 1949. *Into the Wind*. Hodder and Stoughton, London

Rex, J. and Moore, R., 1967. *Race, Community and Conflict*. Oxford University Press

Rhodes, J. and Kan, A., 1971. *Office Disperal and Regional Policy*. University of Cambridge, Department of Applied Economics Occasional Paper 30. Cambridge University Press

Riddell, P., 1973. 'Foreign Banks and the Property Market', *The Banker*, vol. 123, no. 573

    1975. 'Property Losses – How Far the Bank's Own Fault', *The Banker*, vol. 125, February

Robinson, J., 1951. 'Introduction' to R. Luxemburg, *The Accumulation of Capital*. Routledge, London

Rogow, A. A., 1955. *The Labour Government and British Industry 1945–1951*. Blackwell, Oxford

Rolt, L. T. C., 1958. *Holloways of Millbank*. Newman Neame, London

Rosdolsky, R., 1977. *The Making of Marx's 'Capital'*. Pluto, London

Rosenberg, N., 1960. *Economic Planning in the British Building Industry, 1945–1949*. University of Pennsylvania, Philadelphia

Samuels, J. M. and Wilkes, F. M., 1980. *Management of Company Finance*, third edition. Nelson, Walton-on-Thames

Saunders, P., 1975. 'Who Runs Croydon?'. Unpublished PhD thesis, University of London

    1979. *Urban Politics: a Sociological Interpretation*. Hutchinson, London

Savory Milln and Co., 1970. *Building Book*. London

    1973. *Building Book*. London

1977. *Building Book*. London

1980. *G. Wimpey*. London

Sayers, R. S., 1956. *Financial Policy, 1939–45*. Longman and HMSO, London

Schmidt, A., 1971. *The Concept of Nature in Marx*. New Left Books, London

Schwarz, B., 1977. 'On the Monopoly Capitalist Degradation of Work', *Dialectical Anthropology*, vol. 2, no. 2

Scott, A. J., 1976. 'Land and Land Rent: an Interpretative Review of French Literature', *Progress in Geography*, no. 9

Scrimgeour, 1973. *John Laing and Son Limited*. London

1975. *The Construction Industry*. London

1978. *John Laing Limited*. London

Seaborne, M. and Lowe, R., 1977. *The English School*. Routledge, London

Sebag and Co., Joseph, 1978. *The Property Share Market 1978*. London

1979. *Property Share Guide 1979*. London

Simon and Coates, 1978. *The Leading Contractors*. London

Slough Estates Ltd, *c.* 1970. *Slough Estates Limited, 1920–1970*. Slough

Smith, A., 1970. *The Wealth of Nations*. Penguin, Harmondsworth

Smyth, H. J., 1982a. 'The Historical Growth of Property Companies and the Construction Industry in Britain between 1939 and 1979'. Unpublished PhD thesis, University of Bristol

1982b. *Landbanking, Land Availability and Planning for Private Housebuilding*. School for Advanced Urban Studies Working Paper 23. University of Bristol

Stuart, C. (ed.), 1975. *The Reith Diaries*. Collins, London

Sugden, J. D., 1975. 'The Place of Construction in the Economy'. In *Aspects of the Economics of Construction*, ed. D. A. Turin. Godwin, London

Sunday Times, 1981. 'Top Nuclear Job: Board's Decision Splits Industry', May 31

Taylor, F. W., 1947. *Scientific Management*. Harper, New York

Taylor Woodrow, 1981. *Energy Magazine*. Southall

Times, The, 1939. December 29

1974. 'Key Property in City Fails to Attract Bidders', March 9

Timpanaro, S., 1975. *On Materialism*. New Left Books, London

Tuckman, A., 1980. 'Looking Backwards: Historical Specificity of the Labour Process in Construction'. In *The Production of the Built Environment 2*. Proceedings of the Second Bartlett Summer School, University College, University of London

United Nations, 1970. *Trends in the Industrialisation of Building*. Department of Economic and Social Affairs, New York

Uthwatt, A. 1941. *Interim Report of the Committee on Compensation and Betterment*. Cmd. 6386, HMSO, London

Vickers da Costa, 1980. *Property Quarterly Review*, no. 14, London

Walker, R. A., 1974. 'Urban Ground Rent: Building a New Conceptual Framework', *Antipode*, vol. 6, no. 1

1978. 'The Transformation of Urban Structure in the Nineteenth Century and the Beginnings of Suburbanization'. In *Urbanization and Conflict in Market Societies*, ed. K. Cox. Methuen, London

Walker-Smith, Sir Jonah, *c.* 1948. 'Building'. In *The Industrial Future of Great Britain, Lectures – University of London and Institute of Bankers*. Europa Publishing, London

Ward-Perkins, C. N., 1952. 'Banking Developments'. In *The British Economy 1945–1950*, ed. G. D. N. Worswick and P. H. Ady. Oxford University Press

Whitehouse, B. P., 1964. *Partners in Property*. Birn, Shaw, London

Whittington, G., 1972. 'Changes in the Top 100 Quoted Manufacturing Companies in the United Kingdom 1948 to 1968', *Journal of Industrial Economics*, no. 1, vol. 21

Wigham, E., 1976. *Strikes and Government 1893–1974*. Macmillan, London

Wood, C. R. J., 1948a. 'Phoenix'. In *The Civil Engineer in War*. The Institution of Civil Engineers, London

　1948b. 'Reinforced-Concrete Pier Pontoons and Intermediate Pierhead Pontoons'. In *The Civil Engineer in War*. The Institution of Civil Engineers, London

Working Party on Building Operations, 1950. *Building*. HMSO, London

Wright, J. F., 1962. 'The Capital Market and the Finance of Industry'. In *The British Economy in the Nineteen Fifties*, ed. G. D. N. Worswick and P. H. Ady. Oxford University Press

Yaffe, D., 1973a. 'The Crisis of Profitability: a Critique of the Glyn–Sutcliffe thesis', *New Left Review*, no. 80

　1973b. 'The Marxian Theory of Crisis, Capital and the State', *Economy and Society*, vol. 2, no. 2

Index